jocks2

jocks 2

Coming Out to Play

Dan Woog

alyson books
los angeles | new york

MANUFACTURED IN THE UNITED STATES OF AMERICA..

THIS TRADE PAPERBACK ORIGINAL IS PUBLISHED BY ALYSON PUBLICATIONS,
P.O. BOX 4371, LOS ANGELES, CALIFORNIA 90078-4371.
DISTRIBUTION IN THE UNITED KINGDOM BY TURNAROUND PUBLISHER SERVICES LTD.,
UNIT 3, OLYMPIA TRADING ESTATE, COBURG ROAD, WOOD GREEN,
LONDON N22 6TZ ENGLAND.

FIRST EDITION: OCTOBER 2002

02 03 04 05 06 a 10 9 8 7 6 5 4 3 2 1

ISBN 1-55583-726-3

LIBRARY OF CONGRESS CATALOGING-IN-PUBLICATION DATA
    WOOG, DAN, 1953–
      JOCKS 2 : COMING OUT TO PLAY / DAN WOOG.—1ST ED.
      ISBN 1-55583-726-3
      1. GAY ATHLETES—UNITED STATES—BIOGRAPHY. 2. HOMOSEXUALITY,
    MALE—UNITED STATES—CASE STUDIES. I. TITLE: JOCKS TWO. II. TITLE.
    GV697.A1 W687 2002
    796'.086'642—DC21   2002071671

CREDITS
• COVER PHOTOGRAPHY BY ROBERT JOHN GUTTKE.
• COVER DESIGN BY LOUIS MANDRAPILIAS.

Contents

Introduction

When my book *Jocks: True Stories of America's Gay Male Athletes* was published in 1998, reaction was surprisingly intense. My premise—that there were far more gay athletes and coaches than anyone suspected—proved to be true. The book struck a chord with a broad range of gay men. Some had spent years, even decades, as closeted jocks, always believing they were the only ones; at last they were thrilled to learn they were not alone. Others, younger, drew inspiration from the fact that they might come out and still be able to run, swim, or play hockey or soccer. Still others had liked sports as youngsters but turned away from athletics because the locker room and playing fields were too homophobic to bear. And, of course, there were men who had never thrown a pass or batted a ball but always dreamed about gay jocks. They were excited to discover that some of their fantasies might actually be true.

Much has changed in four years. Perhaps the most important positive event began with a front-page story in *The New York Times*. Robert Lipsyte's piece ran on Sunday, April 30, 2000, the day of the Millennium March on Washington. Sensitively yet powerfully, it told the story of Corey Johnson, a football linebacker at Masconomet High School in Massachusetts who a year earlier had come out to his teammates and coaches.

Corey's story sounded like a made-for-TV movie, except it was true. He was a bright, articulate, popular, and talented athlete who made up in heart and toughness what he lacked in size. But throughout his junior year, tortured by fears of what his same-sex attractions would mean for his future, Corey sank into depression. His grades plummeted. He had no idea how as captain he would lead his team the following fall.

Introduction

Thanks, however, to a fortuitous confluence of circumstances—Corey lived in the most progressive state for gay youth in the country; his school had a thriving gay-straight alliance; his coach was an enlightened, intelligent, and caring man; and Corey followed the advice of parents and other adults who loved and cared about him—his coming-out story was the stuff of legend.

Corey's teammates—boys he had grown up with—did not turn on him. To the contrary, when they realized he was still the same person ("I didn't come on to you last year in the locker room, and I won't do it now—anyway, who says you're good-looking enough?" he joked in the coming-out meeting), they embraced his uniqueness. They asked for T-shirts from the Ramrod bar. They watched his back when opponents made antigay comments. And on the bus home from one important victory, they serenaded him with "YMCA."

After the *Times* story—and Corey's speech that same afternoon in Washington, D.C., in front of half a million people—he was flooded with 10,000 E-mails. He became gay America's most sought-after speaker. And in the months that followed, hundreds of athletes, young and old, gained the courage to come out to their own teams.

The second major gay male athlete–themed story of the past four years was different. In spring 2001, Brendan Lemon, editor in chief of *Out* magazine, described his romance with an unidentified major league baseball player. That quasi-revelation ignited a media frenzy. A few outlets, primarily in the gay press, concentrated on learning the identity of the closeted athlete, and callers to sports radio shows catering to the lowest common denominator spewed a bit more venom than usual. Most coverage, though, took a more balanced tone by exploring the ethics of outing a boyfriend, the reasons an athlete stays in the closet, and the potential impact on team chemistry and endorsements a player's coming-out can have.

One of the best columns was written by Arthur Martone, sports editor of the *Providence Journal*. Comparing Lemon's boyfriend to Jackie Robinson, who broke the color barrier, or Curt Flood, who fought baseball's slave-like reserve clause—men whose suffering smoothed the road for those who follow—Martone wrote: "If certain [judgmental] segments of society can begin to accept gays on our fields and courts and ice surfaces, they may begin to accept them in the workplaces and supermarkets and shopping malls as well."

A similar quote came from St. Louis Cardinals pitcher Mike Timlin. Asked how he would feel about having a gay teammate, he said, "I already have, knowingly, and it wasn't a problem." San Francisco Giants outfielder Shawon Dunston added, "There's a lot of them playing."

Reaction on Internet chat sites was also, for the most part, intelligently nuanced. One contributor to ESPN.com wrote, "I'm interested in athletic accomplishments, not sexual prowess. The only difference it [a favorite athlete coming out] would make to me would be to raise my level of respect for the person. I can't imagine the abuse that guy would suffer." Another said, "For someone to say it is OK for 'heroes' to sleep with dozens or even hundreds of women, abuse women and children, do drugs to no end, commit an endless list of crimes, and then say it is not all right to be with someone of the same sex is both hypocritical and extremely close-minded."

There were, of course, a few postings like this: "Being gay doesn't make [someone] a bad person. Though I would respect his decision, I wouldn't wear his jersey because I don't want to be affiliated with someone whose morals contrast with my own." Or this: "There is no place in the sports world for gay athletes. They need to stay in the closet, or they will hear it. I will openly boo any athlete who acknowledges being gay. Even if that athlete was one of my favorite players, he would turn into an enemy."

Yet, tellingly, no one, within baseball or outside, seemed surprised to learn there is at least one gay man starring in America's national pastime. The country has moved far beyond that delusion and seems ready to accept reality. The prevailing view was articulated well by the man who wrote: "I don't care if the guy is gay. Just win some games is all I ask. Give me a team filled with homos and heteros—whatever, but just give me a team that brings me home a championship."

Those were not, of course, the only post-*Jocks* stories—some positive, others negative—to hit the sports pages. Billy Bean, a journeyman baseball player, came out two years after retiring in 1995. Few people had ever heard of him, but as a symbol of the power of the closet (he spent his career isolated from both the sports and gay worlds, to the point of pretending a lover's death never happened), he fit the bill.

Baseball was in the news again in 2001, when the Cubs bought 10 full-page display ads in a local gay paper. The advertising was believed to be the first ever by an American men's pro sports team in an exclusively gay publication. According to the team's manager of special events and entertainment, "It was a no-brainer. Wrigley Field is smack-dab in the middle of the gay neighborhood." The day before Chicago's annual gay pride parade, the Cubs sponsored a promotion called "Out at the Ball Game," setting aside a special section of the stadium for gay fans.

The Minnesota Twins called a similar promotional event "Out in the Stands." Not to be outdone, the Braves supported Atlanta's bid to host the 2006 Gay Games by providing their own section for tickets sold by a local gay group. The same day, the Atlanta Gay Men's Chorus sang the national anthem.

The Cubs, however, took a step backward when pitcher Julian Tavarez lost his cool after Giants fans booed him in San Francisco. They remembered a spring training fight Tavarez (a former Giant) had gotten into with one Giants player as well as when Tavarez had tagged another player tag hard on the forearm. Tavarez replied by saying, "Why should I care about the fans? They're a bunch of ass-holes and faggots here." The media, Cubs president Andy MacPhail, and manager Don Baylor all roundly criticized Tavarez, who quickly apologized.

That was still a step forward from previous "faggot" controversies, such as when Atlanta Braves pitcher John Rocker had mentioned "some queer with AIDS" in a diatribe against New York Mets fans. Likewise, Allen Iverson of basketball's Philadelphia 76ers had included antigay lyrics in his rap album and later called an Indiana fan who heckled him a "faggot," and Sacramento Kings star Jason Williams had said the same about an Asian-American fan. In all three instances it took longer for the sports stars to apologize—and their words seemed less sincere. Williams, for example, could not even utter the word "gay." (He announced he intended no disrespect for "the Asian community or any other community.")

Yet when Wimbledon tennis champion Goran Ivanisevic called a line judge a "faggot" just two months after Tavarez, the remark received little attention. Ivanisevic was a media darling; his derring-do on the court, and charming Croatian accent off it, won over most sports reporters. This was not an isolated incident; earlier in 2001, Ivanisevic likened racket-throwers to "faggots."

A stranger controversy erupted at the University of Virginia over, of all things, a football fight song. For years it has included the line, "We come from Old Vir-Gin-I-A, where all is bright and gay." Since the late 1970s, however, students have emphatically declared their heterosexuality by yelling "Not gay!" In 2000 a group of students drew attention to the homophobic, ignorant, juvenile, and stupid nature of the "Not gay!" chorus. Others quickly defended their right to yell "Not gay!"for a variety of

xii stock reasons: freedom of speech, the importance of fighting the PC police, the tradition of college students saying idiotic things.

The debate soon embraced such topics as the effect the cheer had on gay students, athletes, and coaches at the school, as well as its effect on public perceptions of the highly respected university. There was even a panel discussion with, among others, the soccer goalkeeper who organized a petition drive against the chant. Nothing was decided, of course, but supporters of both sides kept the controversy alive for months in the pages of the *Cavalier Daily*, raising consciousness all across campus.

Other events have also shown how the landscape for gay issues in athletics is changing. In 2000, Rudy Galindo, the openly gay ice skating champion whose routines often include elements from the Village People, Judy Garland, and *The Rocky Horror Picture Show*, revealed that he was HIV-positive. The media reacted with concern and encouragement. The focus was almost entirely on his skating and health, not his sexuality.

Such changes have been noticed by Frank Deford, whom *GQ* magazine has called "the world's greatest sportswriter." His work appears everywhere, including in *Sports Illustrated* and on HBO's *Real Sports with Bryant Gumbel* and National Public Radio's *Morning Edition*. In 1976, Deford wrote a groundbreaking biography of 1920s tennis superstar Bill Tilden. Flamboyant both in public and private, Tilden was eventually arrested—and shunned—as a pedophile. He died, penniless and alone, years before his election into the International Tennis Hall of Fame.

When it was first published, *Big Bill Tilden: The Triumphs and the Tragedy* opened many readers' eyes. Few knew that such a great athlete could have been so "different." Tilden's sexuality had been talked about when he was still a tennis star, yet people forgot about it after he went to jail. The reason, Deford says, is that the subject was taboo.

The fact that there are no openly gay male professional team
sports stars 70 years later does not surprise Deford. "Are there any
openly gay chairmen of the board of Fortune 500 companies? Any
openly gay movie stars?" he counters. "It is still something of a
taboo to talk publicly about."

But, Deford adds, professional athletes have other worries that
chief executives and matinee idols do not: the reactions of teammates and fans. "I think a gay athlete would say, 'Do I need this?
Why take a chance? If I drop a pass, the things I'll have to hear
aren't worth it.'" He also mentions earning power. "Advertisers
don't look for trouble. They follow the path of least resistance, and
signing a gay athlete is not that path."

Deford says that gay athletes are saddled with the public's perception of them as All-American men who always get the prettiest
girls. Though gays in other professions may also fear coming out,
they do not have such a "jarring image" to deal with.

But much has changed from Bill Tilden's days. People are more
aware and accepting of homosexuality. And, Deford notes paradoxi-
cally, if the first pro athlete to come out has a great personality, he
could become a media sensation. "He'll make personal appearances
and be on *David Letterman*. And if he does that, the numskulls in the
crowd will have a tougher time. If he is up-front about himself, how
can anyone hurt him?"

Phil Mushnick, a self-described "radical moderate" who serves
up trenchant analyses of media sports coverage, fan behavior, and
social criticism in the rabidly conservative *New York Post*, carries
Deford's thoughts in a different direction. "The same reason we
ask 'Why are there no openly gay pro sports athletes?' is the
answer to the question: because it's athletics. We're not talking
about accountants or musicians or dry cleaners. There's so much
association with machismo, bravado, and courage, even if most of
that is misdirected."

Still, Mushnick says, the world is ready for a major sports figure to come out. When the AIDS crisis first hit, he says, "everyone had a joke. Then they found out or realized they knew one gay person, or five, and the jokes ended. Today, everyone is comfortable with homosexuality, except for one or two lunkheads who think their kid will get raped. And of course the drunks will always yell things from the stands, but that's because they're drunks."

America, Mushnick says, "is ready for some guy to say, 'I'm gay. I'm not here to change the world. I just want to go to Disney World with my lover.' And if he's batting .320 and in his free agent year, everyone except one Neanderthal owner will want to sign him. Are fans going to boo the gay guy who hits the home run to beat your hated rival? I don't think so. They're going to want his autograph."

There may be a backlash from "Christian right-wing evangelical Anita Bryant–type players" who demand a trade, he says. But eventually, the pro-gay forces will win. "It's like women's suffragists who eventually won. And they won for the right reason: because it's right."

Robert Lipsyte, the man who broke the Corey Johnson story in the mainstream media, has seen vast social changes both inside and outside sports since his first stories appeared. Lipsyte has had a varied career in which he has written about Muhammad Ali, automobile racing, and cancer, as well as award-winning young-adult literature. He is a vocal opponent of coaches who demean young male athletes by calling them "girls," "sissies," or "faggots." The current generation of athletes, he says, does not respond to such negative motivation, and good coaches no longer talk that way.

He calls the attractive, winning Corey Johnson a poster boy for social changes. But Lipsyte is aware that his groundbreaking story may have contributed to a false sense of security among some young athletes. "It's not suddenly easy to come out everywhere. And the media has not really handled gay issues well. Even with Corey and

Billy Bean, there has not been a lot of follow-up. There's been no real attempt to see what's going on. We cover sports in a hack, celebratory, fan 'zine, jock-sniffing, ass-kissing way. There's very little room for realism."

But, Lipsyte says, the sports world has been moving away from its previous position as a character builder, whose role was to prepare American boys for business, the army, and the farm. Sports is now seen entertainment. As such, it includes more women, minorities—and gays.

That's welcome news for all America. It's especially good news for Americans who are gay. Finally, they are being acknowledged— if not by name, at least by presence. Their issues are being discussed, usually rationally. And that affects hundreds of thousands, perhaps even millions, of gay men who are not professional athletes. They are the ones who every day and everywhere in this country swim, run, play hockey, row, shoot hoops, and hit baseballs. Some are in their early teens; others are much older. All share a love of physical activity, a delight in pushing their bodies to the limit, and an attraction to other men that kept them for too long out of locker rooms and off athletic fields. Or else it pushed them into closets even deeper and darker than those in which other gay men cowered.

Now these same gay men are coming out to play. Here are their stories.

Dan Woog
Westport, Conn.

Quadriplegic Football Player Ed Gallagher

When football players Mike Utley and Dennis Byrd suffered devastating spinal cord injuries, sports fans across America prayed for them, followed their progress, and exulted in their smallest victories.

Ed Gallagher was a football player with a similar paralyzing injury. Far fewer fans heard of his plight, however. The national media offered no updates on his condition, never chronicled his battle to reclaim control over his life. Politicians and ordinary Americans did not send flowers, leave encouraging messages, or organize fund-raisers. In fact, very few teammates or opponents even bothered to write.

One reason may be that Mike Utley and Dennis Boyd were professional football linemen for the Detroit Lions and New York Jets, respectively, while Ed Gallagher's career peaked as a scholarship athlete for the University of Pittsburgh.

Another reason, however, might relate to the injuries themselves. In 1991 Mike Utley fractured his sixth and seventh cervical vertebrae in a regular season game against the Los Angeles Rams. A year later, Dennis Byrd was partially paralyzed in a collision with a teammate during a game against Kansas City.

Ed Gallagher's story was different. In 1985 he threw himself off a dam in a desperate suicide attempt, 12 days after having the first same-sex experience of his life.

The steps Ed climbed to the top of the 110-foot-high Kensico Dam in Valhalla, New York, were swift and sure. The road he has traveled since then—after becoming the first person ever to survive a leap off that Westchester County structure—has been long, slow, and hard. Ed, paralyzed for life from his chest down, has taken his wheelchair to places he never imagined he would go. He visits gay bars in New York City, where for the first time in his life he is meeting men who find him attractive and who turn him on too. But he spends far more time talking to schools and civic organizations throughout the tri-state region, encouraging people of all ages to face their feelings rather than repress them. With full openness and brutal honesty, he discusses three important elements of his life: suicide, disability, and homosexuality.

As different as Ed's life is today, it is a stroll in the park compared with his first 27 years. And his perpetual smile tells all who meet him that the quadriplegic, openly gay Ed Gallagher of today is a far happier human being than yesterday's confused, closeted, perpetually frightened football player.

His story begins in North White Plains, a leafy suburb half an hour north of Manhattan where Ed grew up. His father, a World War II pilot, met his mother, a dental hygienist, on V-E Day. After the war his father entered the hardware and appliance business, while his mother stayed home to raise three children. As the youngest child, and only son, Ed admits he was spoiled. He was in many ways a typical boy, wild at times, with girls on his mind. He loved Gale Storm and Loretta Young—any woman, really, with red lipstick and nail polish—and often pleaded with a sister to put on lipstick, so he could kiss her the way Hercules kissed his women in the movies. At 14, when he discovered the joys of masturbation, he was turned on by "everything and everyone." His first fantasies were of females, but after he developed a crush on a male friend, Ed began masturbating to images of men too.

The early 1970s were a confusing time for Ed. He was growing quite tall but remained very skinny, so he felt awkward. He could not talk in class without blushing. No one in his family discussed the one subject constantly on his mind—sex—and none of the boys in the neighborhood did either. "I hear people talk all the time about how they did circle jerks when they were kids," he says today. "I never knew anything about that. All I did was go home after school, close the door, and jerk off alone."

Though Ed's sports background had been limited to Little League baseball, one of the first things he did after entering Valhalla High School was join the football team. "Like most kids at that age, I needed an identity," he explains. "I also think I wanted to fulfill people's expectations of me. I was big, lanky, and uncoordinated, but the coaches thought I might develop."

As a sophomore defensive end in 1972, he played on the 0-7 junior varsity team. The next year, when varsity coach Ron Berlingo took him under his wing, matters improved. Moved to defensive tackle, Ed felt more confident. The varsity team was only 1-7, but Ron was an excellent coach. The next year, Ed's senior season, the Vikings went 7-2. His personal achievements mirrored his team's: Ed earned All-County and All-State honors.

Football provided many things Ed needed: an encouraging mentor in Ron Berlingo, friendship and camaraderie, physical activity, physical fitness, self-confidence and self-esteem, recognition from classmates. And something just as important, but at the time less recognizable, than all that.

"When I was struggling with my sexuality, football was a great way to tackle gorgeous running backs and get away with it," Ed laughs. "I admit it, football was part sexual for me, even though I didn't think of it that way then. I know I had crushes on guys across the line from me."

Those feelings, however, terrified Ed. He heard Coach Berlingo, a man he admired, try to motivate his team by saying, "Come on, don't block like a faggot." He knew his teammates wondered why such a strong, good-looking, well-respected athlete seldom dated. And the more confused Ed got, the more he shut down.

"I still had crushes on girls, but I was more and more attracted to guys," he says. "Of course, I had no idea what I would have done

4 if I ever got a chance with any of them. I don't even know how much I actually even wanted to be with them. It was more like they were part of my fantasy world when I masturbated. Now I know lots of kids have feelings like that, but at the time I was so worried, I made sure that if I ejaculated thinking about a guy, the next time I came I had to be thinking about a female. That doesn't make a lot of sense, until you realize all I was trying to do was organize my own chaos."

Ed felt accepted as part of the Valhalla football team, but he also knew an invisible wall separated him from everyone else on the squad. He never felt complete. "I always wore a Halloween mask," he says. "That's OK one day a year, but I had mine on every day of the year."

He feared that if anyone discovered his fantasies—"found out I was headed in that direction," he calls it—his life would be destroyed. "Football can be a brutal sport for kids," he says. "You have to be like everyone else, or suffer the consequences. I think a lot of kids, at my high school and every other one, shared some of what I was going through, but we all shared it alone. The biggest orgasm in the world for me would have been if I was able to talk about what I was feeling, but I knew I couldn't. I saw all the jocks on the light beer commercials, and I knew that was what I had to emulate."

His saving grace, he says, is that he was not effeminate. He knew he did not want to wear dresses, so in his mind he rationalized he was not "one of them." At the same time, he crawled into bed many nights with his stomach tied in knots. Over and over he asked himself, *What the fuck am I going to do?*

Somehow he got through senior year. He joined the track team as a shot putter and discus thrower. He went to the prom with a girl who liked him. He had no sexual contact with anyone, and graduated from high school a virgin.

After gaining All-State recognition Ed was recruited by some of the nation's top football colleges, including Boston College,

Syracuse, Penn State, Maryland, and Duke. He chose the University of Pittsburgh, in part because head coach Johnny Majors and three assistants came to his house and showed highlight films of current star (and future Heisman Trophy winner) Tony Dorsett. The economy played a role too. Ed's father had suffered business reversals, and was ill. Pitt's offer of a full scholarship was hard to turn down.

Ed's worries about his father's health were not new. For years—ever since a fourth grade classmate's father died—Ed had been preoccupied with death. He watched *Marcus Welby, M.D.* religiously and spent two years convinced that a cyst in his armpit meant he had terminal cancer. As with his same-sex feelings, however, Ed could not imagine anyone in whom he could confide his fears.

He entered Pitt in the fall of 1975 consumed with worries. He asked himself, *How can I keep playing this game?* The "game," of course, was really two: football and pretending not to be attracted to men. He worried about his health, and the health of those around him. And he worried about being a virgin.

He describes his four years at Pitt as "good and bad." The bad part came on days when all he wanted was to stand outside and yell "Homosexual!" He had no idea how that would feel, but he was desperate to try. One March day in 1976, in the middle of spring football, he walked off campus, found a phone booth, and called a counseling office in downtown Pittsburgh. Choking on each word, he told the woman who answered, "I think I might be a little bit queer."

"That was all I said," he recalls. "I didn't continue the conversation. But it felt so good to know that someone—even some anonymous person—knew about me and didn't keel over and die." That day, Ed says, he "popped an internal balloon with a verbal pin." That tiny act of desperation helped get him through the rest of spring.

Still, he did not consider himself gay, for one reason: He had never even touched another male. Looking back, he knows there were opportunities—in fact, he could have had flings with several

6   teammates—but he could not imagine the consequences. He feared admitting he was gay even to himself. He feared social isolation, if anyone found out. And he feared the loss of his scholarship.

On the field, Ed had a checkered career. His junior year, standing 6-6 and weighing 275, he started 11 games at left offensive tackle. He was benched for the nationally televised Penn State contest—the coaches claimed he had missed some blocks against Army—but regained his starting spot for the post-season Tangerine Bowl.

On the second day of training camp as a senior, however, Ed ripped calf muscles doing a seven-man sled drill. Three weeks later, favoring that side, he did the same thing to the other calf. There was also a new line coach, and he and Ed clashed. Needless to say, his senior football season was disappointing.

His last year in college, Ed found a girlfriend. They had good times, he says, but their sex was more of a release for him than anything else. In fact, he compares it to lifting weights. "It was a physical outlet, really. I tried so hard to act cool, be detached, that even when I had an orgasm, it was not a totally orgasmic feeling." However, he admits, "I don't know if things would have been any different with a guy. I've always been a loner."

On the other hand, Ed regrets missed opportunities. "I had the physical balls, but not the psychological balls, to make it happen. It would have been nice to play both sides of the fence, and find out where I was really going." He regrets never giving himself the chance. "I was just too caught up in the whole jock image," he says.

Still, Ed was not through with football. The year after he graduated, an agent called to arrange a tryout with the New York Jets. Ed spent nearly three weeks in camp, going against the likes of Mark Gastineau, before Coach Walt Michaels released him. "I had to try it," Ed says. "I had gone from being a horrible jayvee player to getting an NFL tryout. That's a pretty good accomplishment, I think."

When he was cut by the Jets, Ed felt almost gleeful. Now, he told himself, he could live the life he was always meant to live. He looked forward to going places, meeting men, experimenting sexually.

But it did not happen. Instead, Ed went right back to his old ways. He found comfort doing physical, nonintellectual work, first as a bouncer, then in moving and storage. Those were not bad jobs—Ed got along with his coworkers, and knew he was not cut out for a suit-and-tie position—but at the same time it was not what he wanted to do with his life.

In addition to hiding his sexuality, Ed felt suffocated by another closet: No one knew he was a writer. An English writing major in college, he began composing poems. After John Lennon's murder, he tried songwriting. For Ed, those were important ways of communicating. Still, he remained somewhat silent. He never spoke or wrote the word "gay."

Not until 1985, when Ed was 27 years old—and after several girlfriends—did he have his first same-sex experience. It started when he signed up for Saturday morning songwriting classes in New York City. This was not something he told his fellow movers about, but he enjoyed going in to the city. His classmates and teachers appreciated his writing, and in class and afterward, wandering around New York, he saw people he thought might be gay. He was still too frightened to approach any of them, but simply knowing they were there was a source of comfort.

On February 16, Ed ate dinner by himself, then walked around Greenwich Village. He gathered enough courage to enter a gay club, and ordered a drink. It was only his second time in a gay establishment—he had walked into a bar once to use the bathroom—and although he did not want to talk to anyone, he felt at peace. Seeing other gay people who were at ease with themselves, he felt less alone. A young man struck up a conversation. Ed was so naïve he did not realize he was being cruised.

After a few drinks, the man invited Ed home. Ed said no, but the

8   man persisted. Finally, he told the former football player: "Come on. I'll just suck you off, if that's all you want."

Ed told him he had never done anything with a guy, but the man was relentless. Finally, Ed says, "My emotions overruled my intellect. I figured, yeah, it'll be nice to get my dick sucked. I'm 27. I ought to do it."

Until that night, Ed had never kissed a man. He had never played with a man's penis. In fact, other than brief glimpses in locker rooms, he had never seen another penis up close. The man who took Ed home was true to his word, and limited himself to oral sex. Later, Ed reciprocated. Everything was new.

The next morning around 8, Ed felt strange. He told the man, "I gotta go lift weights," and abruptly left. He wanted to return as soon as possible to his familiar, secure way of life.

In Grand Central Station, Ed felt lonely. He told himself he had deceived many people. Looking back, he says, those feelings were wrong. "What had I really done?" he asks rhetorically. "I was a guy trying to have fun, just like anybody else. But ever since adolescence I'd had this self-punishing side to me, and waiting there in the station I got more and more nervous."

Inside the train, things were no better. A *Village Voice* lay on the seat, and the headline screamed out at him. "What's Wrong With the AIDS Blood Test?" it asked. The night before, Ed had not worried about AIDS—in fact, his partner had assured him "I'm OK"—but suddenly Ed convinced himself that he had been infected with the deadly virus.

Guilt and grief overwhelmed him. How, he wondered, would he ever be able to hug his mother again? How could he use the same toilet seat as his roommates? And how could he live without being able to tell anyone about those powerful fears? He rode the train home terrified.

Back in White Plains, things got worse. "Holy fucking shit, what have I done?" Ed asked himself. "I'm a pariah, poison, a bastard who deceived everyone." He shakes his head in wonderment, recalling those dark days. "It was all so wrong," he says. "I didn't have AIDS. I had oral sex. And even if I had tested positive, what was the big deal?"

Suicide, Ed says, is a sign of immaturity. It represents an inability to look at life's problems in more than one way. It is the worst, most cowardly way of running away.

But Ed ran. He was petrified of the future. He could not imagine dealing with the headlines he thought were imminent: "Bud Gallagher's Son, A Faggot, Dies of AIDS." There was, he thought, a way to prevent that. Another headline might look better: "Ed Gallagher, Former Pitt Football Player, Despondent, Commits Suicide."

"Twisted, isn't it?" he asks. "But I was so scared of hurting other people. And I so did not want to be gay. Nowadays people ask me why I didn't talk to someone. Well, even if knew who to talk to, what would I have said? 'How can I take my blow job back?' I couldn't say that. In my mind, I was now one of 'them.' "

Eleven days after that first encounter, on February 28, Ed picked up a baseball bat, swung it against the side of his head, and dazed himself. His heart fluttered, and he tasted blood. He went upstairs, watched television—and could not believe he did not have even a slight headache. ("I guess football gave me a hard head," he jokes.) However, he told himself he was dying, so he wrote a series of please-forgive-me notes, placed them under his bed, lay down, and waited for death.

That night he had the strangest dream of his life. Beautiful, angelic figures surrounded him and told him everything would be fine. He should have taken it as a positive sign, he says, but he did not. Instead, when a ringing telephone woke him the next morning, he was still alive. He could not have been more angry, or depressed.

"It's March 1," he remembers telling himself. "You've gotta start the month out right." He knew his sister, brother-in-law, and nephew would arrive soon from upstate. If he died that day, they would be together to console each other.

Ed drove to a cemetery, intending to cut his wrists. But he couldn't do it; it would take too long to die. So he drove to the nearby Kensico Dam. Once he jumped, he knew he would be unable to change his mind.

The choice of the dam was also symbolic. Just a mile away stood Valhalla High School, the place he had become an All-County and All-State football player. *Yeah, spit on this fuckin' reputation,* he said to himself. *I don't want it. Football is part of the reason I'm in this situation.* That was not true, he says now, but at the time he thought it was.

"In a twisted, cowardly way," he notes, "I thought I would be sending a positive message to parents, to talk to their kids about feelings. I realize a much better way to do it is the way I've done for the last 15 years—in person, face-to-face—but I was scared out of my mind. A voice inside kept telling me I had to jump."

March 1 was a beautiful day. Ed walked past a lovely picnic area. A medical student, feeling lonely and depressed himself, saw Ed mount the steps. The student wanted to say something but did not. Instead he sat down to eat lunch. Suddenly he heard an awful noise. Looking up in horror, he watched Ed bounce off the dam, 20 and 30 feet at a time. Finally, after what seemed an eternity, he landed, 90 feet from where he started.

Despite a broken wrist, ankle, and neck, Ed was alive. His spinal injuries were the worst. His vertebrae snapped at the C6-C7 levels, rendering him a quadriplegic. Incredibly, however, Ed was not only conscious, but coherent. "Did I do it?" he asked, when the medical student reached him.

"Yeah," the man said.

"Am I going to die?" Ed asked.

"I don't think so," replied the man.

Ed spent the next five months at Westchester Medical Center in Valhalla, punching doctors, nurses, and anyone else he could. With a tracheotomy tube in his throat and metal rods in his head, that was no easy task. Most of the time he lay flat on his back, counting tiles in the ceiling. He was still suicidal, but now faced an added worry: how to explain his botched attempt. It was a horrible situation. He loved his parents but hated having them see him like that—and being unable to tell them why. He still thought he had AIDS, was worried now that they would find out, and lay immobilized with a spinal cord injury as well. More than ever he wanted to die.

As he had for so many years, Ed remained silent. One nurse, however, chipped away with questions and drew a bit of information out of him. She told Ed that, based on the evidence she saw, he did not have AIDS. In 1985, however, there was limited information on the disease, so he remained unassured.

Finally, after half a year of agony, Ed's life changed in an unexpected way. Bedsores on his left heel led to osteomyelitis, and Ed asked what kind of drugs would help. A doctor, tired of Ed's belligerent manner, snarled, "Hey, Gallagher, what we're talking about is amputation." He pointed to Ed's knee. "Amputation up to here."

Ed panicked. He had spent several months paralyzed from his chest down, cursing God. Suddenly, however, he realized he did not want to make his life any worse than it was. Somehow, he said to himself, he had to keep his broken body whole. In a flash, he understood he had already done enough damage, to himself and others. Silently, he prayed: *Please God—if you're there—don't let them take my leg. I'll try again. Come on, God!*

His prayers were answered. Infectious disease specialists removed a small part of the bone (without anesthesia, for all Ed feels from his

12 chest down is pins and needles), and prescribed antibiotics. "That was it," Ed says simply. "All of a sudden I was jolted back to reality."

In September 1985 he entered The Burke Rehabilitation Hospital in White Plains, vowing to be a bit more open about who he was. He could not yet talk about homosexuality—the subject still frightened him—but at least he knew he had time. He began writing poems, and books of aphorisms. He spoke on a radio show, discussing suicide prevention. He made friends at the hospital and gradually felt better about himself.

As with any recovery process there were peaks and valleys, but in February 1986—11 months after throwing himself off the dam—Ed left the hospital and moved into his parents' apartment. Life was odd there—his parents still did not know the reasons behind Ed's suicide attempt—but he started the process of building a new life.

It was not easy. Ed still thought he might be dying of AIDS; he continued to punish himself for his homosexual feelings ("Even after breaking my friggin' neck!" he marvels today), but slowly he opened up. A year and a half after his suicide attempt, he told a psychiatrist about the same-sex experience that precipitated it. Ed realized that he needed to find a purpose in life, and gradually he found it. That purpose was to help people through their own crises. Ed learned he had a talent for that. He found too that by helping others, he helped himself.

In 1991 HBO aired a documentary, *Suicide Notes*. For the first time, Ed talked publicly about how his gay experience contributed to his suicide attempt. To his surprise, he received excellent feedback from across the country. That represented another turning point in his life. "We all need self-esteem, a sense of purpose, something to keep up going," he says. "I needed to know that, after such a catastrophic blunder, what I was doing counted. Otherwise, I probably would have just sat around and spun my wheels—and I don't mean in my wheelchair."

Despite the positive response to his openness, however, Ed has heard from very few teammates and coaches. In fact, during his entire ordeal, the football world basically stayed away. Attempted suicide, he surmises, was too frightening for big, tough jocks to handle. (His former high school coach, Ron Berlingo, did visit him in the hospital as soon as he could. His first words to Ed were: "What was it, a girl?" All Ed could croak was, "No.")

In fact, since coming out publicly, only one ex-teammate has confided in Ed about his own same-sex feelings. Today the two men joke about which former players were cute. Otherwise, when old teammate calls, the conversation never touches on anything personal. Especially, Ed says, something as personal as sexuality.

Nevertheless, sex is always part of their lives. Ed notes, "Sports in itself is very sexual. Practicing and playing are a great release. I think many guys struggle with their sexuality, and for them sports is their orgasm. They can be silent, strong, and detached—and get off not with guys, but with games."

When he talks in schools, Ed watches athletic-looking students for their reactions. Most seem friendly. Often, they hang around when he is finished and shake his hand. "I think when I say that I had straight fantasies and gay fantasies, that might relieve some of their own personal struggles," Ed says. "I know it's not true for everyone, but I think I'm touching some nerves. And those are the nerves I wish I could have touched when I was 14, 15, 16 years old. All I do is try to say we're all human, we're all sexual, and labels do nothing but pigeonhole people. Labeling is so destructive. A human being is not a label, he's a vast array of talent and potential. That's all I'm trying to get across."

Unfortunately, Ed says, while understanding looks in the classroom are one thing, it is entirely different trying to change the culture of the football field and locker room. "I just don't think people can be totally open in the football world. Someone who came out

14 would probably get ridiculed. There's still that phony Joe Jock atmosphere: 'Be a warrior, kill whoever you can, be detached about everything.' I know there's a lot more than 'a football player' in any one person, but getting football players and coaches to understand that is not easy."

That does not mean Ed will stop trying. "I think what's needed is someone like myself to keep knocking on the door, saying, 'It's OK to be gay. I've learned a lot. I almost killed myself out of fear and desperation, trying to fulfill other people's expectations and win their approval.' It would be nice if someone said, 'Screw this million-dollar contract, this is who I am and I'm proud of it,' but I don't think it's going to happen. So myself and people like me just have to keep saying it's OK to be who you are, don't worry about it, your life will still be OK."

Despite those harsh words, Ed still considers himself a football fan—to a point. He likes watching games, knowing how hard it is to compete and what it takes to win. At the same time, however, he is annoyed at "the superficial narcissism, the whole jock mentality" of the sport. On the other hand, he says, "I also get annoyed with certain members of the gay community, from time to time. They're not perfect either. I get tired of guys who are only out to get their dicks sucked, guys who are totally self-pleasing without any regard for anyone else."

Part of that annoyance might stem from jealousy. "Every part of me doesn't feel the way it used to," he admits. "I've had plenty of good experiences with men since I've been paralyzed, and it's good—I'm glad people are still attracted to me in my wheelchair, and that I'm attracted to them—but I do have a lack of sensation. People say, 'Well, an orgasm isn't just in your dick, it's in your head too,' but I ask them, 'When was the last time your head exploded?' Something good has come of all this: I've learned not to measure every aspect of sexuality by my dick, but my dick is still a part of me."

While Ed does not consider himself a member of the gay community, neither does he identify with the disabled community. "I'm Ed Gallagher," he says simply. "I express my views as a man who is gay and a man who has a disability, but I don't like to put myself in any clubs or cliques. We're all human beings, apart from any labels. That's what life is all about."

For over a decade, Ed has tried to get that message out to as many people as possible. He has written three books, including the very graphic, semi-autobiographical novel *Johnny in the Spot*. In 1989 he formed Alive to Thrive, an organization promoting suicide prevention, emotional and sexual health, creativity, and the free expression and rights of all individuals. The group includes Hector Del Valle, a former drug and alcohol abuser who became a quadriplegic in a 1982 automobile accident, and Lisa Tarricone, paralyzed in 1985 during a hiking trip when she slipped off a 100-foot cliff. In addition to speaking, the organization maintains an informational and inspirational Web site (www.alivetothrive.org).

Ed has spoken nationally. He has appeared on *20/20 Downtown* and Howard Stern's radio show. *Mr. Ed's Corral*, his Westchester County cable access TV show, "explores such topics as rape, intimacy, and body fitness. As often as possible, Ed ties sexuality in with other issues, in a nonthreatening way. "It's not about 'me, me, me,' but about what's going on with you, you, you," he explains. "Everyone has unique feelings, and they should feel comfortable with them. But at the same time, having feelings is universal. We should all know that too."

A decade and a half after inner demons chased him to the top of an enormous dam, Ed Gallagher is at peace—with the world he inhabits and, more importantly, his inner self. He has a simple philosophy on life, and his role in it. "I'm going to say what I feel, and what I feel needs to be said," he explains. "If I drop dead tomorrow, I want to go out knowing I'm somewhere on the path I want to be.

16 "Through all I've been through, I've learned that human beings are very complex. All of us need to find someone we can talk to and trust. At the same time, we all need to look in the mirror and accept who and what we see there. We can't punish ourselves for the reflection, or for what we think we should see. That isn't what life is about."

And no one on earth knows better than Ed Gallagher what it means to live.

Ironman
Christopher Bergland

In the mid 1980s, Christopher Bergland was a student at the exclusive Choate boarding school—John F. Kennedy's alma mater—and hating every minute there. He was drinking seven days a week, depressed beyond belief, and completely asexual.

Ten years later he completed—and won—a Triple Ironman in Hawaii. He swam 7.2 miles, bicycled 336 miles, and completed a 78.6 mile run in 38 hours and 46 minutes.

That feat—which translates into swimming the Hudson River from Ground Zero all the way north to Grant's Tomb; hopping on a bike and pedaling down to Richmond, then running all the way to the University of Virginia at Charlottesville, a couple of hours away by car—makes Christopher Bergland arguably the greatest athlete in the world.

Of course, he no longer drinks; instead, he fills his days eating healthy food and maintaining a rigorous training routine. The demons of depression have not been completely exorcised—much of that disease is genetic and can be controlled but not eliminated—yet the endorphin rush he enjoys from physical exertion overwhelms the negative chemicals, enabling him to embrace life with confidence and enthusiasm. And today Christopher is hardly asexual.

In fact, the Triple Ironman champion—the man who symbolizes pushing the human body to its absolute limit and facing the ultimate physical challenges and overcoming them, the man who "out-machos" the most macho of men—is gay.

Talk about turning stereotypes on their head.

For Christopher, the Triple Ironman and other events like the triathlon may be a mere stroll through the park, although for

18 most people they would be unfathomably difficult. Christopher even characterizes the events and training for them as "super-sexy." He adds, "We train hard, we're in good shape, and yeah, I see a hot guy on the beach and I fantasize about him. But there's more to it than just sex. Behind the veneer of someone's face and body is the knowledge that he's been through a lot; he's trained incredibly hard to get where he is. I find those interior landscapes amazingly intriguing. I know that if someone is attracted to me, it's partly because there's a mystery surrounding me and my intense physical quest. Well, I see that in others. I want to get inside them and find out what makes them tick. And if it's an elite athlete who's really cute, I want to figure out even more how he got where he is."

Christopher is really cute himself. He has shining eyes, curly blond hair, and a sculpted body that actually gets used outside the gym. And the story of how he got where he is today is at least as interesting as any competitor's tale.

A New York City native, Christopher was born to a neurosurgeon father and microbiology researcher mother who divorced when he was young. His first masturbation magazines featured women because those were publications most readily available. When a year or so later he saw photographs of naked men, he began fantasizing about them. That caused no shame—in fact, he felt quite comfortable with who he was—but for many years he had no compulsion to act on his desires.

Christopher describes his Choate years bleakly. "My friends and I hovered in dark places. We were cynical, jaded, and self-destructive. I didn't give a shit about anything. I spent lots of time alone, listening to music. I was very introverted and introspective." Christopher is unsure how much his behavior had to do with sexuality issues, how much was related to his depression, and how much was normal teenage angst. Whatever the reason, he says that he "shut down" at boarding school, curling up into a protective ball against a fierce outside world.

He had no sexual experiences of any kind at Choate. He drank every day during his final two years, and although he did not smoke much pot, he earned a reputation as a burnout. Teachers and administrators, he says, basically threw up their hands and tried to ignore him.

To his amazement, Christopher managed to get into college. He calls Hampshire College, an ultra-liberal school in western Massachusetts, "a godsend. For the first time in my life I had freedom to create my own thing." That led to a newfound passion for learning.

Despite his growth in certain intellectual areas, Christopher was still not ready to embrace other people or even make his own emotional acquaintance. He rose early, spent much of his time studying alone, and ate sparse vegetarian meals. "I was cracking a whip over my monkish self," he says. His major—philosophy—was well-suited to a solitary lifestyle.

Hampshire had a thriving intramural program and a noted ultimate Frisbee team, but the physical activity Christopher chose was typically solitary: He ran.

One reason he started running, he says, was to purify himself from all his boarding-school abuses. Combined with his healthy diet and the pure New England air, for the first time he felt physically good. But running was also, he says, "part of my attempt to be perfect in every way. I'd gone from a reckless, unmotivated, self-destructive person to someone who was the exact opposite. I started out so maniacally, it took me a while to find a happy medium."

When he found that balance, he was enthralled. He discovered the bliss of achieving a flowing, all-encompassing state; dreamful yet awake, he was conscious of every part of the world around him. He was able to work through much of his "life stuff" without consciously thinking about it. He still bore the scars of his Choate

20 experience—it had crushed him into the ground, he says, making him feel useless and worthless—but running came naturally to him, and it made him feel good. On one level, running to a certain point and then returning was tangible proof he could do whatever he wanted. On another level, it was beyond explanation. When Christopher ran he felt connected with the sky, the earth, the entire universe.

But he still did not feel connected to any form of sexuality. As radical as Hampshire was, he says it was also an "asexual" place—and running, to him, was the ultimate asexual activity. So the bright, articulate, sensitive young man remained sexually dead. He derived a strange sort of steely ascetic pleasure from denying himself sex. He took a perverse pride in not having crushes on anyone. And he certainly did not identify with any type of gay community.

Then came Provincetown.

Christopher had graduated from Hampshire in three years, then spent the next three in Los Angeles. But in 1988 he returned to New York, and that summer traveled to Cape Cod's gay mecca. There, he finally raced out of the closet.

Back in New York that fall, he worked as a waiter in a chic West Village restaurant and joined a trendy gym. He did not realize how fast he could run on a treadmill, but another man did. Jonathan Cane was completing a Ph.D. program in exercise physiology, and asked Christopher for permission to test his lung capacity. Jonathan was amazed by Christopher's score: The numbers suggested he had the potential to be an elite runner. Jonathan offered to coach Christopher, and make him a superstar. "We're friends now, but for a while I thought he was living vicariously through me," Christopher says. "I'm not a win-win-win guy, but he was. I did win a lot of Central Park races, but he was way more into it than I was." Even today, with all his success, Christopher says that the act of training is more important to him than the accumulation of trophies.

Despite his disavowal of competition, Christopher continued to race. In 1992 in Washington, D.C., he entered his first marathon He completed the 26.2 mile course in 2:41, an excellent time for anyone but phenomenal for a first-time marathoner. A race of that distance often takes even veteran runners by surprise. Particularly difficult is "the wall," an almost physical barrier that strikes even experienced athletes around the 20-mile mark. But, as Christopher explains, "I enjoyed it. People gravitate to what they do well, and I finally learned what my talent is. I'm blessed genetically, I have good bio-mechanics, and I have the right 'system.'"

Those gifts also made Christopher an excellent triathlete. In 1994 he won a Gay Games gold medal in that grueling sport, which combines a 0.9-mile swim, a 25-mile bike ride and a 6.2-mile run. (Because New York's EMTs never showed up to provide coverage for the swim, that portion was replaced with another run.) His closest competitor trailed three minutes behind.

Within a year, Christopher was ready to tackle a breathtakingly more demanding event. The Ironman begins with a 2.4-mile swim, continues with a 112-mile bike ride, and ends with a full marathon. A world-class time is eight hours. Christopher finished his inaugural Ironman in 10:41, remarkable for a rookie.

But Christopher was not content to stop at that level. Three years later he entered a Double Ironman—a 4.8-mile swim, 224-mile bike ride, and 52.4-mile run—and placed third. Then in the fall of 2000 he accepted the ultimate challenge: a Triple Ironman. Contemplating such an event is hard enough; actually finishing is a spectacular achievement. Winning a Triple Ironman defies belief.

Christopher, however, downplays even that achievement. "It's pretty exciting and terrifying to compete, but after I finished, I didn't think it was that hard. I always want to raise the bar and prove I can do something harder. When I'm in the middle of an Ironman, even though I want to stop, I push my body to the max, and I transcend those thoughts. I plow through them, and in the end I come out a stronger person."

Because his father is a neuroscientist, Christopher grew up surrounded by discussions of mind mechanics and brain chemistry. Today, he understands firsthand exactly what his father meant. "Exercise is so good for my head. I think my brain has been rewired over the years," Christopher explains. "From that rewiring, endurance sports have fostered my ability to choose the perspective from which I view reality. Now I'm in the driver's seat. I've learned from doing Ironman races how, in the face of adversity, I can anchor myself to the place inside me where I feel safe, where pain and suffering are inconsequential, where no matter what obstacles are thrown at me, I just keep moving forward and ride it out."

But chemicals and brain rewiring go only so far to explain Ironman's almost mystical hold on Christopher. There is another element to Christopher's passion, and the former philosophy major thinks often about the link between his athletic accomplishments and his sexuality. "I don't know exactly how close the connection is between my intense training and my being gay, but I do know the stereotype that gay people are wimp sissies is untrue. We actually are very tough—we've got a lot of tenacity. For myself, I set up every day of training based on my belief that the human will can prevail over any circumstance. I know that if I want something bad enough I can achieve it.

"Not to get too psychoanalytical, but I think that most gay people develop a real mental toughness to survive in a predominantly heterosexual world. Some of my coworkers jokingly call me 'Ironman Barbie,' because to them being a gay Ironman seems like a contradiction or oxymoron. But to me it seems so painfully obvious how I, as a gay person, would choose this sport, and how I will always feel a need to prove myself by going further, being stronger, and running faster."

Still, Christopher is not ready to be a poster boy for gay athletes. When he meets new people he never mentions his Ironman feats. He has seen the reactions—it takes others a long time to reconcile the ideas that he is both a world-class athlete and gay—and it gets tiring trying to help them understand that.

"I don't talk about it a lot," he says. "A lot of triathletes can be pretty geeky people: 'I'm a stockbroker by day, a triathlete by night.' It sounds like a personal ad. I don't want to be like that. What I do is so important to me, I don't want to use it just to get some guy. The sport of triathlon is sacred to me. I don't feel right parading it around."

There is another reason: Despite his amazing accomplishments, Christopher still has difficulty thinking of himself as an icon. "I'm in good shape, but I'm not a big G.I. Joe muscle boy like you see at the gym. I know my body type is not a lot of gay people's choice for what a hot, sexy guy is."

He knows too that his workouts are different from most other men's. At the Chelsea Piers Gym, where he works out "insanely," he looks around at the pumped bodies, none of them sweating, and understands that he is there for a different reason. "I'm hyperfocused, drenched in sweat, on the bike for three hours, and I'm not cruising." To draw less attention to himself, he belongs to three gyms. "That way, people don't think I'm crazy," he says. "They don't know I spend two or three hours a day at two or three different gyms." A typical day might include a two-hour bike ride, 30-minute run, hour-long swim and one hour of weight lifting. When he is in serious training for an Ironman—and Christopher has competed in nearly a dozen, as far away as Germany, South Africa, Australia and New Zealand—he spends up to eight hours a day, six days a week, on cardiovascular work alone.

He also works three days a week at Kiehl's, a 150-year-old East Village shop owned by a former Olympic skier. ("I'm a triathlete

24 who sells soap and eye cream," he laughs. "How gay is that?"). Nonetheless, he finds time for an active social life. "It's weird how many hours there are in a day," Christopher says. "My energy level can be an issue after working out all day, but I have lots of friends."

What he does not have is a boyfriend. "I probably could find time for that too, but it just hasn't happened. It's taken a long time, but I've finally gotten very good at fulfilling my life. I like my life so much now and have so much joy in what I do. I like being a free agent. Boyfriends bring me headaches. They tie me down. Don't get the wrong idea: I'm a hopeless romantic, but it's hard to find people I really, really like."

It is also hard to find other gay triathletes. In that rarefied world, Christopher says, he has no idea who else is gay. In fact, he does not even know how many fellow competitors know about him. "I'd like to have 'gay' be identified with me, but I don't know how to go about it," he confesses. "My big fantasy is to bring someone I'm dating to the Triple Ironman in Hawaii and hold hands at the awards banquet. It would be romantic for me, and I'd like to see everyone's reactions."

One reason Christopher is not fully out has to do with the background of most triathletes. The white upper-class world of triathlons attracts very driven people who have succeeded in many other areas of life. They have plenty of money to spend on equipment, lots of time to train alone, and although they are friendly, they are not used to spending time talking about personal issues. When they gather for competitive events, they are too focused to talk about anything beyond their sport.

The Gay Games, where Christopher has won two gold medals, are in some ways different but in other ways not. He was proud to compete, and he enjoyed the camaraderie, excitement, and spirited opening and closing ceremonies, but he never felt a need to go beyond the games and truly bond with anyone. He explains: "Being the fastest gay person—that's not really significant to me. It almost feels like the Special Olympics. Not to sound like a jerk, but why are we separated from straight athletes?"

Ideally, Christopher says, he would like to see openly gay people competing with and against straight people at the Olympics. He does not know when or if that will happen, but he would love being part—even though he has no idea how. The conflicts return as he says, "I don't know how to tell people who it is I sleep with. And I don't know how appropriate that would be in the sports environment."

Ultimately, for Christopher, sports transcend sexuality. Running, biking, and swimming carry him to a mystical place. He arrives there unmotivated by money, consumerism, the desire to win or the fear of losing. It is a place where he can be philosophical and meditative, where he feels peace and joy. It is a place far removed from Choate, where Christopher felt so dark and alone, and from Hampshire, where he turned so inward he took pleasure in denying himself the joy of sexuality.

Former philosophy major Christopher Bergland still lacks a full, complete explanation as to where, how and why his athletic passions intersect with his carnal desires. But he is far less concerned about finding the answers than he once was. "I feel a great deal of energy, almost a joie de vivre, when I am around triathletes. I just like being surrounded by people with zeal," he says.

He smiles broadly. "Besides, many of them are really, really cute."

Swimmers
Matt Young and Jim Jordan

Many gay athletes say that when they were growing up the locker room was a place of terror. Contrary to popular image, it was not a home away from home, somewhere they could hang out for hours on end, snapping towels and bonding with teammates. In recent years, in fact, the locker room has almost gone the way of the typewriter and rotary phone. Few physical education teachers require showers after gym class, and even sweaty, smelly varsity athletes like football players have taken to changing in the privacy of their bedrooms.

But Matt Young's story is different. His first locker room memories are enjoyable; not until he grew older did the experiences became uncomfortable. Now, at age 28, he has rediscovered swimming, and once again he revels in stripping down with teammates.

It was in Gardner, a small town in north-central Massachusetts, that Matt first fooled around in locker rooms. At age 7 he started swimming with the Greenwood Memorial Swim Club, a very competitive program, and within a couple of years he and his teammates found a fun way to relax following the intense, daily three-hour practices. The boys ran around the locker room hanging towels off their erections, making jokes about each other's penis size, and generally enjoying prepubescent horseplay. Matt and his friends did not think it abnormal or shameful; it was simply a way to have fun.

Matt notes that at those ages—8 to 11—most American boys do not run around naked following practices and athletic events. He also played soccer and ice hockey, and no matter how grungy they were, players in those sports did not shower together. On the few occasions they changed in front of teammates, no one ever stripped all the way down. They took off their uniforms (except their underwear), put on their clothes, then went home to clean up.

In seventh grade, however, Matt's gym teacher required everyone to shower, and for the first time Matt realized that running around naked, comparing erections, was "not normal." That lesson was first learned when a friend noticed that Matt was semihard and asked if he was gay. The tone was curious, not malicious, but Matt answered forcefully, "No!"

"The reason I got hard in the locker room wasn't because of guys," Matt says. "It was because I had all this adrenaline rushing through my body after a good workout. Then erections became a conditioned response to taking off my clothes. There was never a situation—at that age anyway—where I was looking at other boys. It was just horseplay we did together, and no one cared." But seventh grade social pressures can be brutal, and Matt soon taught himself to walk through the locker room without becoming aroused.

Matt continued swimming—and earned New England rankings—until he burned out at 14. In high school he ran cross-country as well as indoor and outdoor track; he also got involved in theater. There were gay people in the drama program, but he did not identify with them. He was not effeminate; besides, he dated girls.

In 1990 he entered New York University, where he got back into swimming. NYU's less-than-competitive program suited him fine. He stood out as a freshman less for his skill than because he was the only swimmer whose girlfriend came to meets.

But that spring, after the season ended, he had his first gay experience. For a while he had realized men were attractive, though not in a sexual way; it was, he says, "more a feeling like I want to *be* that guy, to attain his body, rather than be *with* him." Yet when he took a writing course called "The Rhetoric of AIDS," he began reexamining what he calls "my Catholic perceptions of sexuality." It dawned

28   on him that it was all right for people to be gay, and that it might be possible to have sex with a male.

"So I did it," he says simply. "Wow—it was great!" Over the next couple of years he dated both men and women. That did not cause any internal conflicts, but during his second year on the NYU swim team, his feelings for the sport shifted. As he reflected on the previous year, he saw homoerotic behavior everywhere he looked.

For example, at a hotel before a championship meet, he and three teammates shaved down together in a bathroom. That was not unusual—swimmers often remove excess hair, believing less resistance will save precious thousandths of seconds—but the quartet did it while completely naked. "At the time, none of us thought it was bizarre," Matt says. "I realize now we found it titillating. It was like a tribal ritual for us. Then afterward we made sure to go hang out with girls, probably to reaffirm ourselves, but we kept talking about how smooth our legs felt."

Many male swimmers, he laughs, were "dorky. We hung out with each other and with the girls swim team. That was our main social thing. We knew each other so well. We were not cool or high-profile, like the basketball team. We existed, but no one cared about us. So we did these things, and no one thought anything about it."

After his first gay experiences, afraid his secret would be discovered, Matt felt estranged from his teammates. The swimmers were not into macho posturing, but that did not ease his discomfort. By his third year he had a boyfriend and needed to make money, so he got a job and left the team. He lost contact with most swimmers. The following year Matt ran into a former teammate, who casually mentioned that another swimmer had come out, adding that he was campy and funny and made the team laugh. Matt was stunned for two reasons: one, because he had not known the swimmer was gay; two, because his teammate had told him. To this day Matt still has no idea what prompted his teammate to say that. Did Matt's teammate know he was gay? Was the teammate trying to come out to Matt? Or was he simply passing along a bit of intriguing news?

After graduating as a music major, Matt spent eight months with the national company of *A Chorus Line*. (He played Don, the straight dancer. "That's so funny, because male chorus dancers are so gay," he laughs.) When the tour ended he wanted to stay physically active, so he returned to competitive swimming. This time he joined a gay team: New York Aquatics. And this time the locker-room environment was very different.

Before his first practice Matt wondered if he, as the new gay guy, would get checked out by everyone. He changed into his Speedos, said hello to a few swimmers, and walked onto the deck. Some of his new teammates did give him the once-over, but as soon as the workout began he was like—well, a fish in water. The Aquatics acted just like all the other swimmers he'd known. They had the same workout routines and joked around the same way. It was as if he'd never left the sport and forsaken a straight team for a gay one.

He realized that swimming with the New York Aquatics was far better than with Greenwood or NYU. His previous teams trained six days a week, which made swimming a job. The luxury of working out one evening a week helped Matt rediscover the pure joy of his sport.

Gone too was the uncomfortable feeling he'd had since puberty whenever he found himself among other naked swimmers. In its place he felt an easy comfort. Matt says, "We all know we're gay, and we all want to have a good look. No one has to shield their eyes. We're adults; we can be naked, and enjoy it. We had a jokey pig pile the other day. It's not scary or shameful or offensive—it's not even sexy. It's just fun."

For the first time since he was 10 or 11, Matt feels free to hang out in the locker room after practice. He relaxes, laughs, catches up with his friends' lives. Afterward, he joins a group heading out to dinner.

The team provides an excellent way to meet people with similar interests in a nonthreatening atmosphere. It also extends Matt's circle of gay acquaintances. He is among the youngest of all 180 Aquatics; the oldest is 60. Most have interesting, good-paying jobs. There are more men than women; most have swimming backgrounds, though a few are beginners. Dating other team members is not uncommon (Matt did it himself), but one-night hookups are rare. That would be too incestuous, he says.

Matt, who is now in a relationship with a nonswimmer, continues to enjoy the camaraderie the team provides. Swimming with the Aquatics has also allowed him to feel comfortable again, not only in the water but the locker room too. In fact, he feels so comfortable, he knows he could now go back to a straight team if he so wanted. (Many of his teammates, however, compete only in gay meets. The "straight" atmosphere, with wives and children cheering competitors on, is too intimidating for them.)

"The important thing to me now is not whether the team or meet is gay or straight but just the fact that I'm swimming," he says. "It was hard getting back in the pool, but I'm really glad I did it." And that holds true even if Matt is nowhere near as hard now as when he and his teammates romped in the swim-club locker room, having a blissful 10-year-old's blast.

• • •

Jim Jordan always felt at home in locker rooms and pools. Beginning in 1970, when he was 5 and swimming the 25-yard backstroke in mini-meets against swimmers age 10 and under in his hometown of San Diego, it seemed as natural as breathing. Most of his family swam, his friends were swimmers, and besides, Jim was good. By the time he was 10, his relay team was ranked nationally.

"I loved it," Jim explains. "You can always measure how much better you're getting. I felt comfortable in the water, and there's a certain amount of independence there too. A lot of swimmers are pretty self-motivated, and I was too. I just enjoyed being in that situation. It was the world I knew. I never questioned it."

He swam competitively in high school—the private Bishop's School in La Jolla—primarily the 100- and 200-meter butterfly, as well as some backstroke. In 11th grade he qualified for his first national meet and traveled to Fort Lauderdale. The first time he felt a true team bond, however, was at Williams College in Massachusetts. The Ephmen, Williams's swim team, were perennial New England champions, and one of the country's top NCAA Division III teams. The swimmers were a close-knit group, in and out of the pool.

They were so tight, in fact, that they thought nothing of holding shaving parties. Because swimmers cannot shave their own backs, the Williams athletes gathered in the showers and did each other's. "When I try to explain it to nonswimmers, they go, 'Oh, God, what's with that?'" Jim says. "But it seemed completely natural to me."

One swimmer was a model, whose contract stipulated he could not shave his head. In the spirit of bonding, the team suggested he shave his genitals, and he agreed. "There was nothing strange about any of that," Jim notes. "It was just something we did, and we all joked about it very easily."

The Williams team also swam naked in the dark. "It's incredibly relaxing," Jim says. "But people would walk through the area, hear us, peer down, and see a white ass in the darkness and say, 'What's going on here?' "

After Jim graduated in 1987 he entered a masters degree program in biology at the University of Oregon and put swimming on hold. He was too competitive to simply swim laps in a YMCA pool. He also spent two enjoyable summers teaching biology at the Hotchkiss School in Lakeville, Conn. His sister, a prep-school teacher and

32 coach, encouraged him to apply for a full-time job somewhere. He settled on Lawrenceville, a prestigious boarding school near Princeton, N.J. He was attracted by its high academic standards, $350 million endowment, and strong swimming tradition.

He has been there, teaching science and coaching swimming, ever since. During his first eight years he lived in dorms. "It's a lot of work when you're in your 20s, gay or straight, to be a parent to 20 or 30 ninth grade boys," Jim says. "You have to handle all their needs, and you're so wrapped up in school, you have no time for your own social life." That is one reason it took him so long to come out. He had known he was gay for a long time but assumed all through college and beyond that the type of athletic man he was interested in would always be straight.

When he moved out of the dorms and had a bit of free time, he began exploring the gay scene in Philadelphia, 40 minutes away. At first he thought that was the only place he could "be gay"; he could not imagine any gay life in Princeton, let alone Lawrenceville. But after several months, when he made a few solid relationships, he began to understand he was not as alone as he thought. He met gay teachers who hung out at the same places he did and had the same friends.

Jim also met people who, like he, were athletically inclined. It was good that they felt open and comfortable, but some of their stories stunned him. He learned of a swimmer on the West Coast who lost his athletic scholarship after getting drunk and ending up in bed with another male. He returned home humiliated, unable to tell his parents why he was no longer in school, and joined a club team to train for the upcoming Olympic trials. The coach was a homophobe, however, who routinely used the word "faggot." Distraught and unable to concentrate, the young man abandoned his Olympic dream.

Hearing that tale and seeing the plight of gay youth motivated

Jim to act. He joined the Philadelphia chapter of the Gay, Lesbian, and Straight Education Network (GLSEN), planning to volunteer there. Jim's younger brother urged him to work closer to home: at Lawrenceville itself.

"I had never thought of it [Lawrenceville] as a welcoming place for gay kids," Jim says. "But I knew there was a need for it, and I was in a unique position to make things happen. But I was also the head boys swim coach. What would all the close-minded and shortsighted people say and think?"

Jim was paralyzed with indecision. One day, however, he saw a former swimmer in a gay bar, and realized that people much younger than he were meeting such issues head-on. He knew Lawrenceville far better than Philadelphia and decided to act. He attended GLSEN workshops, met inspirational people working hard for change and, excitedly, talked to several trusted faculty members about addressing gay issues.

Jim persuaded Lawrenceville to hold an in-service training day focusing on gay youth. Several straight students heard about the initiative and sent an E-mail requesting a Gay-Straight Alliance. The headmaster asked Jim to help, and in the spring of 2000 it was formed. Through such activities as National Coming Out Day and a speech by GLSEN founder Kevin Jennings, gay issues gained visibility on campus. Jim became more visible too.

There was none of the backlash he had feared. In his role as coach, gay issues seldom arose. Jim has found, however, that people's attitudes toward him have changed—positively. Several swimmers have joined the GSA, not because their coach is gay, but because they support the club's stands and activities.

Jim does not go into locker rooms, but then again he never did. He also coaches girls teams, and he realized long ago there is no need for a coach to enter a locker room. "I think it's too bad so many gay people focus on issues like 'the locker room,'" he says. "Fears like that keep people from expressing themselves. The issues aren't about locker rooms; they're about teaching kids to be respectful of everyone and accept all their teammates, whether they're gay or straight, fast or slow."

In his years at Lawrenceville, Jim has come to understand that prep schools differ from public high schools. Living together, boys grow close; with that comes a comfort level that allows them to break down the barriers that teens often construct as defenses. Prep school boys are willing to show affection; they wrestle playfully in the halls at a moment's notice.

However, Jim continues, that comfort level does not extend to gay students. There are no out athletes at Lawrenceville, nor any nonathletes who are out to the school at large. (Some have come out to privately to teachers or friends.) "If a kid came out, then maybe the other guys wouldn't hug or wrestle him or walk around the hall in boxers. I don't think kids are willing to risk that loss of friendship and interpersonal relationship," Jim says.

Jim's personal comfort level, which did not begin to rise until he was 30, was raised immeasurably when he joined the Philadelphia Fins Aquatic Club, a gay team. That was where he met people he had never known existed—other gay athletes—and learned he was not the only swimmer to have grown up gay.

Yet it took meeting someone he was interested in before Jim truly came out. When he did, his competitive juices again flowed. He found he had much in common with gay swimmers; when he swam in a gay meet during Philadelphia Gay Pride weekend, it was the first time he truly connected with gay people. He met men who were physical and athletic. He did not have to worry about being uncomfortable; he was in his element.

In the summer of 1999, Jim competed at a major meet in Atlanta. Warming up with 700 others—virtually all men, most between 30 and 40 years old, and fast—he spotted a familiar face. It was a man he had swum with in college. Neither had known the other was gay.

They spent a long time catching up. The other man spoke about his gay life in San Francisco, then mentioned another teammate Jim once had a huge crush on. When he returned home, Jim called him. The man had had a similar experience at Williams; he too thought he was the only gay swimmer in the world. Together, they recalled the many homoerotic incidents on their team, including shaving parties and naked swims. Now, in one of life's little ironies, Jim is dating the man's younger brother—also a swimmer.

"Swimming has triggered all this," Jim says. "Most of my friends I've met since coming out have come through swimming. And I'm still finding more and more Williams swimming alums."

So how gay is swimming? Jim is unsure. He does note, though, that it is an activity anyone can do on his own. "People growing up gay can escape the world through swimming. It's a sport where you can be who you are; there's not a lot of being forced into certain roles. You hear fewer macho-type comments than in other sports— the things that are so tough to listen to if you're a gay kid. Football, wrestling, hockey can be intimidating for a young person just realizing his sexuality. There's a certain amount of forced expression of masculinity there."

Coming out has added to Jim's confidence in the pool. He won a masters national championship for his age group (30 to 34) in the 50-meter backstroke and placed in the top 10 in five different events. He is driven by several imperatives. He wants to stay in shape and look good; he wants to meet men, and he wants to succeed in order to prove to himself he can reach the potential his coaches always talked about. When he works out and races well, he feels better about himself. And swimming remains an escape of sorts. In the water, it is impossible to talk to anyone; the constant motion is relaxing, almost therapeutic.

Having said all that, however, Jim admits that if he did not have a gay team, he would no longer swim. Of all the pleasure he gets from swimming, the most important is feeling comfortable. At this point in his life, enjoying common interests is most important. The gay team environment—meeting people and forming solid relationships; sharing common experiences, without having to explain so many things—keeps Jim coming back. "Having these two parts of my life—my sexuality and my swimming—merge together, is magical," Jim says. "It gives me a very comfortable, unifying feeling about my life."

The Philadelphia Fins are good; several members hold national masters records. As a result, they attract straight swimmers too. Jim admires their courage. But he saves his highest accolades for the entire sport of swimming. "We have some amazing, phenomenal gay swimmers, and they've gained us some great acceptance in the entire masters swimming community," he says. "Swimming has always been a sport that accepts people for what they do. Every swimmer knows it's not just about talent. They all appreciate that to succeed you have to put an incredible number of hours into the pool, and that has nothing to do with being gay or straight. Today, nearly every swimmer in the country knows someone they've swum with or against that's gay, and they respect those people for their dedication, hard work, and talent. I don't think you can say that about nearly every football or basketball or hockey player. But it's one more reason I'm proud to say I'm a swimmer."

Gay Sports Web Site Developer Jim Buzinski

Males are visual creatures. Many enjoy staring at female bodies; that's why, in the athletic world, *Sports Illustrated*'s most popular issue bulges with women wearing scanty swim suits, and perhaps the most popular National Football League "team" is the Dallas Cowboy Cheerleaders.

Some men, of course, prefer gazing at the male physique. Thanks to companies like Abercrombie & Fitch, which plaster images of buff guys all over magazines, catalogs, billboards, and bus stops, finding eye candy is easier than ever. But it is still hard for gay men to admit they lust after America's idols: athletes. Speaking publicly about one's attraction to an Olympic swimmer or a Dallas Cowboy is still risky. Even some segments of the gay community view that admission as violating an unspoken code of social conduct.

That's absurd, says Jim Buzinski. "What's wrong with saying Brady Anderson is a great baseball player *and* he has a great body?" asks the 43-year-old Californian about the Baltimore Oriole outfielder. "How can that be offensive? Sports is a visual game. When was the last time you saw a picture of (New York Giants defensive back) Jason Sehorn *without* his shirt on? Everyone notices who's hot and who's ripped. The difference is we're not afraid to say it. That's what makes our site so lively."

"We" is Outsports.com, and "our site" is the Web's premier destination for men who love both sports and the men who play them. It offers breaking news, columns, chat rooms, links, and plenty of visual stimulation. As Jim, the site's cofounder, notes, "If *Sports Illustrated* put out a gay sports magazine, it would be Outsports. We're ESPN for homos."

He quickly adds, however, "We're not offensive. We never talk about penis size. We know our sports, and we write about it well. That's our true strength. We're a place gay men can go and feel comfortable talking about any aspect of sports."

Plenty of gay men do just that. Its traffic—hundreds of thousands of page views a month—more than doubled from June 2001 through March 2002. That was without any advertising or marketing; people found it through Web searches or word of mouth. Some stumble across it by accident—perhaps they've done a search using a key word like "Aikman," and the site just pops up—but most are actively seeking a gay sports site.

The site's users are overwhelmingly male, between the ages of 20 and 50. They come from cities, towns, and villages across America, and around the globe. Some are athletes themselves, others just fans, but many are both. Most are college educated.

The most popular page is "Picture This," a photo link updated daily. The shot can be of an athlete, coach, or team. It is always, however, visually appealing. If the athlete is not hot, then the action is. The photos are as eclectic as possible, ranging as far afield as track, biking, and rugby. Jim, who shares daily selection duties with cofounder Cyd Zeigler, says that the most popular shot ever showed 25 Stanford University swimmers in Speedos. Countless users downloaded it as wallpaper.

Another popular feature is "Clubhouse," where users post profiles and find others with similar interests. It is not, Jim emphasizes, a "personals" section, but rather a place to find a tennis partner or flag football team member. "People really do say, 'If you're traveling to Pittsburgh, let's go the Y and shoot hoops,'" he says. "And there's a huge variety of interests. One guy found another man who was into technical scuba diving, which I had never heard of."

The variety of interests extends all the way to NASCAR racing, a sport even less associated with gay men than football or rugby. "I

never thought automobile racing would be popular, but people 39
jumped into that discussion," Jim says. "I think it's especially important in sports like that for people to understand they're not alone.
And it's important to realize that gay sports are broader than any of
us know."

As at most sites, Outsports's discussion boards take on lives of
their own. The threads are often gay-oriented but not always. One
was filled with reactions to a *Penthouse* article in which a Pittsburgh
Pirate talked about sex with his wife; another, a bit more thoughtful,
concerned racism in tennis. Memorable gay-themed discussions
include whether straight people should be allowed to play on gay
teams, Allen Iverson's use of the word "faggot" on the court and in
his rap music, the pros and cons of coming out as an Olympic athlete, and which athletes would make great porn stars.

The "Tops and Bottoms" feature is a bit more straightforward
than it sounds, simply listing the best and worst of that day's sports
news ("A way to provide daily content without having to write it,"
Jim says candidly). But with features like former Denver Broncos
running back Reggie Rivers's condemnation of homophobia, alerts
about upcoming events like a college panel on gays in sports and a
TV profile of Greg Louganis, and provocative columns ("The Best
Sports Films for Gay Men"), users do not have to look hard for gay-
related items.

The "Week in Review" usually offers a gay perspective. Jim
points out, "It's amazing how much stuff has a gay angle." Stories
include professional athletes' treatment of gay fans (the San Diego
Padres' Brad Ausmus respects them; many Seattle Mariners do not),
antigay comments on sports talk radio, and how a group of Turkish
oil wrestlers (burly men in leather trousers who cover themselves in
olive oil) tried to stop gay men from watching.

Outsports's brief bios of openly gay athletes and coaches is considered the most extensive list anywhere, with an impact far beyond

titillation. Ricki Lake's producer mined it for information while researching a show about an openly lesbian athlete who lost a scholarship opportunity.

Also popular are the listings, which are sorted by types of sports and geography. Teams and clubs representing a broad variety of sports—softball, basketball, volleyball, bowling, rowing, biking—post announcements and information with hyperlinks to their sites. "We want to become the repository for anything having to do with gay sports at the local level," Jim says. "If the local papers can cover high school sports and Little League baseball, we might as well have similar services for a gay audience. I never understood why the gay media covers the Academy Awards but not the Super Bowl or even the local gay flag football team. Plenty of people want that information."

Not every page succeeds, of course. Essays on general sports themes fail to arouse much interest, for example. Jim notes, "You can find those anywhere. People look to us to supplement their sports diet, not fill it completely. We can't compete with CNNSI.com and ESPN, so we shouldn't try. Whatever we do should have something of interest to gay people." That is why the annual NCAA basketball tournament preview includes a "Hot Factor," and columnist Charlie in the Trees previewed the major league baseball season by picking his favorite player on each team and including their photos.

Interestingly, though Outsports never hesitates to name straight athletes whose looks and bodies turn gay men on, no sports figure has ever demanded his picture be removed from the site, or his name stricken from a discussion board. Jim has received fake E-mails from people claiming to be out collegiate athletes ("Fraternity pranks," he calls them), but overall the reception has been good. Some of the site's biggest fans, Jim laughs, are straight women who appreciate his and Cyd's taste in men.

Outsports is a labor of love for Jim, who traces his involvement in sports back to his working-class hometown of Wilkes-Barre, Pa. He and six siblings played everything—football, basketball, baseball, Wiffle Ball—as well as board games like Strat-O-Matic. Organized sports never appealed to Jim, who was too tall and thin until college, but he loved covering games for the Coughlin High School newspaper.

He was "happily, ignorantly clueless" about his sexuality all through high school. He preferred looking at guys to girls, but because he never heard the term "faggot" that attraction did not worry or frustrate him. He came out at 18 when, drunk in a basement, a friend from Penn State Wilkes-Barre suddenly kissed him. A jolt ran through his body, and from that moment on Jim understood what he was. He and his friend stayed together for nearly nine years in an easy, relaxed relationship.

When Jim transferred to Penn State's University Park campus he reported on politics and general news for the local *Centre Daily Times*, then after graduation became assistant city editor. After breaking up with his boyfriend Jim moved to California, and landed a job with the *Pasadena Star-News*, first in news and later sports. In 1987 the *Long Beach Press-Telegram* hired him away as sports editor. He remained there for 11 years.

He was completely out at that paper, a situation that seems noteworthy—in fact, he was the only openly gay sports editor in the United States—but Jim took it in stride. His openness spurred the paper to cover thoroughly and well such difficult stories as Magic Johnson's HIV-positive revelation and Greg Louganis's coming-out. Jim says with pride that sports was the *Press-Telegram*'s best section, the only area where it could compete with the larger *Los Angeles Times*. "It's important to be out in the newsroom because of the impact you make," he says. "Being open forces people to think about issues they otherwise might ignore or gloss over."

In 1998 Jim accepted a buyout package and spent eight months deciding on a new career path. When fighting broke out in Kosovo he took up a friend's offer to help on the *Los Angeles Times*'s international desk. Despite his many years as a sports editor, Jim always considered politics and foreign affairs his primary interest; sports was an avocation. He notes, almost as an afterthought, that he quarterbacked Team Los Angeles to a flag football silver medal at the 1990 Gay Games and a gold in 1994, then played tennis "badly" at the 1998 Games.

But a year after Jim joined the *Times*, he and Cyd, a friend he met through flag football, vacationed together on Cape Cod. In Provincetown they argued passionately about the NFL. There were few gay men Jim could do that with, and when Cyd mentioned a Yahoo club for gay football fans—one of Yahoo's most popular sports sites—an idea was born.

In the fall of 1999 Jim and Cyd brainstormed for a good domain name. Outsports fit the bill; it signaled "gay" without screaming it. In November the site went live, with Jim and Cyd posting a few thoughts about the NFL.

Within a couple of days, Yahoo listed Outsports in its search directory. Jim still does not know how that happened, but traffic surged. As users posted questions and comments about other sports, the site grew organically.

By late spring of 2000, Jim and Cyd realized they had a viable Web site. It had morphed from a hobby into an important nexus between gay men and sports. But success came at a price. Jim and Cyd (who works full-time for the Disney Channel) were putting 20 to 30 hours a week into Outsports. A year later it still was not a moneymaker; then again, neither was Amazon.com.

In fact, to a certain segment of Internet users, Outsports is far more valuable than the mammoth bookseller. Anyone can sell goods online, but to fill a niche no one knew needed filling is truly rewarding. Jim describes with satisfaction a man who through Outsports discovered a gay flag football team and for the first time realized he could play sports *and* be gay. Meeting other men like him enabled him to come out. Jim calls that story "the highest compliment I could get."

Outsports has been good for himself too, Jim says. He has been amazed to learn of the variety of activities gay men participate in. Hearing the tales of openly gay high school and college athletes has convinced him that America will soon see the first out male professional in a major sport. And he has been heartened to find out how similar gay and straight men are, at least in the world of sports. "We get just as turned on by a game and just as pissed off at a team as anyone else," he says.

But, when it comes to other kinds of turn-ons, gay men and straights are decidedly different. "We do enjoy looking at the athletes themselves a bit more," Jim Buzinski admits. So, for male sports fans who prefer Jason Sehorn's chest to Dallas Cowboy Cheerleaders' breasts, Outsports.com offers the best seat in the stadium.

Rugby
John Daly, Scott, Anthony Frederick

They come in every imaginable body shape, size, and type. Some are scrawny speed demons; others are hulking, heavy-hitting he-men. Their faces—even the cutest and most handsome—are marred by black eyes and bruises. They sing politically incorrect songs that get louder and less on-key as the hours pass, then they slide naked along beer-covered floors.

They sound like the most nongay group this side of a Tailhook convention. But the Renegades Rugby Football Club has attracted a large cult following in and around their hometown of Washington, D.C. And their fans sometimes express adoration in bizarre ways: Though only 40 men are listed on the team roster, an estimated 300 Washington-area residents claim to be Renegades in their online profiles.

Rugby is an odd vehicle for gaining glory. It is not a glamorous sport; in fact, it is dirty, muddy, sweaty, slimy, and strange. There are no crowds to speak of, and *The Washington Post* does not cover rugby games. One player notes, "If you love your body, this is probably not your sport." In the body-conscious bars and bookstores of Dupont Circle, that is hardly a ringing endorsement.

Yet the Renegades thrive. And just a few years after their founding by a couple of self-professed "rugby junkies," they have become one of gay Washington's most intriguing success stories.

Part of the interest stems from the team's eclectic makeup. The Renegades call themselves "America's first multicultural men's rugby club," and diversity across lines of age, race, and ethnicity is prized. Organizers actively seek minorities. The percentage of Latinos and Afro-Caribbeans—who, like gay men, are underrepresented on traditional rugby teams—is high. Half the team speaks Spanish. Many players are professionals: doctors, lawyers, CEOs, and CFOs. While it is a gay team (and the Renegades are proud of spearheading the creation of the International Gay Rugby Association and Board), straight men are welcome. Three have "come out" so far as heterosexual; several others keep their sexual orientation private. (In the parallel universe of gay sports, some straight men might not want their teammates to know.)

Men are attracted to rugby—and the Renegades—for many reasons. For some, it is the difficulty of mastering a new game's physical skills and learning its esoteric rules. For others, it is the chance to bang bodies together while wearing the skimpiest of pads. There are men who are drawn to the task of melding 15 players into one cohesive unit, and men who find pleasure in the sport's improvisational nature.

For many gay men, however, rugby's appeal transcends those physical challenges or psychic rewards. "This is like climbing a mountain," says Anthony Frederick, an avid Renegade. "Many guys on the team never played sports in high school. They felt threatened by athletes, or they worried about getting 'found out.' They see this as a second chance—it's the football team they never got a chance to join." The mountain metaphor is apt. After playing against an English team, one of Anthony's teammates proudly proclaimed, "I just climbed Kilimanjaro!"

The sport is hardly for everyone. Anthony says, "You can't love your body and play rugby. A lot of guys, after one practice we never see them again. They go to the gym, but they don't want to walk around Dupont Circle with bumps and bruises. They're test-tube athletes, not rugby players."

A teammate adds, "It takes guts and determination to come out for rugby. It's not easy to do in a culture that's so focused on looks. I come out of every game with a bruise somewhere or cleat marks

46   on my forehead. You don't see a lot of gay men willing to put themselves in that position. But the feeling of utter exhaustion after a game—even if you can't turn your head—outweighs all the black eyes."

Every Renegade has felt that strange brew of battered body and otherworldly elation. Those feelings bind the team together, both on the dirt field and afterward in their beer-soaked socials. Yet every Renegade's path to rugby is uniquely his own.

John Daly's began as the oldest of six children in a traditional Irish Catholic family. He was yearbook editor, performed theater and community service, played soccer and swam, but claims to have not done any of them particularly well. Skinny and physically inse- cure in high school, he did not start coming out until 1991, his freshman year at Georgetown University. Up to that point, he was "a gay agnostic." He knew he was not like Billy Crystal on *Soap*, but because he had no other gay role models, he had no idea who he was. He did not deny his homosexuality; he simply never asked himself "the question."

Then, in college, John met a gay man and asked about his life. As they talked about homosexuality, John began a coded journal. "I think I might be 'g,'" he wrote.

"How stupid was that?" he laughs, cringing at the memory. "If someone saw it, would they think I was German? Geriatric?"

Late on New Year's Eve of sophomore year, after four bottles of champagne, John described his confused feelings to a friend. She was fine with his revelations and offered to help—when she was less drunk. He fell asleep "30 pounds lighter."

For six months, John went on a tear. He came out to everyone he knew, although he still had not had a date with a man. When he told his parents, his mother cried. His father—a "methodical sur- geon"—thought the situation could be negotiated to a mutually agreeable conclusion. But both parents worked through their fears and worries, and John calls their current attitude wonderful. His 16-year-old brother actually tried to fix John up with his prom date's gay brother. "Even though he smoked, I thought that was so cute," John says.

At Georgetown, John he played intramural soccer, flag football, basketball, and volleyball. After graduation in 1995 he stayed in Washington, teaching in an inner-city school and organizing an informal Sunday morning flag football league.

One night at a party, a football friend who also played on the Renegades suggested John try rugby. He laughed, pointing to his size—"5 foot 10, 160 pounds soaking wet"—but the friend persisted. John went to a practice. He liked the players and loved the sport. His thirst for rugby knowledge quickly became insatiable. He spent Friday nights renting rugby videos and studying rule books.

John was enthralled by rugby's competitive aspect, creative strategy, and intriguing combination of his two favorite sports: football (tackling and aggression) and soccer (skill, teamwork, and nonstop action). He started as a wing, where his speed, agility, and kicking talents proved potent weapons. After gaining experience he moved up to scrum half, a play-calling position of leadership. Soon he was named captain.

John benefited from and contributed to the fraternal feeling so vital to rugby success. "You need all 15 pistons firing," he explains. "One or two stars can't do it." The Renegades' 15 starters—and 25 others—include three types of players: men who have played rugby before; those who have played other sports but not rugby, and men who had never played anything at all. John respects the third group the most. "They're what this team is all about," he says. "Watching them find their passion really stokes my fire."

His teammate Scott (who, because he is not out to his extended family, asked that his last name not be used) belongs to the second group. Although his father had been a college football star, Scott's sport from age 4 onward was soccer. He reached the Olympic Development Program level in North Carolina before a severe knee injury in college ended his Division I career.

Like John, Scott realized relatively late that he was gay. As a Duke University graduate student in anthropology, he was walking in Chapel Hill one night when he became separated from all but one of his friends. The other man suddenly grabbed Scott and kissed him. "Part of me wanted him to stop. The other part wanted him to go on forever," he recalls. The man could not believe it was Scott's first kiss. He was sure Scott had been flirting with him all night.

Over the next few days they talked, and Scott realized he was gay. He was not traumatized. "It was more like 'I should have been more aware of this before,' but I never had a reference point. The only gay person I had known was slight and feminine, and I like more masculine, rugged guys."

A few months later, attending the University of Kentucky for two more masters degrees, in social work and public policy, Scott began exploring Lexington's surprisingly active gay scene. He wanted to stay active athletically too, so when he could not find a soccer team he took up field hockey. Its technical demands and arcane rules made it challenging to learn, but because he could outrun, outreach, and outhit most women, the novelty soon wore off.

In the summer of 2000, a year after Scott moved to Washington to work for an HIV/AIDS organization, he met a former college lacrosse player now with the Renegades. After 12 knee surgeries Scott was hesitant to try such a physical sport, but—like John—one training session changed his mind. "I instantly saw gay men who had the same sense of camaraderie and friendship as my college soccer team," Scott says. "There was the same good feeling, the same 'your mama' jokes. They took the sport seriously, but they didn't just disperse after practice." The second day, while running sprints and doing agility work, he realized he was pushing himself as hard as he ever had in college. He was eager to return for more.

At 6 foot 3 and 210 pounds Scott was one of the biggest players, yet also among the fastest. Moving through several positions, including wing, inside center, and lock, he learned the game thoroughly. He especially enjoys fullback because—as he did as a soccer sweeper—he roams the backfield, directing play while shouldering enormous defensive responsibilities.

A third Renegade, Anthony Frederick, has a football background. He played in high school, already knowing he was gay. Despite growing up in a Lutheran small town in western Nebraska, being a gay athlete was not stressful. "Kids didn't really date," he says. "And because it's the most German community I've seen outside of Germany, no one poked their nose into other people's business."

His father had spent 30 years in the military, so Anthony enlisted too. Trained as a linguist, he learned German, Polish, and Arabic. He served in the Gulf War ("chairborne, not airborne") but after eight years in that homophobic environment got out to preserve his own mental health. He enrolled at Centenary College in Shreveport, La., where his parents then lived, and in 1999 graduated summa cum laude (with a double degree in English and German literature). His next step was Georgetown University graduate school, studying communications, culture, and technology.

That fall his boyfriend—who knew Anthony had played rugby in the military—brought him to a Renegades recruitment party. Like John and Scott, he soon succumbed to the team and sport's allure.

Anthony calls his position of lock addictive. As he describes his role, his enthusiasm almost overwhelms him. "You have to be tall, strong, and heavy, and deliver fierce hits. You're the engine of the scrum, the filling in the middle of the cake. It's such an adrenaline rush, I can hardly wait to get to the next tackle. In football you wear so much padding you almost don't feel the hits. But in rugby you've got only a few soft pads, just enough to keep your bones from breaking. It's by far the most physical sport I know—hard contact, bone on bone. A friend of mine plays hockey, and he wears a hard helmet, all these hard pads. I can't imagine playing with all that.

"Rugby is so pleasurable to play," Anthony continues. "We're not that good, but we put in so much effort. We hit hard right to the end and never give up. There are 69 teams in the Potomac Rugby Union, and a lot of them take only college athletes or experienced players. We're different. But every practice we grow. One of the most exciting things I know is watching us move the ball and score."

Though hardly the best team in the Potomac Union, the Renegades boast perhaps the most ardent fans. Some are gay men who cannot believe there actually *is* a gay rugby team; others mythologize any man who plays such a stereotypically macho sport.

Occasionally that attention oversteps the bounds of propriety. One player had his photo and America Online profile stolen by a man who claimed he was a Renegade in order to find dates. Mostly, however, the players—the genuine ones, anyway—seem amused by their cult status. One day they wore their jerseys to a local bar fundraiser and were treated like rock stars.

Yet despite its rough-and-tough image, Anthony says, rugby is not a fighting sport. The violence is so close to the surface, there is no need to lash out beyond and punch. Instead, players talk—actual conversation, not trash. That is because, when you come right down to it, rugby is as social as any sport gets.

That social aspect explains why the Renegades traveled to England in the summer of 2000 to compete in the International Gay Sports Festival. They faced London's King's Cross Steelers and the Manchester Village Spartans, Britain's two gay rugby teams, and bunked in their opponents' homes. Reciprocal visits followed, and along the way John Daly learned of the University of Manchester's Ph.D. program in counseling psychology. He enrolled in September

2001. "I never would have done that unless I had a base of friends there and a team to play with," John says.

But for all of the sport's camaraderie, the Renegades serve an important function by being a gay team. Scott says, "Even in Washington, I don't think any of us could play on a straight rugby team as an out gay man. It's *the* macho game played by guys who don't take shit from anyone. I couldn't put up with all the antigay, anti-female, anti-everything remarks you hear during any practice. Even if it's unintended, it would make that team unenjoyable for me. We don't have that here, so it allows us to focus more."

John has a similar perspective. "Given my trepidation about rugby because of my size and misconceptions about the game, I never would have joined a straight team. I've learned to tune out the two most common forms of abuse on the athletic field—'fag' and 'pussy'—but knowing I'd hear them would have prevented me from trying a new sport like rugby. A gay team is a safe place to learn because you don't have to worry about your teammates' reactions."

Reactions of opponents are, of course, a different matter entirely. One of rugby's most cherished traditions is the "third half." John explains: "After 80 minutes of beating the piss out of each other, you spend the next two hours joined together swilling beer."

Teams approach third halves with the gay squad in a variety of ways. Two clubs—University of Maryland–Baltimore County and Western Suburbs—are particularly supportive of the Renegades; predictably, their socials are the best. Other sides are unsure how to act around a bunch of gay rugby players. When North Bay, a team with a well-earned hard-partying reputation, hosted the third half, several Renegades sensed an intentionally toned-down mood. After a while, John approached the North Bay captain and said, "You know, we usually do a 'Man of the Match'"—a celebration in which the game's best player drinks a quart of beer, while everyone sings.

"We do too!" the captain replied. Suddenly, amid copious beer-drinking and raucous singing, both teams let loose. Soon it was time for the "Zulu Warrior," another rugby tradition. Zulus are reserved for players who have just scored their first try (carrying the ball into the goal or grounding it there). The honoree celebrates by running naked during the third half. At this particular Zulu a North Bay player ran the length of the bar, then returned by sliding along the beer-soaked floor. Both squads roared with delight.

"Our socials are a little more high-quality than most," John says, meaning there is better food and beer. The Renegades' songs, however, would never be sung at a Human Rights Campaign dinner.

Though most third halves end happily, and most games are played without incident, there are occasional reminders that old habits die hard. John recalls tackling the Maryland-Baltimore County captain hard, then landing atop him. "Get off me, faggot!" John's opponent blurted. Instantly he realized what he said and turned pale. John flipped him on his back, looked him in the eye, and said calmly, "Come on now, let's not call each other names." The Maryland captain spent the rest of the match apologizing every chance he got. John reassured him that words slip out and it was OK.

Anthony notes that moments like that are rare. "A lot of teams don't know what to expect with us," he says. "But they see pretty quickly that we look like them and we play like them. They're shocked, but everything's fine."

Still, no one denies reality: The Renegades are a gay team. That can cause problems, even for a gay athlete. Compared to his college soccer squad, Scott says, "A lot of guys don't have the 'sport mentality.' I get frustrated when they have social time during practice. With 30 gay men you're bound to have some catty conversations, and that drives me nuts. So I bark at people. I don't mind being the asshole."

He is annoyed too when someone goes out for the team because of fantasies about big, burly men. "They come to practice, they get 53 muddy and hurt but not laid, and we never see them again," he says. "I just laugh."

Then there are the men who stick with the team, but believe that because they are gay they cannot tackle strongly or hit head-on. Scott says, "People have to understand that if you play full-speed, you won't get hurt. You can't play a sport like this halfway. I'm amazed when I see guys with that attitude, or guys without an athletic background who don't even know the fundamentals of running. To me, that stuff is innate."

Scott gets frustrated because he wants the Renegades to play better. But his annoyance is tempered by the realization that the club's mission is to do more than just play rugby. It is important, he knows, to give men traditionally underrepresented on the field a chance to play, have fun, and feel part of a close-knit group.

He acknowledges, "It's a constant balancing act between being a team, and being a gay team. If we were a straight team we'd probably be more competitive. I know we won't win much for a while. So I've learned to get satisfaction just from doing my best."

John has also the given the "gay sports" issue a great deal of thought. "I don't like hearing people talk about 'that gay rugby team,' " he says. "Am I a gay rugby player, or a player who is gay? Which of those identities influences me most? I think of myself as a rugby player who happens to be gay. But I know different players might have different perspectives."

Noting that the Renegades are not entirely gay, he adds, "It's not the be-all and end-all to be a 'gay team.' But it would be nice if people recognized us as a good team, most of whose players happen to be gay."

Scott says, "There is a fascination in the gay community with the fact that we play rugby. People see it as an incredibly brutal sport. They don't know it's really just a wonderful, physical game. If played

54 right, it won't hurt you. In fact, it will provide all kinds of satisfaction through exertion, power, and finesse. The aches, bruises, bumps, and other pain makes you feel like you can't go on on Monday. But they diminish, and Saturday can't come soon enough."

This fascination with a high-intensity, low-profile sport draws men like Scott, John, and Anthony together, knocking heads on the worn fields of Washington and drinking beer at the rowdy gatherings that follow. The aggressively straight yet relentlessly social world of rugby has welcomed the Renegades with—at least most of the time—open arms.

And if any opponent has a problem playing a primarily gay team? Scott answers for the rest of the Renegades: "I guess we'd just have to go out and kick their ass."

Snowboarding
Ryan Miller

Snowboarders revel in their status as anti-jocks. From the sport's birth two decades ago, when boarders were so detested they had to sneak onto ski slopes long after dark, to the dawn of the 21st century, when the image is still baggy pants, multiple piercings, and a devil-may-care disregard for the downhill skiers with whom they finally share mountains, snowboarders have stood apart from mainstream athletes. Their sport—celebrating creativity, courting danger, thumbing noses at regimentation—welcomes anyone with energy, guts, a good sense of balance, and a desire to live life outside of society's mainstream.

You would think that the snowboarding world couldn't care less if a boarder is gay, bisexual, straight, or a eunuch.

As Ryan Miller found out, however, you would be wrong. This may be the 21st century, but that means sports—even alternative or extreme sports—are big business. Big business means media coverage, television contracts, sponsorship deals. And those things mean keeping quiet about homosexuality, or risking the consequences.

Ryan learned that lesson firsthand. In the winter of 1998 he was in the fifth year of a long-term relationship with a snowboard-related company. They treated the national-level competitor well; he, in turn, brought them visibility and prestige. But one day a company representative noticed a gay pride sticker on Ryan's bumper, and suddenly the relationship changed. Ryan's contract was not renewed. A major sponsor—crucial in a sport that, despite its grassroots image, involves costly equipment and travel expenses—was lost.

At the same time, Ryan realized the snowboard circuit is not exactly a wintertime version of the Summer of Love. Fellow com-

56 petitors—the guys he traveled with, trained with, and hung out with—routinely told antigay, anti-Semitic, and racist jokes. No one, as far as he knew, was out as a professional snowboarder. Lacking parental support too, Ryan decided to keep his homosexuality quiet.

But he was out in every other aspect of his life—as a college student, ski instructor, marketing professional, you name it—and hiding an important part of himself became more and more difficult. In the spring of 2000, when he made a U.S. professional team, he looked ahead. He realized he would spend the next several months working out and bunking with a small group of people. Keeping silent would be harder than ever. He knew he could no longer hide.

Ryan's unique coming-out process epitomizes the peculiar position snowboarding holds at the turn of the millennium. In keeping with the sport's emphasis on individuality, he did it by emphasizing sexuality as just one part of his personality. But, mindful of the importance of sponsors, he also came out by creating a marketing proposal. Ryan pitched himself as an openly gay professional snowboarder.

Drawing on his knowledge of sports marketing, Ryan made phone calls to a dozen companies. He followed up by sending professional-looking portfolios that noted his accomplishments, and emphasized the demographic markets he could reach and the number of impressions their company logos would make. He supported his pitch with statistics on gay consumers and their spending habits.

Several companies responded. Nidecker offered to provide him with boards; Swany said they would give him free gloves for the season, and Bomber offered deeply discounted bindings. The responses were heartening, but not enough to offset the $15,000 to $20,000 he needed to eat, train, compete, and travel.

By Thanksgiving 2000, Ryan was ready to quit. But when a gay friend in Philadelphia heard the news, he wrote a check for $5,000. Two weeks later, a gay bar in Chicago raised $7,000 more. Ryan

moved to Colorado to train with the team, and at last his career
seemed back on track.

But on a trip to Whistler Mountain in British Columbia, a few of his teammates badgered Ryan to go to a strip club. He told them that was not his idea of a good time. Over the next week, guys he had been friendly with the season before grew aloof. Subtly but clearly, they stopped including him in social activities. Though he had come out on his own terms, Ryan again felt depressed. Once more, he was ready to quit.

Then he received a phone call from Tim Gill. In addition to his fame as a gay philanthropist, the founder of the Colorado-based Quark software company runs Outboard, the world's largest gay and lesbian snowboarding event. He invited Ryan to Denver for dinner. Inspired, but without any promises, Ryan committed himself to a few more weeks of snowboarding.

With a new coach, Mike Mallon, and two new locations—Steamboat Springs, Colo., and Park City, Utah—Ryan's riding took off. He had a good race in Quebec, scored a few more high finishes, and then got a follow-up E-mail from Tim Gill. Outboard agreed to finance the rest of his season.

Free of financial concerns, Ryan concentrated on training. He moved to Steamboat and—helped by the coach's easy acceptance of Ryan's homosexuality—immediately hit it off with a new group of snowboarders. His eight teammates, most of them still in their teens, bombarded him with questions they were genuinely eager to learn the answers to. They asked about nondiscrimination laws, emotional attractions, even the appeal of the leather community (of which Ryan is a member).

When racers on other teams made derogatory comments, Ryan's new teammates leaped to his defense. It was the first time any boarder ever stood up for him. After an injury caused him to miss a road trip, the group stuck a gay pride sticker on their van to remind them of him. At last, the image of snowboarders as chill, accepting people matched reality.

Ryan's path to that point of acceptance was filled with more pitfalls than merely his coming-out and sponsorship travails. It started in the Valley Forge area, the demarcation between suburban Philadelphia and Amish farmland, where he was born and raised. In the Spring-Ford School District he tried soccer and baseball but never enjoyed them or any other team games. In high school he learned that all males occasionally have feelings for and fantasies about other men. However, he was taught, those thoughts soon end, and men eventually marry women and have children. He figured one day he would do that himself. He dated a girl for four years; ironically, she later came out too. (The topic of lesbianism had never been broached in sex ed, he says wryly.)

After graduation he attended three colleges before landing at Ursinus, five minutes from home. There, in choir, he met his first openly gay person. They became friendly, and one night the man asked Ryan how long he had been gay. Ryan was stunned. They talked, and as the friend described all the gay people of all ages he knew, Ryan realized something important was missing from his life. After several weeks of introspection and contemplation, his process of self-acceptance began.

He came out a year later. His mother said she had suspected for years. (Ryan explains, "I guess it was because I wasn't a partier, I didn't sleep around, I played four musical instruments, spoke five languages, and was in the marching band!") However, the news blindsided his father, a white-collar worker in the construction industry. Having never imagined his only child would be gay, he took the news hard.

His parents suggested a therapist. Ryan countered that he would go on one condition: They go first. Surprisingly, they agreed. After one visit his parents told Ryan they realized he was normal; they, however, would continue to see the doctor to work through their own issues. Over time they came to accept their son. One of his proudest moments came when they helped him move in with his boyfriend. These days, his mother cheers him on at meets wearing Ryan's sponsors' logos—including Outboard.

Despite his aversion to team sports (not helped, he says, by breaking both eye sockets and one cheekbone in baseball), Ryan always loved skiing. He started at age 5 at Spring Mountain, a tiny slope a few minutes from his house. It was such a friendly place; parents had no qualms dropping their children off for hours on end. From age 9 to 13, Ryan skied happily until 9 or 10 at night, five days a week, then returned for more on weekends.

Skiing proved to be his salvation. "I was the school outcast," he says. "I was never good at gym, so I was always labeled 'gay' and 'fag.' Kids didn't know what that meant; they just said it because I wasn't a football player, which was popular, or a wrestler, which was God."

However, he was coordinated and had good balance. As he excelled at skiing—and added jumps, spins, and aerial moves to his repertoire—he gained some measure of revenge on the youngsters who had heckled him. Now they simply left him alone.

At 14, Ryan started teaching skiing at Spring Mountain. Within two years he was assistant director of the ski school. By the time he was a high school senior, snowboarding was becoming an accepted winter activity there. A course was needed—and Ryan was the only staff member who knew how to snowboard. He seized the opportunity by designing methodology, writing training materials, hiring staff, even marketing the course. He continued those pursuits all the way through college, and along the way earned a Professional Ski Instructors of America Level II certification with specialties in biomechanical analysis and sports psychology. He traveled throughout the Pocono Mountains and New England, teaching teachers how to teach both skiing and snowboarding.

All that activity did not interfere with his education. At Ursinus he changed his major from music to economics and business administration. The department chairman saw Ryan's work as an extension of his studies. Because he was learning management skills and running his own business, he was allowed to design a flexible class schedule.

During that hectic period—studying, teaching skiing and snowboarding, training 300 instructors, marketing his courses, coming out—Ryan also began competing. Snowboard races were challenging yet fun. He snowboarded throughout the Mid-Atlantic region from Maryland to New York. When he began, he did not even realize he was earning points to qualify for national championships in slalom and grand slalom. In 1996 at Mount Snow in Vermont, he finished 12th out of 100 snowboard racers. That shocked him, but he was even more stunned to place fourth in the college national championships at Killington.

He was completely self-taught. Then he replied to an ad for a training camp at New York's Hunter Mountain. An Olympic snowboard team coach, Nick Colavito, served as guest instructor. On the second day he asked Ryan to join his private team full-time. Ryan went to Park City to participate in the highest-caliber race he'd ever seen. In training he finished just two seconds behind the best snowboarder in the world. But during the first official run he hit a gate. It did not release properly, and slingshotted him 60 feet in the air. He blew out every ligament and tendon from mid calf to his toes.

Fortunately, nothing was broken. Unfortunately, soft tissue heals quite slowly. His foot was still in an air cast when the International Snowboard Federation nationals rolled around at Waterville Valley, N.H. Ryan removed the cast, and though he could barely push off, he still finished 17th.

When he finally came out, with his new team in Colorado, Ryan's stature and fame grew. *Hero* magazine profiled him; so did

Snowboarding magazine in a story on diversity in the sport. *The* **61** *Advocate* gave him a prestigious honor: "Innovator."

Ryan certainly presents a striking figure on the mountain. His tricolor Outboard logo, which festoons his speedsuit, outerwear, and fleece, attracts plenty of attention. In the close-knit world of snowboarding, few people have seen or heard about the organization. "People ask me or my mom, and we just say, 'It's a gay snowboard group. You should check it out.' Most people say, 'Cool.' Some of them say they'll tell their gay friends about it."

Professional ranks aside, Ryan says that gay people are well-represented in snowboarding—as they are, he points out, in most sports. Outboard's major event, held each year at Colorado's Copper Mountain, draws several hundred snowboarders. As far as he knows, however, Ryan is the only out competitor. No teammate has ever talked to him about it, not even anonymously.

Ryan is unsure why that is, or why he heard so many homophobic and antiminority comments in the past. Perhaps, he says, it is because the money needed to compete at a high level limits snowboarders to wealthy conservative backgrounds. Perhaps they come from isolated training academies, where they spend so much time on the mountain they have little chance to meet diverse people.

Ryan's loneliness as the only out gay professional snowboarder has steeled two resolves. One is to make the United States Olympic team in 2006. The other is to help any gay teammate by being a positive role model. He has already begun speaking publicly. A recent appearance at the University of Delaware showed him he has a future in that area too.

There is a down side to his dedication, he admits. Because being a world-class athlete demands total determination and dedication, he has not had a stable relationship in years. "People can't hack that I'm gone 90% of seven months," he says. He also puts his marketing career as a project-planning consultant on hold for most of each year. "If I did that year-round," he says, "I'd be out of debt in a few months."

But because Ryan loves snowboarding, he makes those sacrifices gladly. As for the future of gay professional snowboarding, he says, "I'm not sure. I'm out there doing it, but is anybody else following, willing to put themselves on the line? I don't know. Most pro athletes who come out do it after they retire. I'm out now, and that's rare. But I think it's important, whatever sport you're in, to go for your goals as yourself, without lying, and maybe try to change some attitudes along the way."

He knows snowboarding is not pro football or basketball, but Ryan says those lucrative team sports are connected in important ways. "Sports is all about money now. It's what you can do for the sponsor. That drives every decision. Do corporations these days want to exclude 10% of the population? On the other hand, do they include them and risk alienating other fans?"

He concludes with an intriguing thought: "If corporate sponsors 'came out' as gay-friendly, maybe more athletes would too. Money is a very strong oppressor. I think it will take one of two things to change the attitude of sports: either a paradigm shift, or one or two individuals willing to make a change." In the once alternative but now mainstream, corporate-sponsored sport of snowboarding, one individual at least is making that change. And someday soon, Ryan Miller hopes, he can ride that paradigm shift all the way down the mountain—to glory and gold.

College Athletic Director
Michael Muska

For more than a century and a half, Oberlin has earned fame as one of America's most liberal colleges. In 1841, when it was just eight years old, the Ohio school became the first to grant undergraduate degrees to women; throughout the 19th century it was a leader in educating blacks. More recently, in 1972, Jack Scott—the activist-author who helped shelter Patty Hearst from the FBI—arrived on the bucolic campus 35 miles west of Cleveland to serve as athletic director.

His tenure and those of succeeding ADs were widely regarded as failures. Oberlin's once-proud athletic program—which as far back as 1892 boasted a 7-0 football team led by legendary player-coach John Heisman—lay in shambles. Only a couple of teams patched together winning records; the football squad, headed for the longest losing streak in the nation, was particularly pathetic. No one doubted a dramatic change was needed.

Michael Muska seemed like a godsend. With a background that included coaching, sports administration, admissions work, and college counseling; a dynamic personality that motivated the most cynical coaches, athletes, and (especially important) alumni donors; a reverence for Oberlin's often contradictory athletic and social justice traditions, and an eagerness to plunge into all aspects of campus life, he seemed just the man to get the school's sports program back on track.

There was only one problem: Michael was openly gay. And even at liberal Oberlin—a place where, by some estimates, a quarter of the students are queer and the gay alumni association boasts more than 1,200 members—there were doubts about hiring the nation's first openly gay male athletic director. Members of the search committee raised the initial questions; later, several coaches voiced more pointed concerns.

But Oberlin proved true to its pioneering spirit, and in 1998 Michael Muska came to Philips Gym to begin work. He planned to ease into his new job, slowly building bridges with important constituencies and laying the groundwork for renewed athletic success. When the time was right, he thought, the world beyond the Oberlin bubble could learn that the school's athletic revitalization had been engineered by a gay man.

Within a few weeks, however, Michael's plans were shattered. An educational journal outed him to the world. Suddenly, Oberlin's gay AD was national news. The Rev. Fred Phelps threatened to disrupt the first day of classes. To everyone's dismay, the academic year began with the media spotlight shining on Michael's sexuality, not the Yeomen's football prospects.

The campus survived. Reverend Phelps postponed his visit, and for the next three years Michael quietly, steadily, yet energetically set about rebuilding Oberlin's teams. He hired new coaches, including a football coach. He made Philips Gym a more welcoming place for everyone: faculty, staff, nonathletes, even townspeople. He taught courses, sat on student committees, wove himself into the fabric of Oberlin life. Along the way, he won over some of his strongest critics. Veteran coaches had to admit that Oberlin sports were once more on the move; crotchety alumni pulled out their checkbooks and began donating again.

And then in December 2000, another article appeared. This one, the cover story of the *Cleveland Plain Dealer Sunday Magazine*, lauded Michael for the vigor he brought to Oberlin athletics. But it also delved deep into his past, revealing details about his romance with an athlete decades earlier, when he coached track and cross-country at Northwestern University. It was information no one at Oberlin had known. "We're dead," one coach wailed. "We'll never get 65 another player from Ohio again."

Oberlin's gay athletic director was back at the staring gate. It was a place Michael Muska had been many times before.

Born 50 years earlier and educated at St. John's Prep, an all-boys Catholic boarding school in Massachusetts, Michael earned his first headlines as a track and field and cross country star. He accepted an athletic scholarship to the University of Connecticut—not a Catholic college, as his parents preferred—because, he says, "part of me wanted to figure things out."

It took a while. Michael dated women until he was 23, about the time he earned his master's in sports administration from the University of Massachusetts. When he finally admitted he was gay, he paid a price. He did not think he could be out in the hypermasculine sports world, so he vowed no one would ever know.

Michael coached track and field and cross-country at Cornell University for two years, then moved to Auburn University, where he coached 16 All-Americans and was twice named Southeastern Conference Coach of the Year. In 1982 he was hired by Northwestern, located in Evanston, Ill., just outside Chicago; four years later he was selected Big Ten Coach of the Year. Finding Chicago's gay scene a bit more inviting and anonymous than small-town Alabama's, he edged a tiny bit out of the closet. However, when he was outed by a supervisor he scuttled back in. He filed a grievance against her, claiming her defamation of his name could hurt his career.

He was, at the same time, coming out to his family. His father—an ex-marine who owned a construction company—took the news poorly but eventually made tremendous progress. It helped that Michael's partner was a runner from Michigan who slung a mean chain saw. (The same man won over Michael's mother because he could sew.)

66   But work remained difficult. At Auburn Michael had risen at
dawn to train runners, then stayed in the office until 11 P.M. recruiting West Coast athletes. It was, he says, "the perfect excuse not to
have a social life." At Northwestern, by contrast, he had a social life,
and the result was disquieting.

One day a recruit asked if something he had heard from a rival
school was true: Was Michael gay? "I beat around the bush and
didn't answer," he recalls. "I probably implied I was, and in the end
I didn't get the kid." Michael was beginning to realize that if he
remained at Northwestern, the gay issue would hang over him and
his team like a heavy cloud.

In 1986 three members of a relay team told Michael they did not
want a fourth man—a gay athlete—to run with them. Michael held
a team meeting and stood up for the gay runner. He said his team
would not discriminate against anyone, for any reason. Yet the
minute he spoke those words he realized he had signed his death
warrant as coach.

The situation turned ugly. He received obscene, late-night
phone calls that were traced back to team members. He knew he had
to leave, and a year later, when a position opened up at Brown
University in Providence, R.I., he seized it. He was out from the
start and found no problems at the liberal Ivy League school. His
first job was coaching women; then he moved into administration,
as an assistant athletic director, and admissions, as associate director.

Michael remembers, "Brown set the tone for me to be who I was.
I was 36, and I was no longer going to let anyone do that for me."
He became a gay activist, successfully lobbying the Rhode Island
governor and Providence mayor to help pass a statewide gay civil
rights bill.

In 1993 Michael was hired as track and field coach and college
counselor at prestigious Phillips Andover Academy. He also served
as faculty liaison for gay issues, the first such paid position at any pri-

vate school. Those various worlds intersected easily. One day at 67 practice, one runner asked a teammate if he ran without a shirt to impress the girls. "No, the coach!" the boy replied.

In 1996 Michael moved to another prep school, Milton Academy, as track coach, college counselor, and faculty adviser to GASP (Gay And Straight People).

Two years after that, while Michael was preparing for a sabbatical teaching history at the American School in London, the athletic director job at Oberlin came open. It appealed to Michael for several reasons, not the least of which was the circumstances under which he had left Northwestern. Oberlin represented "an opportunity to be who I am, yet at a college. The liberal Eastern prep schools were safe—I could be out and no one cared—while Oberlin was special and different. Of course, I went into it with the idea that if they wouldn't take me for who I was, I wouldn't go."

The search committee winnowed the field of candidates from several dozen down to about eight. During Michael's interview, just after he was asked how he would handle a dispute between a coach and a player with green hair ("Depends on the kid's batting average," Michael joked), he was asked if there was anything else the committee should know about him.

He replied matter-of-factly that he was gay and wondered if that would lead to problems. "No one fell of their chair or called 911," Michael says, and the interview proceeded to other matters.

When the committee narrowed the list to three final candidates, however, Michael's sexuality was on some members' minds. Blake New, the men's soccer coach, asked pointedly, "Does this guy want the job in order to be athletic director and help Oberlin, or because Oberlin is an environment where he can feel comfortable being openly gay?" It was, members agreed, an important question, and one they wrestled with for some time.

In the end, however, Michael's sexuality was not the overriding

68   issue. History professor Heather Hogan, who cochaired the committee, says, "My priority was finding the best AD we could for a program that was in a lot of trouble. Some people were hesitant about Mike, but I think they were also uneasy about hiring anyone from the outside, based on past experience."

Clayton Koppes, vice president for academic affairs and dean of the College of Arts and Sciences, adds, "We thought Mike was best qualified to build our athletic program. Of course, for 30 years Oberlin has included sexual orientation in our antidiscrimination clauses, so it would be a violation of our own standards not to hire him on that basis. Oberlin has historically taken forward-looking, progressive stances on social issues, so we said we ought to do that in this case too."

When Michael arrived on campus the following June, he was prepared to deal with hostile questions from certain coaches. In his first staff meeting, questions arose about his sexuality. Michael responded directly, asking why his being gay had anything to do with the daily workings of the department. It became clear that some coaches worried that if the word got out, it would perpetuate the stereotype of Oberlin as a "gay" school and make recruiting even harder than it already was. "That was, and is, a valid concern," Michael says. "But I'm a firm believer that any kid who wants to come to Oberlin has to come here with his eyes open."

The football coach was particularly confrontational. He pressed Michael not just about homosexuality but other issues as well. "He wanted to let me know he was in charge," Michael says. "Other people in the department listened to what I said and gave me a chance, but I don't think he ever did."

The football coach was quoted as saying his concerns about Michael's homosexuality were irrelevant to "whether I love gays or I hate gays. What he does behind closed doors doesn't bother me. He can play with chickens for all I care. It has to do with the realities of

Division III football. Recruiting is difficult, and when you're zero **69**
for a zillion, it's really difficult. To have an openly gay athletic director does not help." The football team was not zero for a zillion that
fall—just zero and 10—and Michael met little resistance when he set
about finding a new coach.

Blake New, the soccer coach, says the football coach's continued
opposition was an isolated case. Two other veteran coaches who initially opposed Michael's hiring have, he says, become the AD's
"biggest supporters. He's given them responsibility, kept them
involved, and they appreciate that."

It was not long after that first meeting with his coaches, however, that Michael's casual attitude toward his homosexuality was
severely tested. An Oberlin staff member, while discussing another
story with a reporter from *The Chronicle of Higher Education*, said
casually, "We're so liberal, we just hired a gay athletic director." The
reporter, sniffing a good lead, ran with it, and soon the preeminent
weekly magazine for university faculty members and administrators
broke the story. No one from the *Chronicle* had ever called Michael
for a quote—or even to verify that he was in fact gay.

Yet he found himself, barely one week after being hired, the talk
of the college world. And when every gay periodical in the nation
picked up the story, he was soon the talk of America's gay community as well. Michael joined Billie Jean King and several other lesbians on a Provincetown, Mass., panel exploring gay issue in athletics. *USA Today* printed quotes from the event, and soon Reverend
Phelps was faxing threats to appear at the opening of school. Alumni
began calling administrators, wondering what the hell was going on
at Oberlin; admissions officers braced for the fallout. Despite his
earlier denials, it seemed to some people that Michael was indeed
using Oberlin as a bully pulpit for gay activism.

Unbowed, Michael dove into his work. He began motivating
coaches who needed it and weeding out those who did not

respond. He worked with the alumni and admissions offices, speaking forthrightly not on gay topics but about the challenges of turning the moribund athletic program around. He was, it seemed, everywhere; no challenge was too small, no group too insignificant, to care about.

"From prep school life I knew the importance of being involved in many areas," Michael notes. "I decided I needed to build as many bridges as I could." He reached out to the school paper, *The Oberlin Review*, writing a weekly column that put a human face on athletes (one memorable column highlighted a very devout Christian). He helped create a seminar course, "Homophobia in Sport," as part of the fledgling Comparative American Studies program. He joined the Student Life Committee and eventually chaired it.

People at Oberlin—including many who seldom cared about athletics, or had always thought about it in negative terms—took notice. "Philips Gym became a more welcoming place for everyone," says Dean Koppes. "In the past some students and faculty felt unwelcome there—there was a tinge of homophobia. Now it is seen as a place for the whole community. Mike has broken down stereotypes, to show that academics and athletics can fit together."

Professor Hogan echoes those sentiments. "Mike is readily accessible to lots of students. The athletics operation is physically separate from the rest of campus. He provided needed integration, energy, and the articulation of the values of Division III athletics."

Professor Jan Cooper, who teaches expository writing, adds, "Mike's presence undercuts all the assumptions about athletics. He crosses lots of categories, in very interesting ways. And with his history background, he brings an academic cachet. His being out disrupts the sense of what athletes and ADs are. It makes people pause and listen carefully to whatever he says."

In class, Professor Cooper has seen a "huge difference" in how football players deal with sexuality. She attributes the change to two men: Jeff Ramsey, the new coach Michael hired, and to the AD him-self. "Everyone knows Mike and thinks he's cool," she says. "That's helped make the football players more curious. They're open to exploring, and not afraid to ask provocative questions."

Professor Cooper lauds Michael for his awareness of gender dynamics. "He knows what it's like to come through a system that has the potential to discriminate, and he acts in a way I have not seen other male coaches or administrators do. He's not ashamed of the fact that the women's teams are doing better than the men. And when an alumnus wanted to give money to reinstitute a men's golf team, Mike insisted it include women too."

But, Dean Koppes notes, there have been bumps in the road. A few alumni and others still think it would be easier if Oberlin did not have to deal with one more sexuality issue. To them, the dean replies, "Sure, it's always easier to never take risks. But that's boring, and it's not the type of institution Oberlin is." Fortunately, he says, "Michael is resilient. He always bounces back from adversity. That is the only way he can survive and flourish in a culture that is not always supportive."

One example of that adversity occurred early in Michael's tenure, when Reverend Phelps announced he would arrive on the first day of classes to "educate and warn Oberlin to repent and flee the wrath to come." On his Web site, the Baptist minister described the athletic director as a "filthy fag lying in his own feces." It took Reverend Phelps a year and a half to finally appear at Oberlin. When he did, with a dozen supporters singing hymns and waving signs saying THANK GOD FOR AIDS, the campus responded in typi-cal Oberlin style. "Fun With Fred Day" featured clowns, balloons, kiss-ins, face painting, and a pagan ritual to banish negative energy. Hundreds of people had a great time ignoring the protesters, who left after half an hour.

Another moment of adversity came when a group of students

petitioned the Student Life Committee, on which Michael sat, to form a Sadism and Masochism Bondage and Discipline Club (for discussion purposes only, they noted). Plans for the club had been raised several times before. The previous time, the faculty told the students to come back with answers about how the organization would run. They did, and the ball was now in the Student Life Committee's court.

"No club had ever been turned down at Oberlin before," Michael says. "I felt we couldn't put our value judgment on this. It was not about whether I am pro- or anti-S/M B&D; it was about students doing exactly what they were asked to. It probably was not great for our image, and probably as AD I shouldn't have voiced support for it. But I could not in good conscience have voted against it." The proposal ultimately failed, by one vote.

The *Plain Dealer* story, including intimate information about past boyfriends, was a third, more public example of adversity. "That was a tough one," Michael admits. "They decided they were going to do it, so it became a question of whether I'd cooperate or not. I did. There were questions that were too personal, yeah, and in the athletic department that rubbed salt in the wounds of some people. But I think that was an overreaction."

Men's soccer coach Blake New says that for two weeks after the article appeared, Michael "walked around like someone shot his mother. He realized he screwed up by trusting a reporter." In the end, however, Michael bounced back—as he had so many times before—and once again faced head-on the many challenges that come with the job.

A major challenge is dealing with the coaches of Oberlin's 10 men's and 11 women's varsity sports. "I think I've made converts of a number of them," Michael says. "One guy suddenly realized he'd never been around gay people before. Most of them now realize my being gay is a nonissue most of the time. Just as some kids might not belong at Oberlin, some coaches might not be right for this place 73 too. But I think most of them have come a long way."

One of Michael's most outspoken supporters is Jeff Ramsey, the man he hired to turn the football program around. "Mike's gayness is not a hindrance to recruiting. Our traditionally poor record is," Jeff says bluntly. "When I'm talking to a recruit, I don't hide anything. I tell them this is a liberal school with a high percentage of gays and lesbians. Then I tell them, whatever they want to accomplish in life, they won't be able to do it by discriminating against anyone."

When asked what Michael has done for Oberlin football, Jeff responds, "Where do I begin? He's opened up the lines of communication with administrators, faculty, students. He's shown that football can be very good for this campus. He's built a relationship with admissions that helps us get athletes. He's made our players and coaches realize it's good to be a well-rounded person."

A second major challenge involves athletes. "I'm very careful not to make people feel uncomfortable," Michael explains. "If the football team wins a game next year, I won't be in the locker room slapping them on the butt. I never close the door in a one-on-one meeting with an athlete, and I never have individual students come over to my house. That's an area I'm a little oversensitive in, based on past experiences elsewhere.

"On the positive side," he continues, "right from day one of the Phelps thing, the captains of every sport told me they'd do anything to help. I didn't know them at all, but they knew I was the AD and what Phelps was doing was wrong."

The football players are among Michael's staunchest advocates. Sam Hobi, captain of the 2001 squad, is an unlikely ally. A Mormon from Utah, married and a father, he pulls no punches: "I don't believe in homosexuality. I feel it's a sin. But for me it's about the sin, not the sinner. When I see someone doing something I don't personally believe in, I try to think of Scripture where the savior said, 'Before you try to take the mote out of your brother's eye, see what's in yours.' For me to not come to an institution because it's gay, or Mr. Muska is a homosexual, would be judgmental on my part. As captain of the football team I speak with him at trustee dinners and other functions. I see him as Mr. Muska, the AD, and he sees me as Sam, the captain. He always treats me with a lot of respect, and I try to do the same."

Football player Brad Mahdi, who sits on the student senate and interacts with Michael on various committees, has another take on the gay AD: "He's part of Oberlin's rich environment, and adds one more view that might not have been there, whether from his sexual preference or where he's worked in the past. And in football, when we finally win a game, that will be in part because of the huge effort he's made to help all of us, and bring the campus together."

One athlete with a unique perspective is Mary Margaret Towey. She is a nontraditional student in every sense: 50 years old, home-schooled her entire life, and an out lesbian who competes on the track team. Michael has coached her in the hammer throw and advises her independent major on the sociology of women in sport. "Even here, at what may be the safest school in the country for gays, athletics is the last bastion of homophobia," Mary Margaret says. "But with Mike I know my concerns will be addressed, my problems won't be shunted off to the side. And it signals to me that it is possible to be an openly gay coach, which is something I want to do."

Michael faces few challenges with non-athletes, for several reasons. One is that Oberlin attracts students comfortable with homosexuality; another is that because he teaches classes, chairs the Student Life Committee, sits on the judicial board, and helped formulate the school's anti-Nike sweatshop policy, he fits into the mainstream of campus life.

Alumni, however, are a different story. They wrote letters to the president, citing what Dean Koppes calls their "supposed concerns about Mike's ability to recruit athletes and work with other coaches and alums."

Mike's reply, individually and to the Alumni Council, was direct: "Judge me for who I am and what I do." It took a couple of years, but the message sank in. "It became pretty hard for anyone to say I came in here with an agenda. I work my ass off in this job and for this college, and I think people knew it."

Ernie Iseminger, assistant director of alumni affairs with oversight of athletics, and a former Washington State University rower and coach, elaborates on Michael's point. "I field lots of calls about Mike's orientation. The older they are, the more aggressive they get. They say, 'Don't we have enough problems as it is?' My response is, 'Look at the job he's done. Period. The end. Look at the football program, the numbers, the facilities, the support he's made within the administration for athletics.' I get in some very intense discussions, but I will not back down from supporting Mike. He's probably the most successful AD we've had here in 30 years.

"I set these guys straight," Ernie continues passionately. "Sometimes it takes a few phone calls, sometimes many months, but eventually they realize that having a gay AD means nothing, and they're being foolish. One guy, one of the biggest homophobes I've ever met, a World War II vet, was at a football game ranting and raving. Finally I just said, 'Look at how hard those guys are fighting,' and he had to agree. He even told Mike he'd been wrong."

Why is Ernie such a strong supporter? "It has nothing to do with 'pioneer'; that's not my thing," he says. "I'm not doing cartwheels over this. I just look at the job he's doing. What I love about Mike and Oberlin is that we're sometimes complete opposites. As a Christian I have to constantly question and battle all this internally. Based on the strictest church philosophy, homosexuality is wrong. But I also believe God made everybody and loves everybody. Mike and I talk about this a lot. I've asked about his experiences and if he ever wanted to be with a female. We communicate. We have a good relationship. We love to give each other shit."

As with some alumni, the discomfort level among Michael's colleagues is high. At his first NCAA conference after the *Chronicle* article, only one male athletic director—Stanford University's Ted Leland—spoke to him. (In contrast, he says, "the women flocked to me!") The NCAA has never asked him to address gay issues in sports at a national convention.

He does not raise the topic unnecessarily, but when homophobia occurs Michael reacts. A Pennsylvania school taunted Oberlin's baseball team with antigay epithets. Michael immediately called his counterpart there, threatening not only to never play the team again, but to let the gay student group on that campus know what had happened. Similarly, when a football recruit said that another college used homophobic slurs against Oberlin, Michael told the offending school's AD that he would not hesitate to tell that school's "very active gay group" about the coaching staff's tactics.

Recruiting is vital to the success of every college team, and Oberlin is no exception. "There's no question some of my coaches are overly sensitive to how to defend the issue—'It's a gay campus, now there's a gay AD'—when it's raised," Michael says. "Well, I'm a firm believer that if a kid or family has an issue with that, Oberlin may not be the right place for him. Kids have to make these kinds of judgments, and coaches have to accept what Oberlin is about as well." While no openly gay athlete has ever come to Oberlin because of Michael (and he has no way of knowing if any closeted athletes have), he is proud that at least one straight athlete chose Oberlin as a reaction to negative recruiting by a rival coach.

Michael knows that men's college sports are far gayer than nearly anyone imagines. He recalls sitting in a Providence gay bar a decade ago when a young man wearing a Brown hockey jacket walked in. "I said, 'You're fine, but check the coat.' He said, 'But Mr. Muska, you wouldn't believe how it helps me pick up guys!' We started talking, and he told me there were half a dozen other gay guys on the team. But he was the only one—and this was after the season, in spring of his senior year—who could deal with it well. That just confirmed what I already knew: They're out there, no matter what anyone says."

Yet while the universe of openly gay male college athletes is tiny, the list of openly gay male athletic directors is smaller still. It includes just one name: Michael Muska. Of course, that does not mean he is the only gay male athletic director in America. He has received E-mails from two closeted colleagues, and another from a man who is no longer working in athletics but still refuses to come out.

What does it all mean? "What I've done is considered great in some circles, the kiss of death in others," Michael says. "I have been contacted about a couple of AD jobs at bigger schools. I asked one president if they'd really thought this through, and he said the most popular professor on campus was gay. I said, 'A gay professor is nothing like a gay AD.' He called back and admitted they weren't ready to take that step yet."

"Unfortunately, Mike is still the only one," notes Dean Koppes. "Our society should have as a goal allowing and supporting everyone to advance to the best of their abilities. But discrimination against gays and lesbians is still significant in athletics. It's still an area that's seen as different. I'm glad Oberlin could take this step, but—and I'm sure Mike would agree—I look forward to the day it is *not* news."

Olympic Equestrian
Robert Dover

Mention the Olympics, and people think of famous athletes in big-time sports: basketball's Dream Team, for example, or track an field stars like Carl Lewis. But the modern Olympic movement is made up of 31 summer and 15 winter sports. Many are little known beyond their specialized worlds; they attract passionate, dedicated men and women whose primary rewards come from the thrill of competition and the joy of camaraderie. Something else is little known too: When thousands of those athletes, most of them unheralded, gather together in an Olympic Village, a surprising number are gay.

That is the matter-of-fact opinion of Robert Dover. He is at ease discussing the joys of strolling the Village grounds with his boyfriend; of gay barhopping in cities like Los Angeles, Barcelona, and Sydney; of being an out and proud Olympian, and knowing he is far from alone.

Robert should know. He is a five-time captain of the U.S. equestrian team, a three-time bronze medal winner, and the most honored American dressage competitor ever. Most Americans have never heard of Robert Dover, or of the specialized sport of dressage. But he is as much a part of the Olympic tradition as Jim Thorpe, Mark Spitz, or Nadia Comaneci.

Since 1984, Robert has served the Olympic movement well. In addition to his horseback riding (more on that later), he spent two terms on the United States Olympic Committee's Athletes' Advisory Council, which meets three times a year and acts as the competitors' watchdog. Members of the powerful group discuss issues like doping and selection procedures. Gay issues arise only when an athlete's

right to compete has been jeopardized by allegations of homosexuality or impropriety, as has happened in diving. The council—which,
Robert says, always includes at least one other gay athlete—takes the
athlete's side, so "the gay issue becomes a nonissue."

Olympic athletes, whatever their sport, share similar traits.
Marathon runners, rowers, and soccer or field hockey players—all
have spent enormous energy and astonishing amounts of time
reaching the pinnacle of success. Many surmounted unfathomable
obstacles along the way.

"To be an Olympian, and have such incredible heart and focus,
you must also be extremely intelligent," Robert says. "Many of
the athletes in sports you don't always hear about, like archery or
sailing, are doctors and lawyers and accountants. Because of that
and because of their good education, many of them are also very
open-minded." That is one reason, he says, that he has felt no
fears and encountered no problems as an out athlete, and why he
knows of no negative experiences among other openly gay
Olympic athletes either.

Robert's pleasure is heightened because his sport attracts an
inordinate number of gay men. Dressage—the word is French for
"training"—is equal parts arts and athletics. It originated in ancient
Greece, when war horses were taught to leap high in the air, kicking
out and striking with their front feet, to avoid foot soldiers. Later,
those wartime movements were transformed into equine ballet
dances to entertain royalty. In the 1500s the French elevated dressage into a popular activity, breeding horses with small heads and
highly developed hindquarters.

Riders adopted top hats and tails. The sport grew elegant. The
ideal horses appeared to dance of their own volition; riders were
expected to use as little hand pressure as possible. Like compulsory
skaters, dressage riders are judged and scored on the correctness and
exactness of their figures. Victory or defeat—including the final

event, a six-minute musical freestyle devised and choreographed by the rider—depends on the horse's expression of brilliance.

Unlike most sports, in dressage men and women compete together. Most are long-legged—that is part of the elegance—and, Robert says, many are analytical, cool under pressure, and purposefully single-minded

So how gay is dressage? In the United States, according to Robert, "a large percentage" of male riders are attracted to other men. In Europe—including Germany, where dressage is almost a national sport, and crowds of 60,000 fill stadiums for competitions—the percentage is lower, but still substantial: from 25% to 40%, Robert estimates.

Why are so many gay men attracted to dressage? "Probably for the same reason you find gay men in the arts or on Broadway," Robert says. "We tend to gravitate toward artistic, beautiful things. Dressage allows us to be both sportsmen and sensitive men." Family background helps too. Parents with an aversion to homosexuality might steer a budding horseman away from riding, to a different kind of sport—say, football—while those who are more broadminded encourage young riders.

Until he was 13, little in Robert's life indicated future Olympic stardom. He and his three older siblings moved often; his father's work for an automotive headlight company took them to Chicago, Toronto, the Bahamas, Florida, and Georgia. It was, Robert says playfully, "a typical middle-class Jewish upbringing."

At age 5, however, he was abused by the older son of next-door neighbors. This created for Robert an aversion to men that lasted through high school. For an entire year, he recalls, he did not talk to anyone except those he met at stables—people who shared his love of riding.

Robert's introduction to horses came just before his 13th birthday, when the girl next door took him to a ring. By whim or fate (he is not sure which), the Toronto-area stable was filled with fine German horses bred specially for dressage. An instructor hoisted Robert up and, when he saw Robert ride, predicted he would become a dressage athlete.

The attraction for Robert was immediate. "Horses are fantastic animals," he says. "They weigh anywhere from one to two thousand pounds, but they have great acceleration. When they gallop at 30 miles an hour you need tremendous balance just to stay on." A good rider must feel comfortable despite ceding control. "When a horse—even a pony—decides what he's going to do, you're at his mercy," he explains. While dressage is not as dangerous as jumping over fences, it is risky. Robert is lucky: In 30 years of riding, his worst injuries have been a broken leg and back problems.

Until he entered the University of Georgia, Robert's social life was limited. He spent most of his time with horses, not humans. Finally, in college he began dating women. During his junior year after a long relationship had ended, he went drinking with a man who kept his horse at the same stable. "I woke up the next morning, and there this guy was," Robert says cryptically. "That was pretty scary."

For two weeks he was a mess. The encounter shocked him, because for years he had stowed his same-sex feelings in the recesses of his mind. He wondered whether the night represented a one-time thing, or if it would lead to permanent gay behavior. And he had no idea where to turn for support.

But Robert continued to see his new friend. When the man took him to The Circus—at the time the only gay bar in Athens, Ga.— Robert saw many other men who looked and acted just like him. Men, in turn, noticed the new, young face. Robert enjoyed the attention, and before long the "emotional wreck" had turned into a happy gay man.

Robert came out as easily to his family as he did on campus.

"They're fantastic," he says. "One of my sisters just said, 'So?' And my parents like my boyfriend a lot better than they like me."

It took Robert longer to come out in the dressage world, where he was gaining increasing renown (and where, he says parenthetically, it is harder to be Jewish than gay). Dressage is expensive. An Olympic-level horse costs between $500,000 and $4 million; care, transportation, and equipment are additional expenses. Robert's father paid $1,000 for his first horse; to make money the young rider trained it, sold it for a profit, then did the same with other horses. To make more money, he also began teaching dressage.

Many of his students were women. "I felt it was important to my business that they see me as a sexual being," he says. "I wanted them to want me to teach them." To demonstrate technique, he put his hands on their knees. They shivered; he felt nothing.

By his first Olympics, in 1984, Robert was more comfortable being an out rider. "I had become successful enough that I knew most people would accept me. If they didn't, I knew they weren't really my friends," he says. His boyfriend attended the '84 Games in Los Angeles, and the two men appeared in public together. In the Olympic Village Robert met other gay athletes but sensed he was more open than they.

The '84 Olympics were also where a British swimmer cruised Robert in the gym shower following a workout. The tall, handsome Brit followed him out the door and all the way back to Robert's room. When Robert finally turned and asked, "Do you want to talk?" the man grinned, and pushed him into the room. "That was my introduction to gay people in sports," Robert says. "The Olympic Village is just a smaller version of the world. I'm sure at least 10% of the Village is gay, and they're looking for the same thing everyone else is."

The 1988 Olympics in Seoul had a different feel. Part of it was geographic—"We definitely felt like we were on the other side of the world," Robert says—but part was athletic. "I was more businesslike.

I was focused on trying to lead my team to a medal," he adds, explain- ing why the '88 Games were "less gay" than his other four.

Th 1992 Olympics were plenty of fun, in part because gay friends accompanied him to Barcelona. Four years later, in the familiar city of Atlanta, Robert made a point of being out to everyone. He was not flamboyant—that is not his style—but he felt it was important to be a role model for anyone needing one. There were other gay members of the U.S. equestrian team that year, but at the introductory press conference no one said anything. Robert, who as captain spoke last, described himself as "the token gay Jewish fourtime Olympian." Reporters laughed but did not write much about it.

By 2000 in Sydney, Robert's sexuality was a complete nonissue. The media focused more on his Equestrian AIDS Foundation, an organization he and his lover had founded five years before to help riders and children stricken with AIDS or HIV. That lack of attention to his sexuality suited Robert fine. "While I'm totally proud of who I am, when I compete it's as an athlete," he says. "I'm there to win." He admits it would be a bigger story if a member of the Dream Team came out. However, he insists, the tone of even that coverage would be factual, not sensational.

Of course, Robert's homosexuality has not gone completely unnoticed. In Germany at a major show, several male riders bet an unsuspecting secretary that she could not lure Robert into bed. After two days of fending off her constant come-ons, he learned the truth. "I was mortified and embarrassed," he says. "I thought she was hot for me. I also thought the guys respected me, but they made the whole thing into a joke." After discussing the situation with his boyfriend, Robert told the ringleader he had not been bothered; in fact, he said, he hoped they'd had a few laughs and made a lot of money.

From that moment on, the German riders respected Robert. It did not hurt that he won all his classes there, rare for an American in Europe.

84   He is clearly respected by his Olympic teammates. He calls his five elections as captain "affirmation"—not of himself as a gay man but as someone who holds the highest Olympic ideas to his heart. However, he notes, his idealism cannot be separated from his sexuality. "They know me as a complete human being, and they know I'm not lying about anything."

To Robert, his twin identities as Olympic athlete and gay man are intertwined and inseparable. In his position on the Games Preparation Committee, which oversees every sport's selection venues and trials, he once attended the Paralympic sailing finals. In the moments before the starting gun sounded, he marveled as dozens of athletes tossed their prosthetic arms and legs onto the dock; the artificial limbs only slowed them down. "They were sailors first," Robert explains. "They didn't want to be thought of as disabled, any more than a gay athlete in the heat of competition wants to be thought of as gay."

However, Robert acknowledges, being gay is an integral part of who he is: an Olympic dressage rider. "The way I carry myself, the music I select and the choreography I create for my horse's freestyle—being gay definitely contributes to all that," he says. "But when I compete, like everyone else, I'm there to win."

And win he does—even though he says that, true to the Olympic ideal, the most important victories come simply by competing. It would be hard to find a better poster boy for those ideals than gay Jewish dressage captain Robert Dover.

"Being part of the Olympics is hard to describe," he says. "I don't know that you can fully grasp what it means unless you've walked into an Olympic stadium with your team and 15,000 other athletes, heard your national anthem, and watched someone like Muhammad Ali light the torch." That is a moment anyone—regardless of race, gender, nationality, or sexual orientation—cherishes for life.

Wrestling
Rafael Cruz Rivera

Wrestling—the WWF variety, that is—attracts a fanatical following, thanks to a cleverly outrageous mix of over-the-top personalities, head-banging violence, and envelope-pushing smut and vulgarity.

Its contrast with the original forms of wrestling, freestyle and Greco-Roman—competitions defined by strength, agility, balance, quickness, patience, and intelligence, both of which have endured for centuries—could not be starker. But perhaps the biggest difference between make-believe and "real" wrestling lies in their story lines. The lives of Stone Cold Steve Austin, Triple H, and The Rock, brimming with bogus rivalries, girlfriend intrigues, and feuds with WWF founder and chairman Vince McMahon, are fantasies sprung full-blown from the minds of marketers and writers.

Every word of Rafael Cruz Rivera's story, meanwhile, is true.

Rafael's life is littered with enough obstacles to make even the seven-foot Brothers of Destruction cower: a broken home, drug and alcohol abuse, homophobia. But Rafael's tale ends in triumph. Our hero earns himself an education, finds success and happiness out West, and—in heart-warming fashion worthy of Mick "Mankind" Foley's most incredible victory over adversity—wins a gold medal at the Gay Games.

Score one for the good guys.

Rafael's story began in New York City with his mother, Carmen Cruz, who spoke only Spanish. Lacking marketable skills, she was dependent on a series of boyfriends, most of whom treated her poorly. Living precariously in a series of different apartments, Rafael and his brother, two years younger, witnessed too much of what Rafael simply calls "bad stuff."

When Rafael was 8, a social worker told the boys they would be united with their older sister. That story was a lie; it was the only way the social worker could get the boys into a taxi and away from their mother. The social service workers thought they were doing the right thing for Rafael, who spoke no English and had never attended school.

For the next five years, until she died, Rafael saw his mother infrequently. She led, he says, "a colorful life." She believed in white magic (magic used only for good purposes), and was a devoted wrestling fan. She watched it for hours on Spanish television; her favorite wrestlers included American idol Bob Backlund and Mexican hero Mil Mascaras ("The Man of a Thousand Masks"). When he could, Rafael watched with her. He was enchanted by the action and wanted to emulate professional wrestlers. But when he learned that some of his heroes stood 6 foot 6 and weighed 350 pounds, his hopes sank. Rafael was just a skinny boy.

After being taken from their mother, Rafael and his brother were placed with foster parents in the Bronx. The Puerto Rican couple had already raised two of their own youngsters, along with several foster children. Mr. and Mrs. Rivera were nice, Rafael says, and cared for him and his brother well. When Rafael's mother died, the Riveras adopted the boys officially. As a sign of respect, he took their surname but kept his mother's as well.

The Riveras gave Rafael things he'd never had: discipline, encouragement, an opportunity to go to school. He seized them all, especially education. His first day in school, he was placed at his age-appropriate level: third grade. He lagged far behind his new class-mates, but with the help of demanding yet understanding teachers, he soon caught up. Rafael became a voracious reader; today, two decades later, books remain one of his favorite pleasures.

Though he appreciated the Riveras, Rafael always dreamed of uniting with his mother. Believing one way to do that was through prayer and religion, he attended Catholic services with Mrs. Rivera's mother. But when he discovered certain hypocrisies—for example, the preacher's son smoked marijuana—Rafael decided that to get to heaven and join his mother, he needed a tougher church. At 13, he discovered the Jehovah's Witnesses.

He walked into Kingdom Hall, the local meeting place, on his own. The church provided even more structure and discipline, and Rafael devoured piles of reading material in English and Spanish.

Rafael passed many hours each week with the Jehovah's Witnesses—but he spent many more swimming. As a child, he had almost drowned; now he faced his fears and became a competitive swimmer for the Kips Bay Boys Club and Stevenson High School. His long arms made him a natural backstroker.

Rafael created a life for himself that did not allow any time for trouble. Despite living in the middle of the Bronx, surrounded by drugs, gangs, and violence, he flourished. By the spring of 1988, he was ready to graduate in the top 10 of his class.

But Rafael did not attend graduation. Earlier that year, a few weeks after his 18th birthday, he had come out. Once again his world turned inside out.

For a while his Jehovah's Witnesses brothers had criticized him. They commanded him not to laugh in his usual loud way; it conveyed "the wrong image," they said cryptically. When he ran awkwardly playing basketball—the result of a knee injury—they repeated that same "wrong image" phrase. Rafael did not know what they meant. But one day, a Witness brother read a biblical passage to him. It condemned homosexuality, and suddenly Rafael made the connection. "I left the Catholic Church in part because they let a gay guy preach to the youth group, and now I was being accused of homosexuality," Rafael says. In fact, he says, he felt asexual. He would wake up in horror, then cry, after having wet dreams, convinced he was a sinner destined for hell. Growing up, he had no one to talk to about sex; when his church accused him of being a homosexual, his isolation only deepened. And then he got mad.

Rafael's years of reading had taught him the importance of thinking problems all the way through. He knew he wanted to go to heaven and that homosexuals could not. He knew it was not right for a young person to become angry with someone older. But he also did not know what was really right, or who he really was. He went home, put on his headphones, and started thinking. He thought about male and female parts, how they fit together, and what he wanted to do with his own parts. He boarded a train, got off where he figured he should, walked into a bar, and let a man buy him a drink. Soon he knew where he wanted his parts to fit.

Shortly thereafter, he told the Riveras he was not going back to Kingdom Hall—and why. Mrs. Rivera blamed herself. Mr. Rivera got mad at Rafael for making Mrs. Rivera upset. A week later Rafael moved out.

He lived for a while at a friend's house, then rented a studio apartment in the Bronx. To support himself, he worked the graveyard shift answering phones for the National AIDS Hotline. He snuck into clubs, explored Manhattan life, made new friends to replace all the Witnesses he had lost, and—because he needed only three courses to graduate—somehow managed to complete his schoolwork.

It was not easy. To supplement his income, he says he did "whatever it took to make money. I was 18 in New York City, and I met many very generous strangers. That's all I'll say about that."

By the time the 1988 New York Gay Pride parade was held, he was dating a Radical Faerie who also worked at the Hotline, so Rafael spent the day parading down Fifth Avenue wearing only a satin loincloth. The following day was his high school graduation. Rafael was not there.

But he was not through with school. He enrolled at the State

University of New York at Oswego, north of Syracuse on Lake Ontario. He majored in sociology and his grades were fine, but his main activity was activism. "I was a raging, flaming homosexual afraid of no one," Rafael says. "I was ready to rock the place. One of my first projects was replacing the senior president of GALA (the Gay and Lesbian Alliance) with myself. I had spirit and tenacity, but I was also rambunctious and obnoxious. The only way I knew to be gay was to scream it out. I hadn't learned that coming-out is a process. I'd always been taught that gay equals bad, and all of a sudden I was exploring life with a whole new set of rules."

Rafael dressed in a suit and tie but cut his pants off at the knees and added fairy wings. He walked through the dining hall yelling, "Cocksucker, fudgepacker, queer! I'm not the only gay person here, but I am the loudest! The person sitting next to you might be gay too. And what about you?" As students shot him angry, nervous, or frightened looks, he continued, "But I'm a son, a brother, a man, just like you."

Eventually, however, such activism grew boring, and Rafael followed a boyfriend to the State University of New York's Albany campus. He did not like it there, however, and after he and his boyfriend broke up he decided it was time to move on. Greyhound offered a $69 fare anywhere in the United States, so Rafael stuffed his belongings in a shopping bag and impulsively headed out to a place he'd heard was fun: San Francisco.

Four days before Christmas in 1989—tired, hungry, and a bit dazed—Rafael arrived in the gay capital of the universe. The Radical Faeries welcomed him to their house at 501 Ashbury, offering their traditional gifts: a bed, vegetable-based soup, wine, and pot. "Merry Christmas!" Rafael says.

He stayed in San Francisco for nine years. He loved the city's beauty and its opportunities. He danced at go-go clubs, and for Pansy Division. He sang first tenor with the Golden Gate Men's

Chorus. He worked in a pizza shop, earned his associate's liberal arts degree at San Francisco Community College, spent six years as a Gray Line concierge, went horseback riding and jet skiing, and had several boyfriends.

One was a retired stock manager for Pacific Gas and Electric, a Dutch man 25 years older than Rafael. When his partner was dying of AIDS, Rafael nursed him and fed him his last morsel of food. "It was a beautiful experience for me, being there for someone as he left this world," Rafael says. "It was so gratifying to help make his transition into the unknown a little better. I'm grateful I had that chance. And it was good for me too. It helped me grow up."

One day in 1996, while manning the gay choir booth at the Folsom Street Fair, Rafael learned of an organization he never knew existed: the Golden Gate Wrestling Club. He met some of the wrestlers and realized they were not the behemoths he had seen on television in his mother's apartment. He was intrigued, but it took several months before he summoned enough courage to walk into the club's workout room in the Castro. Feeling scrawny, Rafael was intimidated physically; in addition, two muggings had made him feel very vulnerable.

Gene Dermody, director of Golden Gate Wrestling, had no problem with Rafael's lean body and long arms; his was a perfect physique for the sport.. When Gene learned that Rafael weighed just 128 pounds, he predicted that within a year Rafael would win a gold medal.

Rafael worked out with Gene a few times. Three weeks later the 27-year-old novice entered his first tournament, which was two hours away. His first opponent, a 19-year-old, had been wrestling since he was 5. The younger man won, but Rafael survived to the end and avoided a pin. He felt elated. Prior to his second bout, Gene told him to attack. Rafael went on the offensive, shot, pinned his foe—and earned a silver medal.

"Before that day, I saw wrestling as another temporary thing," Rafael says. "I'm a very adaptable person, and I saw this as something totally new I could learn a bit about, but nothing really more. But after that first tournament I started training with a vengeance."

Wrestling's many positive qualities drew him in. He enjoyed working out, practicing, and learning other men's strengths and weaknesses. He appreciated his teammates' support at tournaments, but realized that wrestling is ultimately an individual sport. Once a match begins, each wrestler is alone, solely responsible for his own success or failure. However, winning or losing can be measured in ways far beyond points and pins. Rafael learned to set personal goals—for example, staying off his back or trying new moves. When he accomplished those goals, he considered that match a victory, regardless of the score.

Rafael—who came late to education—also understood that the best wrestlers are highly intelligent men who never stop learning about their sport. He loved lingering after matches, discussing techniques and tactics with foes.

And even though there is no eroticism associated with wrestling—too much goes on every second to give that a second thought—an intensely physical element still enthralls Rafael. "You are constantly aware of your body and your opponent's," he explains. "Wrestling is not about big gym muscles but being fast and flexible and strong. It's nice, as a 31-year-old, to wrestle these 18- and 19-year-olds and be able to say to myself, 'OK, Rafael, you're smart and strong, and you can handle yourself in combat.' I can feel good about me. It's a form of validation, you could say."

One of Rafael's personal goals was to compete in the 1998 Gay Games in Amsterdam. Training five days a week, he reached that goal—then surpassed it. One week after running the San Francisco Marathon, he and 25 Golden Gate Wrestling Club teammates flew to Holland. To his astonishment, Rafael won a gold medal at 127 pounds.

Characteristically, he downplays that feat. Rafael prefers talking about "the beautiful experience" of hanging out with all kinds of gay people, involved in sports as varied as bodybuilding and martial arts, while soaking up Dutch hospitality. But his coach, Gene Dermody, eagerly puts Rafael's achievements in perspective.

"Rafael's story is really representative of the entire Gay Games movement. He is a poster child for what athletics can accomplish," Gene—a former president of the Federation of Gay Games—says. "Saddled with his past, he could have taken the 'easy road' of entitlements, played up the 'victim' card, and become a bitter bar queen. Instead he chose self-respect, self-discipline, sports, and teamwork."

Gene mentored Rafael in many ways. He taught the young wrestler moves as well as club operations. Rafael learned how to set a budget, raise funds, and run board meetings. So after the Gay Games, when Rafael felt he had outgrown San Francisco and got the urge to move, he took his knowledge about running an organization to Seattle and formed the Kings Wrestling Club. It is the only adult wrestling club in the state of Washington.

Today, the Kings have more than 25 members. They range in age from 19 to 51 and in weight from 127 to 285. Seventy percent are gay; there is one woman. Rafael handles everything from insurance to ground rules ("We are not a dating service" is one). He fills an important role, linking Seattle's gay and sports communities. A favorite "recruiting" tactic is to drag a wrestling mat onto the patio of the Cuff, a popular dance bar, and put on a wrestling exhibition. "People stand around with their drinks and cigarettes, and they're just amazed at our intensity," Rafael says. "Once a big drag queen, a guy who had wrestled in high school, got on the mat with us. We raised $400, and we educated a lot of people."

Rafael is also a full-time student, studying business information technology at Seattle Central Community College. In what he laughingly calls his "spare time" he works as a lead barista at a coffee shop, writes articles for the gay press, and serves as secretary for Team Seattle, the city's Gay Games umbrella organization.

But amid such an active, constructive life, wrestling remains Rafael's true passion. And that is what he does, he insists—he is a wrestler, not a "gay wrestler." Gay wrestling connotes, he says, "lube and latex singlets." His club competes in officially sanctioned Olympic and freestyle tournaments. Members train hard, compete aggressively, and take care of their bodies well. The last thing they think about on the mat is sex.

"You're too busy trying to win for wrestling to be erotic," Rafael notes. "When you grab someone's wrist, it's to get control, nothing else. When there are crowds and coaches yelling and referees jumping around blowing whistles, if you get distracted looking at some guy's great legs, you're going to lose.

"To me, wrestling is a good way to get rid of the aggressiveness that builds up all day inside you. It's an outlet, a way to vent. Afterward you're so exhausted, and you have such respect for your opponent, that the camaraderie just takes over. Wrestlers are like a big family filled with mutual respect. That's another reason the club isn't a dating service—that would be incest!"

Wrestling has shown Rafael how to use his mind and body together in harmony. It has given him courage to pursue goals he might never have dreamed of on his own. It has taught Rafael, the student, how to be a teacher. Most importantly, it has allowed him to feel comfortable in his own skin and luxuriate in being alive. "I feel bad for people who haven't yet seen the light," Rafael says. "It's very sad if you can't be happy with who you are, because then you'll never be able to pursue any dreams. Turning tricks, drinking—that kind of life—is old, simple, and dumb. Setting dreams is new, fresh, and wonderful. That's what wrestling has meant to me."

Today, Rafael describes himself as "a 128-pound gay male who is into life. It would be easy to see me as a certain type—a victim, a

94 bottom, whatever—and because I'm Latino, as someone with a lot of machismo. But wrestling is not about violent punching or kicking. I saw enough of that when I watched my mother get beat up. Now I know a man can use his body for constructive purposes. I enjoy teaching that to other gay men. I love the dance of an over-under tie-up or a fireman's carry. I love the camaraderie of talking afterward with my wrestling friends, analyzing moves, and helping each other succeed.

"For me, life gets better every day," Rafael concludes. "I have wrestling, and I have a partner. My days and nights are full. I feel like I am the luckiest person on earth."

Outed Football Player/Wrestler Greg Congdon

By now, millions of Americans have thrilled to Corey Johnson's story. Thanks to an insightful page one story in *The New York Times*, a positive portrayal on ABC's *20/20*, and a passionate speech Corey gave at the Millennium March on Washington, the tale has achieved almost mythic proportions. With the full backing of his coaches, the Massachusetts high school football star came out to his teammates and received overwhelmingly strong support. Fellow players at Masconomet High School covered his back on the football field; the few times opponents tried to taunt him, the team just played harder. On the bus home after a victory the players serenaded him with "YMCA" and "It's Raining Men"; when he attended gay youth conferences and pride marches, they asked for souvenir T-shirts. Corey became an articulate spokesman for gay civil rights, hung out with senators and movie stars, and even appeared (wearing football pads and eye black) in an ad for the Mitchell Gold furniture company.

Greg Congdon is another football player. He is just a year older than Corey, and lives only a couple of hundred miles away. He is as firm as Corey in his determination that his story be told. Yet it is an entirely different tale. Greg says that its message must be heard by the many gay athletes who may think that because Corey came out to broad acceptance, even reverence, the coast is clear for everyone else to do the same.

Greg's story begins in—and never really leaves—Troy, Pa. A dairy-, pig-, and beef-farming community of about 1,200 in the northeast part of the state, it is a typical American small town. Most residents were born and raised in the area. The high school is regional. The closest gay bar is in the "big city" of Elmira, N.Y. (population 31,000), half an hour away.

Greg's mother, JoAnn, a registered nurse, comes from Elmira; his father, Neil, a construction-site job expediter, was born and raised right in Troy, where most of the Congdon family has always lived. Neil was an excellent wrestler at Troy High School, and when Greg was 10 he followed his dad's footsteps and joined the youth program. Wrestling is big in Pennsylvania, and Greg enjoyed it for several years—at least until high school, when he felt pressured to drop his already-lean weight, 135 pounds on a 5-foot-10 frame, to 119.

He also played football, from Pee Wee to high school. He was a defensive end and center, though small for the latter position. "I liked just going out, hitting, and not worrying about the consequences," Greg says of his love for football. "It was a great way to relieve all the stress. Out on the field, nothing bothered you. You were in your own world. Practices sucked, but playing was so much fun."

Some of that stress related to sexuality. From the time he was 11 and first realized he was "different" from other boys, Greg tried to suppress his feelings of attraction to the same sex. He was successful for a few years. Then, in 1997, his parents bought a computer.

Like many teenagers struggling with homosexuality, the Internet opened up an amazing world. For the first time, Greg learned there were untold numbers of other boys just like him. Many gay youths find this to be an empowering, life-affirming discovery. For Greg, however, the effect was devastating.

Stuck in his small town, he realized how much he was missing. "I saw so many people with boyfriends," he laments. "I didn't know any gay people around here. I didn't think I could ever have what they had, because I was here in Troy." And Troy was not a good place to be. The only time the subject of homosexuality arose was as a joke. It was never discussed in sex education classes. Even the local newspaper, the *Daily Review* in nearby Towanda, ran regular diatribes against homosexuality, sometimes citing the North American Man-Boy Love Association as a representative gay organization.

Adding to Greg's confusion was the fact that for two years, starting at age 13, he had a sexual relationship with his best male friend, who instigated it. However, when they were 15 the other boy said he was straight and ended the encounters. Greg—who was also dating girls, primarily for show, and soon lost his virginity to a girl in an experience he calls "awful"—wondered how his friend could simply say he was straight and change his feelings. Try as Greg might—and he certainly tried hard—he could not become straight as well.

The next year, in a gay chat room, was the first time he typed the words "I am gay." "It felt so odd and weird," he remembers. "I never thought just saying it would be so overwhelming." It was liberating in a way, but also frightening. Greg began withdrawing from friends. He locked himself in his family's computer room, spending every night prowling the Web for information and chatting with other gay youths. He even stopped wrestling junior year, telling the coach he was under too much stress.

His best friend—the boy with whom he had had a sexual relationship—asked why he was spending so much time on his computer. Greg replied vaguely that he was meeting "all kinds of people." Everyone else, including his parents, thought it was simply a new interest that would soon die out.

But 17-year-old Greg had another type of dying in mind: his own. On Sunday, February 1, 1998, he decided that the only way out of his misery was to kill himself. "I just didn't know how to go about being gay," he explains. "I was afraid what would happen if my parents and friends found out. I had no idea how I could live my life. I had no role models. The only gay athlete I knew was Greg Louganis, and he was a swimmer. I couldn't associate with that. There was no *Queer as Folk* or *Will & Grace* on TV. The only gay people I saw were the drag queens on *Birdcage*. I never thought I'd

98 find a boyfriend, like everyone else. If you really believe you'll never find love, you think about killing yourself."

He thought his mother's blood pressure pills would do the job. He downed them, then went online and mentioned what he had done. A boy in California called 911, and from a continent away the Troy police were alerted. "The cop was more interested that the call had come from California than in me," Greg laughs ruefully.

As it turns out, his life was never in danger. The pills were actually diuretics, and they had no effect on Greg's health. But in tiny Troy Community Hospital, while Greg was being treated by a doctor and nurse, the policeman urged him to reveal why he had attempted suicide. He promised the information would remain confidential. Greg, in an emotionally fragile state, worried that his parents would get in trouble if anyone thought they were contributing to his problems. He broke down, told the officer he was gay, and said he could not cope. The nurse noted the information on Greg's medical chart.

He spent a week in an adolescent psychiatric ward at a hospital near State College. The only visitors permitted were his relatives. Meanwhile, his mother had searched his room and found brochures from PFLAG. She thought his homosexual feelings were only a phase.

The night he got home, Greg called his best friend—the boy he had had the relationship with. The friend told him that everyone at school knew Greg was gay. He added that the football quarterback had found out through his mother, a secretary at Troy Community Hospital, who after reading Greg's chart had told her son. The quarterback told friends at Troy High, and the gossip raced through the entire school. Greg was shocked, stunned, and scared, but his friend said soothingly, "Don't worry. No one cares." It was his way of trying to get Greg to come back to school.

When Greg mustered the courage to return, a week later, his best friend—and virtually everyone else—turned against him.

"I lost everything I thought was my life," Greg says. "Kids I'd

grown up with, played backyard football with, been in their houses—it was all gone in the flash of an eye. One guy told me he
couldn't be my friend anymore. My teammates said if I played sports
ever again, my life would be a living hell."

It was not only teenagers who shunned Greg. His coaches
ignored him as well. The wrestling coach talked to Greg's father but
refused to look at Greg standing next to him. When the football
coach was asked why Greg stopped playing, he replied, "I never
thought about it." Greg says sadly, "He was a man I knew well. I
used to hang out with him during my free periods. I was close to all
the coaches."

Only two people in all of Troy High School stuck by Greg's side.
Both were girls. "They were all I had," Greg says.

Even his teachers and counselors seemed unmoved by Greg's
ordeal. He skipped classes, sleeping in his car in the parking lot—or
at a local creek or cemetery—instead of going inside to be tormented. No one called his parents to report that things were amiss.

At home, Greg worked hard to put up a false front. "I was so
used to keeping feelings to myself," he says. "When you're gay and
young, that's what you do. You're scared, but you learn to hide your
emotions. So I'd come home and my mom would ask how school
was, and I'd just say, 'Fine.'"

But it wasn't. One month after his first suicide attempt, Greg
made a second. This time he used pills from an extra-large bottle of
Extra Strength Tylenol. He swallowed 33, then went to bed.

In the morning, his mother woke him up. He was furious that
once again his plan had failed. He put the remaining pills in his varsity jacket, then drove to school and took 10 more. It did not take
long before his stomach knotted up. He threw up, walked out of
school, drove home, and told his mother he did not feel well. She
told him to take a nap. Silently, he took the pills out of his jacket.
She hustled him to the car and drove to the local hospital. Soon, he

100 was in the intensive care unit at a larger one. After four days he was transferred to the teen psychiatric ward of a Wilkes-Barre hospital.

Greg never returned to classes at Troy High School. The principal was not surprised to learn that the quarterback had been a ringleader in Greg's torment. The principal said, however, that while he could protect Greg on school grounds, he could offer no help off them. He advised Greg to get a tutor and finish his junior year at home.

Although the school year ended, Greg's misery did not. After summer football practice his former teammates often drove by his house, yelling obscenities from a truck. His neighbors all heard, yet no one did anything.

That same summer, using the Internet, Greg found a boyfriend: A 16-year-old living 45 minutes away. While reading *XY*, a publication for gay youth, Greg's boyfriend thought it would be a good idea to send a photo of Greg in his football uniform for an upcoming issue. The picture appeared at the same time ESPN was searching for gay athletes to interview for a television show. When that aired, a media frenzy began.

For the first time, the local press looked into Greg's situation. The *Daily Review*'s story on Greg highlighted a lawsuit he had filed against the hospital for breaching his confidentiality.

Today, Greg regrets that newspaper coverage. His uncle and older sister were harassed at work; his cousins, attending a different school, were teased. Another cousin, at Troy High, got it the worst. "It was constant, every day," Greg says. "There was no one to stand up for me, and no one in my family knew what to say." The closest support group for gays and allies was an hour away in Binghamton, N.Y., and no one in the Congdon family knew it existed.

Greg spent his entire senior year "doing basically nothing." He was told to wait until his class graduated before earning his GED. He attended football games and wrestling matches but felt unwelcome. He often stood on the opponents' side, trying not to stand out. He learned later that the ploy did not work. Football players, he 101 was told, would see him and make jokes on the bench. They were the boys he had been friends with all his life.

The murder of Matthew Shepard in October 1998 terrified Greg. Up to that point, he ascribed the reactions of his former friends and teammates to ignorance and small-mindedness. After the gay University of Wyoming student was tied to a fence and left to die, however, Greg wondered whether the hatred he felt in Troy might lead to violence there too. He stopped going out alone.

Despite the hard times, Greg was learning to cope. He traveled nearly two hours to Scranton to visit his first gay club, where he finally met in person some of the friends he had made online. The experience opened a new world for him. "Wow!" he marvels. "It was so beautiful. It was exactly what I'd heard about and looked for for so long. I felt like a 5-year-old kid entering a candy store." As Greg entered the gay community, he tried to build a new life for himself. Still, he acknowledges, it was impossible to replace what he had lost.

"A part of my youth was gone," he says. "Everybody says high school is supposed to be the best time of your life. You've got sports and friends and no worries. But all that stuff was taken away." Missing graduation hurt the most. No longer considered a member of the class of 1999, he did not receive an invitation.

Greg is perceptive enough to realize that despite all his losses, there were some gains. He cites inner strength and a better knowledge of who he is as positive outcomes. "I've been to the bottom of the barrel, and I know what it's like. I don't want to be there again, but at least now I know how to handle it."

If he had the chance to do things differently, Greg says he would have come out to his parents first and would not have tried to commit suicide. After realizing his homosexuality was not a phase, they have become strongly supportive. He would also not try so hard to live two different lives: his straight life and his Internet one. "They just never met," he notes. "If I could do it over, I'd try to integrate them into one. Maybe I'd tell a couple of people I'm gay and let them handle it so there wouldn't be this massive witch-hunt. I think if people didn't have this thrown at them in their face by the quarterback, they wouldn't have freaked out so much."

Greg completed two semesters at Central Pennsylvania College. Yet even at that two-year school across the Susquehanna River from Harrisburg, he found it hard to concentrate. One day someone (he never learned who) got into his dorm room and hung photos of nude girls everywhere.

Today, he works in Elmira for a grocery chain. He is completely out there, and everyone is friendly. He hopes one day to return to college and become a policeman.

He has done some speaking appearances on behalf of the Pennsylvania Department of Health. His messages, he says, are important: letting gay teenagers know they are not alone, and raising awareness that even in the 21st century homophobia exists.

Greg's speaking profile is not as high as Corey Johnson's. He makes it clear that there are other differences between the two openly gay ex-high school athletes as well. "The more I hear Corey's story, the more compelled I am to tell mine," Greg says. "I'm always afraid some teenager will read about Corey, who has a perfect story, and believe things will always be like that. But they have to be careful. Most gay youth live in small towns. When you're older you can move to a city, but when you're a kid you don't have that option. It's great Corey had such a happy ending, but that's not always the case. I think there are two sides to every story. And even though some people have come pretty far in terms of accepting gay people, there's still a long way to go. I'm proof of that."

And so, he might add, are nearly all the 1,200 citizens of small-town Troy, Pa.

Gay Basketball League
Marc Davino

Of the many brutal rituals of childhood, none may be more cruel than picking teams. Unathletic, overweight, scrawny, unpopular, less-than-masculine, and "gay" boys all run the risk of being rejected day after day, sport after sport. For some—including those who actually *do* turn out to be gay—the scars remain well into adulthood. Long after they come out, find their community, and join a gym, they remember the agony of standing in a steadily shrinking line, feeling ever more naked, vulnerable, and unwanted each time they are passed over in favor of a boy more athletic, less disliked, or simply not "different."

Marc Davino remembers those days well. That is why the Boston Gay Basketball League, which he has served as commissioner for nearly a decade, announces only its first five draft picks. The rest are secret.

"We want to avoid gym class syndrome," says Marc. "A lot of us were in that situation in elementary school and junior high. Today our league is the same. We've got geeky guys and athletes." Unlike many school gyms and playgrounds, however, the premise behind picking teams is not popularity but parity. Coaches cannot stack rosters; teams are changed every season, preventing dynasties from forming. The result is sports at its best. People have fun, make friends—and feel good about themselves.

Certainly, basketball has made a difference in Marc's life. A self-described "geek" who graduated sixth in his Long Island high school class, then earned a biochemistry degree from the State University of New York at Stony Brook in 1987 and an MBA from Northeastern University five years later, he now works as assistant director for events and special programs at Boston University's College of Engineering. In high school his only organized sport was tennis; in college it was intramural basketball. He did not come out until age 25. Then, he says, basketball changed his life.

One day, a few months after the 1994 Gay Games in New York City, Marc noticed a small newspaper announcement about the formation of a gay basketball league in Boston. It resonated: He had long felt frustrated by an inability to meet gay men who shared his interests. Because he liked basketball's fast pace, excitement, and team spirit, he gave it a shot.

Founder Buck Bachman had successfully organized a similar league in Minneapolis. After moving to Boston, Buck laid the same groundwork. He found coaches, players, and sponsors; he planned a draft party, and oversaw the first year of competition. Sixty men on six teams played a 10-game schedule.

Marc joined early and was hooked. He was playing a sport he loved; the after-game social gatherings were just as fun. His circle of friends grew. In the third year he was named commissioner, and Boston's gay basketball scene truly became a slam dunk.

The league expanded to over a dozen teams and split into competitive and recreational divisions. The top teams traveled. Spurred by their success in a Chicago tournament, Marc helped form a "Tea Party Classic" that drew teams from as far away as Paris. (The double entendre and historic connotations of the tourney name are brilliant—nearly as clever as certain team names. The Drillers, for example, are sponsored by a gay dentist, while the Outlaws are backed by a law firm.)

"Gay leagues like this are important for a couple of reasons," Marc explains. "One, there are not a lot of opportunities for gay men to meet, outside of bars. This is a way to make friends doing something enjoyable and safe. In a broader sense, though, I think we all have a responsibility to break down stereotypes. Even though the

Gay Games is the biggest sporting event on earth, some people still can't believe there are gay basketball players."

It is not only heterosexuals who are surprised to learn that gay men play hoops. Many gay men grow up thinking fast-paced, fiercely athletic sports like basketball are out of their reach. Marc's mission is to spread the word to all gay men (and lesbians too) that whether they were picked first or last in gym class, this game is for them.

Still, Boston's Gay Basketball League has not succeeded in reaching all segments of society. Only a dozen of the 120 players are black, Hispanic, or Asian. The lack of minority participation concerns Marc. "Boston is not a very racially mixed city, and the gay community is no different," he says. "You can see it in the clubs, the same as in our league. It's very noticeable when we play teams from Washington, Atlanta, Chicago, or Los Angeles—they look like NBA teams. We run notices in the two gay papers here, and we don't say 'White only,' but we definitely don't have a lot of minorities checking out our league."

The league includes women (four at present) as well as heterosexuals. "There's no 'gay test,'" Marc says, referring to sexuality. "I think we have three or four straight guys. They're mostly friends of gay players, and roommates who like basketball." Marc has no idea if the straight players are "out" when talking about the league to others.

But the Boston Gay Basketball League is first and foremost a gay league. Most people join for two reasons: to play and to meet people. Although Marc knows of one couple who met on the court, the average person is not looking to hook up. "I know it happens," Marc says. "But not in the locker room, I'm sure."

The average player, Marc notes, is also an average person. Some are former college athletes, while a few have never touched a ball. Most, however, are 30-something men who enjoyed basketball as youngsters, later felt out of place in the game's hypermasculine, in-your-face environment, and now are reclaiming their rightful place on the court. All share a desire for fun and for healthy action.

"The league has been very good for me," Marc Davino says gratefully. "I'm not a great player, and I definitely would not have felt comfortable spending time in a straight league. Through this league I've met great people, traveled, and felt a lot of camaraderie."

He feels particularly comfortable at the annual draft party, a gala event complete with food, music, an emcee, and just enough gay touches to make it unlike any other basketball league's.

Best of all, team rosters are listed randomly, so no one knows how high or low he was picked. For gay men in Boston, that's reason enough to play ball.

Speed Skating
Rick Swanson

Competitive ice skating can be divided into two sports: figure skating and speed skating. The former is a personality-driven event. Working with a coach, a figure skater creates, develops, and perfects an individual program. That aesthetic performance illustrates exactly who the skater is.

Speed skating, on the other hand, is completely devoid of personality. Each man uses the same technique and stroke. Only one thing matters: crossing the finish line first.

Those differences contribute to a popular stereotype. Many people, including some on the inside, believe that figure skating, with its dance-like leaps and emphasis on showmanship, is filled with gay men. Meanwhile, speed skating—the sport of brute strength, raw power, and bulging muscles—is straight as a finish line.

Not so fast.

Like every other sport in the world, speed skating attracts its share of gay men. In fact, it may be argued that because it is such an inherently conservative, intensely isolating, gotta-prove-your-manhood sport, speed skating may actually appeal to certain males as they work through their own sexuality issues.

That might have been true of Rick Swanson. Coming of age in what he calls "a classic 1980s tractless suburb" of Minneapolis, he did what many Minnesota boys do: play hockey. Soon, however, he wanted to figure skate. But he found that sport less appealing than he thought, and quit. "At 10 it was too flamboyant and prissy for me," he says. "I was always onstage, singing in plays, but figure skating was over the top." Yet in early December his father told him he had to do something outdoors that winter, so he turned to speed skating.

A number of the sport's elements appealed to him. It requires a stupendous amount of self-determination. To succeed, a speed skater must focus all his energy on training and competing, during the long May-to-March season. By age 14, Rick was working out eight to 10 times a week. He Rollerbladed, cycled, ran, and lifted weights, mostly on his own. "Speed skaters are so focused," he notes. "We're a bit off the center of normalcy, as far as how intensely we live our lives. When you work out twice a day, for five or six hours a day, you've got to have a different mind-set."

He worked hard to maximize his physical advantages. Though he stopped growing at 16, when he was 5 foot 6, he developed 21-inch thighs, a 30-inch waist, and a 38-inch chest. He also honed his mental attitude. The strongest body cannot compensate for a loose head, Rick says.

His best race was 1,500 meters; his worst was 10,000 meters. But whatever the distance, he found speed skating fun. "I was young and aggressive, and I liked racing in a pack," he says. "In team sports I was too timid and embarrassed to be any good. Hockey and football had such a 'male attitude' that if you couldn't compete at the top level, it wasn't worth competing at all. But speed skating wasn't like that. I could be somebody, be an athlete, and I didn't have to compete against the other kids in school."

By the time he was in junior high, Rick competed well enough to be ranked nationally. His friends were other skaters from places like Michigan, Illinois, and Missouri, not kids from down the street. Virtually every weekend through high school, Rick traveled somewhere to race. He was fueled, he says, by a desire to be successful, which he believed would lead to acceptance. "If I wasn't an athlete, I knew I could never be accepted by what at that point I expected would be my world," he says. "If you're not an athlete, you have no place in the 'guy world.'"

As a senior, however, returning home after eight months of

international competition, Rick wanted a break. He had always managed to fit plays and choir into his schedule, and he earned a spot in the high school production of *Guys and Dolls*. In the middle of rehearsal, one of the two "jock stud" hockey players he says were "conned into" being in the play asked with an edge if Rick was still speed skating. At that moment, he realized that despite all his accomplishments on the ice, he would never be accepted by his high school peers.

He is not sure where that "superior macho" attitude came from, but he knew where it was aimed: directly at him. Although he was attracted to males, he had never acted on it. All through high school Rick dated girls—and he continued to do so through his early 20s. He struggled with his desire to be part of the same "guy world" he did not particularly like; try as he might, however, acceptance into that world did not follow.

"I gave up a normal teenage life," Rick says. "Every weekend from November to March of senior year, I was off competing somewhere. You can't build long-term friendships that way. I gave up a ton of quintessential Americana, but at the same time I was thankful I didn't have to go through a lot of that. It was so confusing. I was a better athlete than all those skaters on the hockey team who just went around hitting people. I was sick of not being recognized as a good athlete just because I was participating in a nonschool sport."

Rick was more than a good athlete. He was selected for both the junior and senior men's national team. In one important junior world competition he finished runner-up by "an infinite amount— the length of a skate blade."

He was also single a lot. Those dates with girls were infrequent. He knew there were rumors about his sexuality—both in high school and on the international speed skating circuit—because he acted, sang, and was "a Renaissance person." He lived in close quarters with 12 other skaters, nine months a year. "That was my whole

110 life," he says. "You can hide, but they're not stupid. I heard the whispers, but I could never say anything. And I was also a Jesus freak, so no one knew how to figure me out."

Like long-distance running and skiing, speed skating is a very individual sport, Rick says. "It's just you and the clock and the ice, nothing more. If you're good and quiet, people will leave you alone. If you're cocky, you'll never get anywhere socially." Rick was quiet; the other skaters left him alone. But there is a thin line between alone and lonesome.

When he was 20, he fell during a 5,000-meter race. It was the first time he had done that, and for the rest of the season he floundered. He grew tired of "the speed skating womb." A bright man, he needed a more academic environment. He yearned for more friendships, a stronger social life. There was something else going on too: From the time he was 16, he had wanted to be an Episcopal priest. Rick longed for a Christian community.

And there was this as well: Rick finally admitted to himself it was time to figure out if his attraction to men was because he wanted to be like them, or wanted to be with them physically. "By being so alone, those ideas had been stolen from me," he says. "I never understood there was such a thing as deep male friendships. When I was in seventh grade I wanted to be friends with a boy. I knew he was attractive, but I couldn't articulate my deep desire for commitment. No one showed me that was a possibility. In junior and senior high school I was completely excluded from the social scene because I was perceived to be gay. But I didn't have any idea about any of that. All I wanted was to have friends."

He entered the University of Montana. By his sophomore year, he was putting the many pieces of his life—speed skating and the desire to be accepted by other males, his attraction to men, and his deep Christian faith—together. Slowly and quietly, he edged out of the closet. The following year he transferred to a Los Angeles college.

There he found a large and diverse gay community. He joined various gay athletic groups and was mentored by "wonderful men who knew what it meant to be educated, gay, and an athlete." One piece of the puzzle remained unsolved, however. Rick still knew no other gay man who attended church regularly.

"I knew I wanted to be a priest long before I understood my homosexual desires," he recounts. "At 16, my church and youth group were my primary social settings. I gave up that deep, honest place, where I possibly could have come out much earlier, for skating."

The first people Rick came out to, in the summer of 1992, were members of the church. Most understood what he was going through. A few, however, did not. A defining moment in his process came when a conservative evangelical woman, enduring her second decade of a bad marriage, asked Rick to have sex with her. He said he could not because he was gay. She implored him to come to Jesus and be saved.

"I knew she was wrong on so many levels," Rick says. "I knew Jesus loved me already and that any relationship I had with another human would be valid. I told her she had to reexamine her understanding of Scripture and her desire to break her marriage vows."

Rick had little trouble reconciling his religious views with his sexuality. Even in Montana, he says, the Episcopal Church believes that gays and lesbians are children of God, imbued with all the rights and responsibilities of the Christian faith. Through all the pain of figuring out who he was as a gay man, Rick says, he always knew God loved him.

In the 10 years since he graduated from college, the many diverse aspects of Rick's life have melded together. He knows that gay people often segment their lives, fearing the result of bringing different worlds together. He, on the other hand, has never *not* felt that he was an athlete, a Christian, an academic, and a gay man.

So it was not unusual for him to gravitate to ice hockey, a sport he had previously shunned, and play on the Gay Blades team that earned a silver medal at the 1994 Gay Games. He had always dreamed of being in the Olympics; this was close enough. The competition and the ceremony that followed remain one of the highlights of his life.

For the first time, Rick had the male sports friendships he had ached for. He could walk into a locker room where everyone knew he was gay *and* that he wanted to be a priest. "They saw I had guts and balls, and they respected me," he says. "No one there was trying to be someone he's not. The only thing that mattered was we were all trying to do our best."

He plays gay volleyball too. He tried joining straight teams—ice hockey, volleyball, and softball—but found them wanting. "There was nothing there for me. It's great for straight men to build relationships with other guys on those teams, but I wasn't one of them. On those teams, in the dugout or field you're expected to have a girlfriend or wife. If you break those expectations, you're not one of the guys. The other alternative is to pretend to be like them and not say anything. I couldn't do that." He finds the gay dugout and field to be safer havens.

Similarly, when it came to choosing a congregation in Los Angeles, he gravitated to one filled with people who were there for "the right reason": They wanted to know Jesus. They were people who loved all of God's children, instead of looking down on some of them. The members of that congregation became Rick's brothers and sisters, and helped him find the sense of community he had long been seeking.

For years while competing internationally, he lived with people his own age; in college, the pattern repeated itself. Now Rick's church became a place to meet people from a broad array of ages and backgrounds. No matter where they came from or who they were, they accepted him as an athlete, an academic, a gay man—and,

he laughs, a Minnesotan. They taught him how to bring the different pieces of his life together and "how to be an adult."

As he integrated his life, he followed his old dream and became
a priest. He found seminary to be another safe, accepting place. The
church he was assigned to is in a small town beyond the Los Angeles
mountains. As with most gay men in their first jobs, he is allowing
people—in this case, his parishioners—to know him before he
comes all the way out.

Today, as he tries to be the best priest he can, Rick draws on the
lessons he learned from speed skating and accepting his homosexuality. He uses words like "growth" and "advancement." In each
group he has been in, he explains, there has been a healthy desire to
grow. "I wanted to be the best speed skater I could be and to grow
fully and truthfully as a gay person. In a Christian community, it
means to grow into faith and a love of God in a way that our lives
are always centered."

He continues, "'Advancement' in athletics is obvious. In the gay
community, advancement means being seen as full, equal members
of society. In the religious community, advancement does not refer
to the kingdom of heaven, because we all live at the same level. It
means advancing into a unified understanding of humanity, where
everyone is loved for who they are. That's a huge advancement. Too
many people still think God looks down on gay people."

The Rev. Rick Swanson spent much of his life skating in circles.
At the same time he was engaged in a long journey forward, seeking
growth and acceptance. Now he has found it in two places, the rink
and the pulpit. And, to his delight and wonder, both are linked by an
unlikely third: the gay community.

Soccer Manager
Jesse Moyers

Jesse Moyers is proud of many things. He is proud, for example, of his character traits: a strong work ethic, single-minded devotion to any task he takes on, and spectacular attention to detail. He is proud too of the pair of NCAA championship rings he owns. They represent back-to-back national titles won by the Indiana University men's soccer team, a significant accomplishment even for one of the most highly regarded programs in the country.

Yet despite his pride in those rings, they no longer gleam as brightly for Jesse. He still wears them, but these days they remind him of bad times as well as good. The gloss has come off Indiana's storied heritage, and Jesse wonders if he will ever look at his favorite sport—and the IU athletes and coaches he so admired—the same way again.

Jesse did not earn his championship rings as a player, but in the high-powered world of big-time intercollegiate athletics his contributions were just as important. He served two seasons as head student manager, and if that evokes images of a skinny dweeb in glasses handing out jockstraps, then a crash course in Big 10 sports is in order.

Jesse's duties were wide-ranging and crucial to the success of the team. He arrived at the field half an hour before training began, transporting all kinds of equipment: corner flags, cones, balls, ball pumps, practice jerseys, extra whistles, and more. He checked the pressure of 40 balls, filled water bottles, moved goals, set up the field for training according to that day's specifications, then spent two or three hours more attending to thousands of small details that, taken together, added up to the difference between seamless efficiency and hopeless chaos.

On game days Jesse got to Armstrong Stadium three hours 115
before kickoff. He stuck in the corner flags, made sure the field was
properly lined, swept the gutter along the sides, then arranged enormous banners around the stadium. These were the team's pride and
joy, proof positive that Indiana soccer was Number One. The banners boasted of the Hoosiers' many Big 10 championships, NCAA
Final Four appearances and, most impressively, first three national
championships, in 1982, '83, and '88.

Next Jesse made sure both the home and visitors' locker rooms
were stocked with soap, towels, tape, chalk, and water. He greeted
the visiting team and referees when they arrived and attended to
their last-minute requests. He made sure the game balls were in
good shape and always on hand, and arranged and supervised the
squad of ball boys. At half time he set up goals for the small-sided
youth games that entertained the crowd.

When the game was over, Jesse spent another hour closing the
stadium. He stowed the equipment, removed the nets and championship banners, and at long last turned out the lights.

To prepare for away matches—the Hoosiers sometimes traveled
for several days at a time—Jesse packed extra uniforms and all the
video equipment. On the road he organized luggage at airports, set
up film sessions in hotel meeting rooms, polished shoes, changed
studs, even ordered players' pizzas.

There was much, much more. Jesse helped organize summer
camp sessions involving hundreds of youngsters and dozens of
staffers. He was in daily contact with the coach's secretary, making
sure that end of the program ran smoothly. He served as a key liaison between the coaching staff and players, relaying messages, questions, and concerns. Jerry Yeagley, the only head soccer coach
Indiana has ever had (and one of the most respected men in the
intercollegiate soccer ranks) called Jesse far more than a manager.
He was, Jerry said, more like his right-hand man.

"Being a manager is not like being a hang-around groupie," Jesse asserts. "It's more like a full-time job." It is such an important job, in fact, that Indiana University's soccer program provides its head manager with a $3,500 scholarship.

The work is hard, but the rewards are great. For two years Jesse traveled all over the country. Both years, when the final whistles blew he savored the feeling of being an important contributor to national championships. The second time, at Charlotte, N.C.'s 73,000-seat Ericsson Stadium, was particularly memorable. "That atmosphere there, in an NFL stadium, was a great thrill," Jesse recalls. "To see how far the sport had come, from when I started in the mid '80s with parent coaches who knew nothing, was just amazing."

In addition, he formed strong friendships with team members. He was closest to Nick Garcia, an All-America defender now playing professionally. Jesse felt secure knowing that members of two national championship squads respected him because, just as they did, he worked hard every day to make sure the IU program ran perfectly, and achieved its goals.

Jesse went the extra mile because soccer was so important to him. Before he became a manager he was a player. Though not a star, he learned early how good it felt to be associated with a legendary program.

Born in the small town of Campbellsville, Ky., Jesse moved at a young age to Lexington. Both sides of his family were active Southern Baptists, and they passed their faith along to Jesse and his twin sister. But there was plenty of time to be a kid too. When Jesse was 6, his parents signed him up for soccer. He loved everything about the game and played as much as he could.

Beginning at age 11, Jesse was sexually active with neighborhood boys. Even so, he never considered himself "gay" or thought about the social consequences of his experimentation. But one day as a

freshman at Henry Clay High—an affluent school with a well-
deserved good reputation—Jesse grabbed a piece of paper off a
classmate's desk. "Get away from me, faggot!" the boy screamed.
For the first time in his life, Jesse wondered if he might actually be
gay. There was little chance of talking to anyone and finding
answers, however; Henry Clay had, Jesse says, "a very Christian
mentality."

As a sophomore, Jesse tried out for varsity soccer—and got cut. It
was, he says, "a defining moment of my life." He had always played, it
seemed; more than nonstop action and fun, the game provided friends
and support. He wanted to remain involved—as much for the feelings
of camaraderie and inclusion as anything else—but all he could do was
attend his sister's practices and cheer at the boys' and girls' games.

The following year Charles Atinay moved up from girls' assistant
to boys' head coach. Jesse approached him, offering to do whatever
he could to be part of the team. Charles knew of Jesse's failed
attempt to play the previous season and promised to figure something out. What evolved was a manager–administrative assistant
role. Jesse helped Charles organize a booster club, raise funds from
local businesses, and drum up fan support. Together they helped lay
the foundation for the first soccer-specific field at any Lexington-
area high school.

Just as important, whenever Charles planned a team function—
and there were many, including summer camping trips and lake
excursions—he included Jesse.

Charles and Jesse worked well together. In Jesse's junior and
senior seasons, the Blue Devils reached the state semifinals. He
became friendly with goalkeeper Kyle Smith. For two years both
boys also served as editors of the school newspaper, the *Devil's
Advocate*. In high school he was the person Jesse felt closest to—and
the peer to whom he was the most open about his sexuality. To Kyle,
Jesse's gay feelings were never an issue.

Jesse's mentor was Edie Maddox, his sophomore English teacher and the paper's faculty adviser. Divorced from her pastor husband, she had a down-to-earth manner that made Jesse feel comfortable. She was the first adult he confided his gay feelings to. Even his sister and parents did not know.

"I wanted to be open, but it just wasn't a possibility," he says. "I always thought I would spend my life associated with athletics, and in that case I couldn't be openly gay. There was so much locker room talk about faggots and pussy, I didn't see any way I could come out."

Because Jesse was never the most popular boy in school and had a relatively small circle of friends, feeling comfortable in the locker room meant a great deal. "At most high schools and universities, athletes are among the most well-thought-of groups," he says. "I liked being associated with them. I also liked being with a well-respected sport and program. I didn't have the talent or skill to excel in soccer, but I wanted to stick with it. Soccer and the camaraderie I got from a core group of people on the team—those were important to me."

Jesse—whose father once coached high school football in Louisville—explains soccer's attraction: "I never liked rough, stop-and-start sports like football. Soccer was fun, though. It's physically demanding but not violent. You need finesse more than brute power. At first it wasn't about winning and losing, so that was a good way to start. I love the way players are on their own during the game, without a coach telling them what to do all the time. It's a great combination of individual and team play."

In the fall of 1996, Jesse entered Transylvania University in Lexington. Ironically, soccer—the sport that had kept his spirits up throughout high school, when his Baptist upbringing convinced him being gay would doom him to hell—proved to be his collegiate undoing. He remained involved with the Henry Clay soccer pro-

gram, devoting more time to it than his studies. Jesse spent what lit-
tle time he had beyond soccer holed up in his apartment, agonizing over issues like homosexuality, coming out, and his place in the world. For the first time in his life, he skipped classes. Charles, the Henry Clay coach, was concerned, and he probably realized Jesse was dealing with sexuality issues but said nothing.

Charles did, however, talk about Indiana University. He had been a backup goalkeeper on the 1988 national championship team, and spoke often of the Hoosiers' storied history. He described how Coach Jerry Yeagley took IU soccer from club status to the NCAA title. Charles thought the college and its soccer program would be perfect for Jesse. When the Henry Clay team traveled to Bloomington for the Hoosier Cup high school tournament, he made an appointment for Jesse to meet Coach Yeagley.

"I was very intimidated," Jesse recalls. "I'm 5-10. He's 6-1, thickly built, very powerful looking, with a very strong handshake, and he wears dark sunglasses, even inside. But then we talked, and I got excited. He told me his head manager was graduating in December of 1997, and he'd need someone after that. He said he'd try to help me with the admissions office. That really impressed me."

But Jesse was not yet ready for a place like IU. Back in Lexington, he took a full-time position at a bank. A female coworker helped ease him out of the closet. Even though she was one of the very few people who knew he was gay, Jesse felt better. Slowly, he developed a support system.

In the fall of 1997 Jesse came out to his twin sister, Leslie. She cried. Ever since moving out of his house to attend Transylvania, Jesse had been estranged from his family. Finally, Leslie understood why. She thought that telling their parents would explain the distance and bitterness that had developed (in part, Jesse says, because of hearing his father joke about "faggots" and "queers"). Jesse disagreed; the time, he said, was not right. She told them that night.

120 His father said it was OK, while his mother had no reaction. Jesse did not know any of that, however, until two years later. His parents never called.

That same fall of '97 Jesse was accepted at Indiana University, for the semester beginning the following January. Assistant soccer coaches Mike Freitag and John Trask called, encouraging him to keep in touch. He felt almost like a recruit.

Around that time, the Hoosiers were making a drive for the national title. They were undefeated the entire season, until UCLA beat them in the semifinals of the national tournament in Richmond. After that stinging defeat the players vowed to go all the way the next year. Jesse, a month away from enrolling, vowed from afar to be part of that group.

When Jesse arrived at Bloomington, the current head manager took him under his wing. At spring practice he introduced the new-comer to the team. Nick Garcia, Chris Klein, and the returnees from that Final Four team seemed like great stars to him. As he had with Coach Yeagley, Jesse felt intimidated. As Jesse worked that spring, he tried to develop relationships with the team. It took a while. Not until summer did he truly feel comfortable around the players and coaching staff.

From the first day, however, Jesse sensed homophobia in the air. One of the key players was often ridiculed as "faggot" or "gay." Jesse had seen a bit of that at Henry Clay, so he was not shocked, but at the same time he was surprised it occurred on a large college cam-pus. He sensed that the athlete being taunted was at least bisexual—he made a few discreet sexual advances to Jesse, and other times he more crudely exposed himself and asked whether Jesse wanted to suck on his cock—but Jesse did not want to spend time wondering about such things. His first goal was to learn how to be the best manager possible.

Coach Yeagley did all he could to help. Sensing Jesse's insecurity, he went out of his way to praise the new manager. He often put his 121 arm around the young man and told him he was doing a great job.

Still, it took Jesse longer to bond with the players at Indiana than at Henry Clay. He seldom felt included in the "team atmosphere" that was so important to him. Part of the reason was because he spent much of that spring videotaping practices and games, so he had less interaction with players than he would have liked. In addition, many athletes lived together off-campus, while Jesse was stuck in a dormitory. His shy personality also made him different from most of the Hoosiers, who were a vocal, competitive, in-your-face bunch. When Jesse voiced his frustrations to Coach Yeagley, his new mentor assured him he would soon find his team niche.

That summer, he remained in Bloomington to work at the coach's soccer camp. As the newcomer he was assigned the lowliest job—traffic control, helping children cross busy campus roads without being hit—but things turned out well. The World Cup was being held in France, and Jesse spent many hours watching games with the players. He hung out at their houses between sessions, had a fun, laid-back time, and began to sense a bond.

Two-a-day practices began in August. The team ate breakfast together at 7 A.M., then trained, shared lunch, practiced again, and had dinner. At night they viewed tapes, took quizzes, and had meetings. It was all soccer, all the time, and Jesse loved it. He had no time to think about the sexuality issues that had increasingly crowded his mind. Best of all, Jesse was named head manager. The season began, and as he traveled with the Hoosiers to places like Dallas and Los Angeles, new friendships bloomed.

During his two years as manager he felt closest to Nick Garcia, one of IU's biggest stars. The defender from Plano, Tex., was very open-minded. His father was descended from Mexican immigrants, while his mother's family were Scandinavians who settled in the Midwest. "I don't know why, but we clicked from the beginning,"

Jesse says. A few times, Nick even asked if Jesse liked guys. The manager never said yes—but neither did he deny it.

Jesse also grew close to another player. One night, as Jesse drove him to a party, the player leaned over and kissed him on the lips. Then, without saying a word, the player got out of the car. Neither one ever talked about the incident or followed through. "It was an odd experience," Jesse says. "I'm pretty sure he's at least bisexual, but beyond that I don't know what to think."

As he went about his duties as supermanager, Jesse constantly felt on guard. "I'm not a flamer, and I'm not effeminate. I never act any way other than straight," he says. "But I'm human. I am attracted to guys. And if someone scrutinizes my words, my actions, my glances, maybe they might suspect something." Perhaps that is why one day the backup goalkeeper asked Jesse's roommate if Jesse was gay.

"No!" the roommate replied with surprise. "If anyone would know, I would, and he's not." Jesse's roommate believed what he said. But when he recounted that story, chuckling, to Jesse, the manager went into "emergency response mode." He tried, harder than ever, to make sure no one on the outside knew what he was feeling inside.

The goalkeeper was not through, however. At the NCAA tournament in Charlotte, he asked Jesse directly if he was gay. When Jesse reacted defensively, the goalkeeper told him it was no big deal; it would not matter to him one way or another. For the first time in his life, Jesse started thinking that it might be possible to come out and remain part of a soccer team.

But then he thought back to the previous week, when the Hoosiers traveled to the University of Wisconsin. All week long, Coach Yeagley had joked about people in Madison being "very granola." It was obvious, Jesse says, that the coach was talking about "fringe society"—and just as obvious that he was including homosexuals as part of that fringe. The message was even clearer when Coach Yeagley ridiculed the gay pride flags fluttering in downtown Madison.

Those remarks confused Jesse. He had developed a great deal of respect for the five-time National Coach of the Year, a man who had led the Hoosiers to 24 NCAA tournaments and in 1989 been inducted into the United States Soccer Hall of Fame. Like Charles Atinay, Jerry Yeagley had given him a chance to be part of a hugely successful soccer program, honored as well for its high standards. Jesse considered Jerry Yeagley both a mentor and a friend, as he had Charles Atinay too.

"Coach Yeagley always told me I was more an administrative assistant than a manager," Jesse recounts. "By my second year I realized he was very approachable. A lot of times I went into his office unannounced. I talked with him as a good friend about class problems. Soccer was dominating my life. He told me that the team and coaches loved what I did, that I was the best manager they'd ever had, but that school was my first priority."

A few times in the coach's office, Jesse broke down and cried. One time was in early 2000, a few weeks after winning the national title in Charlotte. Jesse described his frustration at not receiving, for the second year in a row, a championship watch. This time the excuse had been that because the athletic director was at the ceremony, it was politically correct to give him the prestigious watch. Again, Coach Yeagley did his best to assure Jesse that the manager was an integral part of the Hoosiers' success.

Jesse could not tell the coach everything, of course. He could not describe, for example, what had happened the previous year—how at Christmastime, visiting a former high school exchange student in the Czech Republic, Jesse had walked into a gay club and saw, for the first time, happy, openly gay people. That night, Jesse realized that although he enjoyed being a soccer manager, life was passing him by. He wanted a boyfriend, just like other gay men.

124   Nor could Jesse tell Coach Yeagley that the previous year he had met an Indianapolis man online and that for several months they had dated. They traveled an hour each way to see each other, but because Jesse did not want him associated with his soccer life, that boyfriend never came to games.

And Jesse certainly could not tell Coach Yeagley that he had recently met another gay person, right on the Bloomington campus. Jesse had found Chase Potter through the IU OUT group's Internet bulletin board.

Chase was much more dynamic than Jesse's first boyfriend, and in the spring of 2000 the two men moved in together. It was becoming more and more difficult for Jesse to walk with his boyfriend on campus without holding his hand, or drive together without kissing. Jesse realized his fears of the team were holding him back from a full relationship—and from what could develop into a turning point of his life.

Around that time, assistant coach John Trask arranged a summer internship for Jesse with the Chicago Fire professional team. He watched a game at Soldier Field, and could scarcely believe his luck: He would be able to shag balls, hear the coaches talk, and prepare for the next step in his sports career.

But despite his great excitement, Jesse felt something else: deep anxiety. He sensed that accepting the internship would mark another step back into the closet. Thanks to Chase and their relationship, Jesse had just started to feel confident in himself as a gay man. Yet he still had not been able to come out to the Indiana soccer team; how could he spend the summer in new surroundings, with professional athletes he did not know? He talked his dilemma over with Chase, and turned the offer down. Instead of interning, he prepared to come out.

In the summer of 2000, Jesse scheduled himself for four weeks at Coach Yeagley's soccer camp. He had worked there before and knew the routine. During the entire first week, however, he thought of 125 nothing except coming out. He obsessed over how best to do it, and tried to imagine each player's response. He was particularly worried about the reaction of Coach Jerry Yeagley, the man whom by that time Jesse considered a second father.

With Nick Garcia off playing for the professional Kansas City Wizards, the player Jesse respected most was Brandon Tauber. A nonstarter from the Gary area, he joined the team in 1998, the same year as Jesse. But Brandon was out of town that summer, so Jesse E-mailed him. Because he valued their friendship, Jesse wrote, he wanted Brandon to know several things: that he was gay, was dating, was happy, and was looking forward to no longer leading a double life.

For nearly a week, Brandon did not respond. Jesse was crazed with fear, but Brandon finally replied. He said he was glad for the E-mail; he valued Jesse as a friend, and in fact respected Jesse more now for his courage than anyone else on the team—or, for that matter, on the entire IU campus. He pledged to give whatever assistance Jesse needed.

The manager did not ask Brandon to keep quiet, and he realized it would not take long before others learned the news. Jesse E-mailed starting goalkeeper T.J. Hannig, who was still in Bloomington, saying he was sure T.J. had already heard through the grapevine. T.J.'s response was, "That's cool," but his actions belied his words. He turned aloof and seemed not to want to talk much with Jesse. The two had planned to get together that summer, but T.J. kept brushing Jesse off, and Jesse felt the friendship dying. All spring, Jesse says, T.J. had talked about having him come to his wedding. After the E-mail, he was not invited.

T.J.'s lukewarm response made Jesse think that continuing to work at Coach Yeagley's camps might be difficult. That thought crystallized when he began receiving E-mails from players he had

126 not contacted directly. The messages were clear: "We don't want you on our team." "We don't want faggots around." "We'd rather you not come back next fall." Jesse had not expected those reactions—especially from people he considered his friends. Distraught, he called Coach Yeagley's secretary. He told her something had come up and that he would not be able to work the final two weeks of soccer camp.

He did receive one encouraging call. It came from Katrin Koch, the university's head strength conditioning coach. For a long time Jesse had known that the tall, powerful German woman had many gay friends. The previous fall, in fact, he had confided in her that he found a player on the soccer team attractive. At that point, she later told him, she knew he was gay. However, she also realized he would have to work through his sexuality issues himself, at his own pace. When she heard that Jesse finally came out, she called and congratulated him. Jesse asked what she had heard from the soccer team. She was evasive, saying only, "Jesse, they're male athletes. What did you expect? They just don't want to deal with this."

In late summer, Jesse decided he would not return to the soccer team. It was a hard decision but one he had always understood to be a possibility. The thought that the Indiana players' homophobic fears or ignorance were stronger than their respect for him as a dedicated, hardworking member of the team's support staff was upsetting, but he believed he was choosing the right way of getting on with his life.

Around the same time, the championship rings from the 2000 season finally arrived. Jesse heard the news midway through dealing with the hurtful E-mails. He called Coach Yeagley's secretary, told her people had been saying things about him, and said he really did not want his ring.

Jesse had not heard from Coach Yeagley since coming out, although Jesse was sure he had been told the news by his players. But after hearing Jesse's comment about the ring, Coach Yeagley left a 127 message for Jesse at his job in customer service at the Monroe County Bank. The coach said he was concerned about Jesse, that he hoped Jesse would reconsider his decision about the ring, and that he wanted him to stop by the office.

Jesse called Coach Yeagley's secretary. Cathy Narey was a nice, friendly woman who had never missed a chance to tell Jesse that, in all her years with the team, he was the best manager they ever had. Now she told Jesse that she was concerned about and for him. He said he felt uncomfortable coming to the office. She parried, asking if Jesse wanted to tell her anything. He responded that he was gay, that most of the players had reacted negatively, and that he no longer wanted to be associated with them. Cathy said she did not think Coach Yeagley had heard about the players' remarks. She added, "It doesn't matter to me that you're gay. You're not the first one on the team, and you won't be the last." She said that Coach Yeagley had dealt with gay players, managers, and staff members in the past, and she offered to talk with her boss about his players' reactions.

The next day, the secretary called again. She said Coach Yeagley was quite concerned. If Jesse felt uneasy meeting him in the office, he would meet Jesse anywhere for lunch.

In mid August, the coach and manager met in a restaurant. At first they avoided the subject of homosexuality. But then Coach Yeagley took off his glasses—something he seldom does—and told Jesse that being gay did not matter to him. He called it a "nonissue" and said he wanted Jesse to be happy. When Jesse said that some players had implied in their E-mails that they spoke on behalf of the coaching staff too, Coach Yeagley asked for names. He repeated that Jesse's sexuality would be a nonissue with everyone in the fall.

Jesse replied that he did not see how he could put himself in an environment with players who had responded so negatively. Coach

Yeagley said he was both disappointed and upset, and several times he asked Jesse to reconsider. Jesse says he is unsure how much of that response was totally sincere and how much was worry about what would happen to the organization of his upcoming two-a-day practices.

Coach Yeagley asked Jesse what specifically concerned him. Jesse said it was not the coaches' reactions but rather what the players thought. He would share locker rooms and hotel rooms with them, and did not want them to feel freaked out or threatened. Throughout the entire discussion, Jesse says, Coach Yeagley never said or implied that he would talk to the players or do anything to ease Jesse's fears. Instead, the coach told Jesse, "There are players who are immature, and that is something you're going to have to deal with." Had Coach Yeagley offered to intercede with the team, Jesse says he does not know how he would have responded. Had Coach Yeagley asked what he could do to help, Jesse does not know what he would have suggested. But the coach never offered or asked, and the conversation ended with Coach Yeagley saying he wanted Jesse to come back but would understand if he did not.

Jesse told the coach he would reconsider his decision but says he did so primarily to appease Coach Yeagley and end what had become a disconcerting discussion. When Jesse called shortly thereafter and said he would not return, Coach Yeagley again said he was disappointed and called it a great loss for the team. "He said a million times that my being gay was not an issue for the coaching staff," Jesse recounts. "But when I talked about the E-mails and asked about the environment with the players, he never offered to say or do anything. He always said it would be up to me to deal with the players on my own."

When the 2000 fall season began, Jesse was not around. Avoiding the game he loved—and the team he had once admired—was one of the most difficult things he had ever done. Around campus, however, Jesse was a happy presence. He was totally open. He and Chase held hands in public, and kissed. At work too Jesse was out. He told all his

colleagues he was gay, and he took his boyfriend to a bank party. Jesse   129
even brought Chase home to meet his parents, from whom he had
long been estranged. They welcomed the couple, and his father even
uttered the word "gay."

Emboldened and confident, Jesse decided to start giving something back to the gay community. He walked into Indiana
University's Gay, Lesbian, Bisexual, and Transgender office to volunteer, and he met coordinator Doug Bauder and assistant Carol
Fischer. He recounted his experiences with the soccer team and
offered to help anyone at IU in a similar situation. Doug, who had
wanted to address gay issues in athletics ever since the GLBT office
opened several years earlier, suggested a campuswide discussion and
panel, similar to a previously successful effort with fraternities.

Jesse assumed Coach Yeagley would want to participate.
However, the coach declined. He said he would always help Jesse,
and was glad to be a "silent supporter"—he even noted that he had
just attended a gay wedding—but explained he had never been the
type of person to talk publicly about homosexuality, and would not
feel comfortable doing so now.

Jesse, Doug, and others at the GLBT office then organized a lecture, open to the public, with a national expert on gay issues in athletics. This time Jesse E-mailed Coach Yeagley. With basketball
coach Bobby Knight gone, Jesse said, Coach Yeagley had become
perhaps the most respected coach on campus. That afforded an
excellent opportunity to start an important dialogue on homosexuality. This time, Coach Yeagley did not respond at all.

Angered, Jesse walked into the coach's office. Coach Yeagley said
he had indeed received the E-mail, but chose to be—he used the
term again—a "silent supporter." He said he knew and respected the
speaker, a noted soccer coach and writer, but did not want to get
involved in a "political issue." He said the topic of homosexuality
had never been talked about in the athletic department and still

130 would not be. He told Jesse the speaker was welcome to come to his office and talk privately, but that would be the extent of his involvement. Coach Yeagley did not respond to repeated E-mail invitations from both the GLBT office and the speaker himself.

The experience has taught him many things, Jesse says. One is that after 2½ years of hard work and supreme dedication to the Indiana University soccer team, in the final analysis nothing mattered except the fact that he was gay. The defining issue for many players was his sexuality, and that was nothing they wanted to deal with or have around them.

That pattern continued long after the 2000 season ended (without a third straight national championship: In their fourth consecutive NCAA semifinal, the Hoosiers fell 2-1 in three overtimes to Creighton). Most players, when they encountered Jesse around campus, continued to ignore him or pretended not to see him.

Jesse has learned that there are other gay and bisexual athletes at Indiana University—including soccer players. "As silly as it sounds, I really thought in high school I was the only one," he says. "But gay people are in every sport, at every level. People think coming out would disrupt the team chemistry and atmosphere, but it's not coming out that does that—it's the reaction to it. That reaction can negate everything positive someone has done. When I came out, all of a sudden that was all that mattered. Nothing I did that was good mattered."

His reaction to Coach Yeagley has been complicated. Prior to coming out, Jesse considered him a good friend, a mentor, even a father figure. While Jesse assumes the coach remains a "silent supporter," his inability to speak out publicly—or even offer to help Jesse with the players—surprises and saddens him. "It's been painful," Jesse admits. "He's a great coach, a great motivator, and he's had great success in everything he's done. But when he had the opportunity to help someone who gave so much to his program— and then help the whole campus too—he passed it by."

Jesse is glad he confronted Coach Yeagley. "Even if he didn't 131 attend the lecture or speak out on my behalf, he has to be thinking about this now," the former manager says. "I know there have been positive moves—20 years ago someone like Coach Yeagley would not have been even privately supportive—but now is the time for someone like Coach Yeagley to take the bull by the horns and admit there's a problem with homophobia. When I was in his office and ran straight into that denial, I realized that even with all the progress, there's still a huge amount of work to be done."

His relationship with soccer is complicated as well. In retrospect, Jesse says, he let the game he loves hold him back from living as an openly gay man. Though he had wonderful soccer experiences at both Henry Clay High School and Indiana University, he wishes he had been able to feel more comfortable with himself at a much earlier age.

Since he left the IU soccer team, Jesse has not attended a single game. He harbors no hard feelings—not even to the players who sent harsh E-mails—and he does not wish the Hoosiers any bad luck. He follows them in the paper but does not yet feel ready to support them from the stands.

"The whole time I've been away from soccer," Jesse Moyers says, "there has not been one day I haven't thought about the great times I had, the big games, and the winning program. I definitely miss all that. If the opportunity arises in the future, I'd like to be involved again in some way with something like that.

"But I don't regret for a day what I did. I hope someday, someone who goes through Indiana University in my situation won't have to go through the same negative experience I did. And I hope the next manager—or player—who comes out to Jerry Yeagley will have a much better experience than I did."

If that happens, then the Indiana Hoosiers can for the first time truly call themselves champions.

Water Polo
Curtis Brown and Mike Crosby

As a therapist with a largely gay clientele, Curtis Brown frequently deals with adult men who, decades after the fact, still feel scarred by the feeling of disappointing their dads. They tell Curtis in sorrowful tones that their fathers always wanted to play catch, toss the football, take them to the big game. All they wanted to do was anything else.

Curtis spends a great deal of time encouraging patients to get in touch with their competitive and aggressive sides. It is good, he tells them, to test yourself in ways you may have shied away from when you were young or in areas you found unwelcoming, even hostile.

Outside his practice too, Curtis must cope with what many people see as an unfathomable paradox: the gay jock. Even today, he says, a number of friends cannot understand why he became an athlete when he was young, and how he as a 45-year-old gay man can remain one now.

Curtis finds nothing unusual in his passion for water polo. He is one of those people, he says, who enjoy a natural affinity for water. He loves the way it feels on his skin; he understands its rhythms and demands, and delights in its gifts. As for the game of water polo, he appreciates its grace, has mastered its techniques, and revels in its roughness. He is the second oldest man on his gay team, the New York Aquatics, and that is both a point of pride and a key to his happiness. "When I play on a Sunday afternoon, I feel like a kid at Disney World," he says. "That one day—putting on a suit, jumping in, competing—makes me feel great and gives me confidence for the rest of the week."

As an experienced therapist, however, Curtis knows that his experience is not the same as everyone else's. Many men have been traumatized by athletics—and swimming can be one of the cruelest 133 of all sports. Sharing pools and showers with other men wearing nothing but Speedos (sometimes nothing at all) can scare away even the physically strongest, emotionally toughest gay boy. Water polo is an exceptionally rough sport, with an enormous amount of underwater kicking, pushing, and grabbing—all illegal, of course, but also undetected—and that can further confuse a young man struggling with sexuality issues.

Curtis feels fortunate he never suffered those problems. Like any good Miami native, he started swimming young. When he was 7 his mother, fearful he would be a chubby child, signed him up for a swim team. Curtis enjoyed the rigorous practices. He swam up to nine miles a day, in early morning and late afternoon sessions, and advanced from AAU age group programs to the Hialeah High School varsity. He discovered water polo at 12 and played that during high school too. The two sports, he says, helped carry him through what might otherwise have been a lonely time.

"I always knew I was gay, but back in the 1960s and '70s there were no outlets for kids like me. Junior high and high school can be rough for any kid, especially if you're gay. Swimming and water polo gave me contact with good people I would not have met otherwise. I worked hard, got in great shape, and hung around with guys in bathing suits. Lots of gay kids can be traumatized by that and by the common purpose and community of a sports team, but it was right for me."

Curtis came out at 20, as a student at Florida International University. By that time he was already a member of the Hialeah city council, having been elected the year before in a race that included 24 other candidates. At the time, he was the youngest elected official in a major Southeastern city. In fact, as the council's second-highest vote-getter, he spent his second year as president. Anita Bryant, Florida's orange juice queen, was at the height of her infa-

134 mous antigay drive, and his revulsion at her rhetoric brought him out of the closet. He did not make a public announcement, but neither was he quiet about his sexuality. Most local politicians knew.

The strain of living two lives—Curtis would chair a city council meeting, then party at a wild club like 13 Buttons—proved difficult, and after four years in office he opted not to run for reelection. "I knew state senator (later governor and U.S. senator) Bob Graham. Claude Pepper was the local congressman, and I could get him on the phone. I knew I had a future in politics, but I also didn't want to invest 10 years being semicloseted, then have it blow up in my face," Curtis says.

So he spent the next decade working for a series of Miami banks—another industry that, at the time, required most gay people to be discreet—before making a second career change. He earned a master's degree in social work at New York University and opened a psychotherapy practice with a primarily gay and lesbian clientele.

Spending each working day dealing with patients' problems is stressful, and water polo provides a perfect release. New York Aquatics is no different from any straight team. There are six players plus a goalkeeper. In a regulation pool it is impossible to touch bottom, so players spend each 15-minute quarter furiously kicking to stay afloat, keeping their elbows high to gain or protect possession. The ball is in constant motion. Water polo players must keep moving too, sprinting forward on fast breaks, then hustling back to retrieve a loose pass. Pushing and physical intimidation are part of the game. Referees, on the lookout for infractions around the ball, often miss peripheral fouls. They see none of the rough play beneath the surface. There is so much grabbing that some players wear two bathing suits.

"The high point of my week is mixing it up with other guys," Curtis says. "The team part is so important. In water polo you can't be an individual star. You have to work with everyone else. You get a great feeling of fellowship and camaraderie that is hard to find in **135** other areas of life. And that feeling is especially important for gay men who may have missed it earlier in life."

Most members of the New York Aquatics played water polo when they were younger. However, Curtis says, the experience of competing with and against other gay men is special. "There is a freedom, an honesty that is missing from most of our everyday lives. Every child deserves those feelings, but many gay kids don't experience them. Being on a team is a lot of fun, and to miss that as a child is very sad. When you find it as an adult, it's incredibly fulfilling and rewarding."

The New York Aquatics are the only gay water polo team in New York. Locally, they play straight teams, including college squads like those of Columbia and St. Francis. The real fun, though, comes at events organized by International Gay and Lesbian Aquatics, a loose confederation of teams from places as varied as Atlanta, Montreal, San Diego, Seattle, Salt Lake City, Vancouver, West Hollywood, and Washington, D.C. Water polo is also part of the Gay Games.

"Our meets are like two- or three-day cocktail parties," Curtis reports. "It's an absolute blast, seeing different cities, meeting new people, hanging out with people we played with and against in the past. As a therapist, I see guys chasing guys all the time. I ask them, 'What are you really passionate about?' Well, I'm passionate about water polo and these guys I play with. To me, it's a real privilege to be able to follow my passion."

Not every member of Curtis's team is gay. One of the coaches is a Chinese-American lawyer; her husband, an Asian physician, plays too. Straight athletes join the Aquatics because they like the team and its atmosphere (and because there are few other water polo teams in New York for nonelite players). Players shower together, dine at gay restaurants, and seldom censor themselves. "I haven't thought much about what it's like for them, because they seem to be fine with it," Curtis says.

One married man exemplifies the team's open spirit. He has brought his children to practices as well as to a way-gay event in Paris (the Aquatics took home a gold medal).

Of course, not every straight player is as clued in. One woman spent several weeks on the team before commenting, "You know, there are a lot of gay guys here." Curtis's response: "Hel-*lo*!"

"Most of them are very good at adapting to who we are," Curtis says of his straight teammates. "For gay people, playing on a gay team, this is one place where we don't have to adapt to the world the way we usually do. There is a great sense of relaxation playing with people who have shared many of the same experiences growing up. We don't necessarily talk about being gay—it's more an unspoken thing—but even though I'm 45 and some of my teammates are 25, we share a commonality. There is something truly special about being on a team with other people who really do 'get it.'"

Curtis's teammates are almost all white. Their professions range from law and real estate to a Pulitzer Prize–winning journalist and personal assistant to Yoko Ono. Most are fairly out. One business executive in his late 20s, however, had been engaged to be married. Curtis says, "He was a big musclehead, and no one knew if he was gay or straight. It's been wonderful to watch, over time, as he grows into his own skin. There's a certain playfulness about him that wasn't there before. He's dating men now, and he's quite a bit more confident about himself. I'm convinced he wouldn't have gotten where he is—at least not as quickly—without gay water polo."

Curtis enjoys watching that transformation from two perspectives: as an athlete and a therapist. "Part of my work is helping guys become more comfortable with themselves, but on the team I can see it from a different angle. I have an opportunity to see their young, fun, cute sides. That's pretty cool, and I consider it an honor to be part of it."

Curtis says that despite the buff environment, romances and hookups between teammates are rare (or perhaps, he jokes, "I'm so old, I don't notice"). Turning serious, he says, "It's nice to be 45, in good shape, hanging around with a bunch of in-shape athletes in Speedos, and I don't mean that in a creepy way. I'm as much an athlete as I ever was. The physical part of the sport is very cool. When you guard a man in the hole, your hands are on him, you grab his foot. That's normal contact, it's part of the game. I enjoy it without feeling bad or uncomfortable, and that makes me feel good too. I like that I can be an athlete, on a team with people who share this important bond with me, and we can be ourselves, have fun, compete, and be friends and feel good about what we're doing."

These days, professionally, Curtis Brown is moving away from psychotherapy into what he calls "old-school psychoanalytic work." As part of his training, he must undergo analysis himself. He finds himself talking often with his analyst about his Sundays in the pool —how much he enjoys the experience and what it means for his well-being the rest of each week.

"As a therapist, I'm often a distant observer in other peoples' lives," he concludes. "When I play water polo, though, I'm in the middle of everything. My only worry is, literally, keeping my head above water. It's nice, a different kind of change from the rest of the stuff I do all week long. It's so good to feel free, let loose, react, and just have fun."

• • •

Mike Crosby is a very different type of gay man than Curtis Brown. For one thing, they represent different generations: At 45, Curtis has lived more than twice as long as 21-year-old Mike. For another, Mike has virtually no interest in politics, gay or otherwise. For a third, he sees no reason to play on a gay sports team. He is

138 perfectly content to compete with a bunch of straight men—in his case, at Harvard University. In fact, just about the only thing the two men share is a passion for water polo.

In many ways, Mike and Curtis represent more than the stories of two generations. Their coming-out stories are vastly different; so too are their post–coming-out experiences. For Curtis, water polo was a way to reconnect with sports and affirm himself as a gay man; today it remains a primary way for him to socialize with other gay men and be proud of himself. For Mike, water polo is neither gay nor straight. It is simply the highlight of his college experience. And the fact that he is out to his teammates—is, in fact, out as an openly gay athlete to the entire Harvard campus—is really nothing more than an interesting part of his life, no more or less important a fact than his being an Eagle Scout or a biology major.

Like Curtis, Mike grew up in an aquatic environment: the affluent Pacific Palisades section of Los Angeles. Like Curtis, Mike gravitated to water polo after first swimming competitively, and he grew to love both the rough environment of the sport and the close camaraderie of his team. For both men, water polo provided important physical and social outlets, allowing them to deal with their sexuality on their own terms, at the right times. However, unlike Curtis—who defines himself as a gay water polo player—Mike thinks of himself first and foremost as a Harvard athlete.

From the first time he played—as a ninth grader at Harvard-Westlake, the elite private school whose coach, Rich Corso, had coached the men's Olympic team—Mike committed himself fully to the game. Each summer he rose daily at 6 A.M. and practiced nearly until noon. During the school year, the commitment was almost as great.

Mike spent so much time training, playing, and studying, he had little time to socialize. His lack of interest in girls was not a problem earlier, at his Episcopal K-8 school; it was so tiny, with only 30 stu-

dents in his entire class, that no one really dated. But as a ninth grader he felt the first waves of same-sex attractions, and over the next
two years he became even surer that he was gay.

At the end of junior year he summoned the courage to mail
another boy an anonymous note. Mike said he liked him and told the
boy that if he was also gay, he should stick something on his locker
as a message to Mike. Unfortunately, the boy never did.

But a few months later, as senior year began, Mike received his
own anonymous letter, with an eerily similar message. This time
Mike was the one asked to put something on his locker—and he did.
It turned out the note came from the same boy Mike had written
first. He did not know Mike had authored the first letter—at that
point he had not been able to admit he liked guys—but when he
used the same words to contact Mike, both their ruses were up.
They began a brief relationship, which ended poorly. "That's OK,"
Mike philosophizes. "It was my first relationship, and that happens
a lot with the first one."

On New Year's Eve, Mike came out to his first good friends, two
boys and a girl. They had no problem with the news, and by spring-
time Mike told several other friends, his parents, and his college
adviser, a gay man named Ed Hu. His peers were fine; Harvard-
Westlake is a liberal, gay-friendly school, and two straight friends
were already involved with the gay-straight alliance. His mother felt
sad and his father confused, but eventually they came around too.

Despite Mike's enormous commitment to water polo, it took
him a while to actually like what he was doing. For the first two
years he and other younger players underwent hazing from older
teammates. "A few of them were real assholes," he says. "One guy
in particular was pretty belligerent, always ripping bathing suits
and grabbing guys' asses. I sometimes wonder if he's a closet case
himself."

But the freshman/sophomore games were fun, and Mike stuck

140 with the sport. He knew he would get better; he did not want to be stigmatized as a quitter, and besides, he says, "I didn't know what else I would do." By junior year he was starting, a not-inconsiderable achievement on a team that consistently ranked in the top five at the high school level nationwide.

"Even when people were mean to me, I still felt a great sense of camaraderie," Mike says. "And I learned to love everything about the game. You play water polo in a pool, so even though it's intense you never get sweaty. It's like a great combination of basketball, with a shot clock and continuous offense and defense; soccer, because it's a ball-and-goal game; and hockey, with lots of goals scored off power plays and subbing on the fly.

"After practice you feel great, and because you burn so many calories you can eat whatever you want. And water polo is also a very social sport. The games are real intense but short, only an hour, so if you're at a tournament with four or five games a weekend, there's a lot of downtime to go to the beach or movies or a restaurant with the rest of the team." When he was an upperclassman his team traveled to Florida, Arizona, and Northern California.

Water polo also challenged his mind, Mike said. Every day he learned something new. There is a great deal of complex team strategy, based on a variety of defenses and offenses.

Mike did not care for much of the violent, underwater contact—elbows to the ribs, kicking feet, and grabbing testicles—but he got used to it. He liked the type of athlete water polo attracts—sociable surfer-types—and enjoyed too the fact that whatever a player looks like in ninth grade, by senior year he develops broad shoulders, a hard chest, and a tight body. "It gets you into what I consider a very attractive male body," he notes.

But despite his happy California upbringing, by graduation Mike was ready for a change. After four years of nonstop water polo, he felt burned out. He did not relish four equally grueling years in college, denying himself the opportunity to try other activities. He knew that 141 water polo programs at schools back east were not as demanding; the national top 10 was always dominated by California.

On Ed Hu's annual college trip east, Mike and his classmates visited 16 schools. He liked Yale, but water polo was just a club sport—a little too casual for him. Brown, Princeton, and Harvard were the only three Ivy League schools with varsity teams, and because he liked the Boston area more than Providence or New Jersey, Mike applied early to Harvard.

It was a decision he never regretted. While he has enjoyed much of his college experience, it is water polo that has made his four years there meaningful and great. He calls his teammates "fun, talented guys," men he respects as athletes and people. "They enabled me to come out to them," he says. "Thanks to them, I did not have to make a decision between water polo and being honest."

Mike arrived in Cambridge thinking he might have to lead a straight life, but after two months on campus—when he wanted to start dating men—he felt ready to start coming out. He told his three roommates, which proved easy: One turned out to be gay himself, while another, though straight, had been president of his high school's gay-straight alliance.

As his first year wore on Mike came out to others, but none were teammates. He did not want them to feel uncomfortable; after all, he says, they were playing a full-contact sport, spending time together in locker rooms, and wearing next to nothing at practice. In addition, a few comments and jokes made by players had an anti-gay edge. More threatening, however, was what he perceived to be the coach's homophobic attitude. "He said as much, if not more, as the team," Mike says. "That was definitely a factor in not coming out." Another element was his desire to gain his teammates' respect before doing anything as potentially threatening as coming out. Luckily, that was easy. Because of Mike's athletic ability, skills, and work ethic, the Crimson athletes liked him as a person from the day he first dove in the pool.

In the fall of Mike's sophomore season, he began coming out to good friends on the team. Surprisingly, he found, most did not know anyone gay. He points out that despite Harvard's left-leaning reputation, the school is filled with all kinds of people—including hardcore Republicans and Christians. Because there are so few openly gay athletes, Mike notes, athletes' presumptions might have gone unchallenged longer than those of other Harvard students.

Although his teammates expressed surprise—most had not thought Mike, or anyone in water polo for that matter, might be gay—they also were completely positive and supportive. After he told eight or nine players individually, and all seemed fine, he decided to tell the remaining dozen or so athletes together. The best chance came at a team photo session, right before everyone left for the summer. Mike had not counted on the coaches being there too, but that did not deter him.

He announced the news, then reassured his teammates that when he played water polo his mind was on the game, not other things. (He did not tell them that, out of the pool, his mind might wander a tiny bit.) He added that he hoped nothing would change between them.

The athletes who had not known before rushed to congratulate him for his "balls." They said they admired his honesty, on top of their respect for him as a player and person. But the best reaction came from head coach Jim Floerchinger, the man he once suspected of homophobia. "He was good!" Mike says. "He came right up to me and said it was his job to make sure I played to the best of my ability, and that meant he would help me solve any problems I had. He said he was surprised, but he liked me a lot and took it well."

Nothing changed that fall, although the incoming freshmen did not know he was gay. Mike had assumed he would never have to

come out again, but as he overheard random comments he realized 143
he would have to. This time he sent an E-mail; once again the reaction was fine. Relaxed and focused, Mike helped lead the Crimson
to a sixth-place finish at the Eastern tournament—their first time
there since 1994—and a 20th-place national ranking.

In the winter following that junior season, Mike participated in
his first bit of gay activism. A friend organized a campuswide panel
on sports and sexuality, and asked him to participate. Mike hesitated, but agreed when he learned he would join such noted names as
former professional football player Dave Kopay and Reggie
Rivers, a straight ex-NFL star who has studied connections
between homophobia and racism.

To an overflow crowd, Mike told his story. Though disappointed that only five water polo players showed up, he was glad he spoke.
"I stay away from a lot of those things," he explains. "I'm not real
educated about gay politics—or any politics—but this was a pleasure. Reggie Rivers is a great speaker, and Dave Kopay was very
inspirational. He came out in 1975. I wasn't even born then!"

But he notes that there were only two Harvard athletes on the
panel: himself and female water polo player Katherine Callaghan. As
far as Mike knew, they were the only out athletes at the entire school.
Why, on a liberal campus with over 1,000 intercollegiate athletes, did
these two represent the entire queer athletic contingent?

"There's this fear of being rejected by the team," he says. "If you
come out to your roommate and it's a problem, you can transfer
rooms. But if your team doesn't accept you, then you have to transfer schools, and even then it might not work. That's a huge risk.
Even if most of the team is cool, what if one coach or one captain is
too rigid or unaccepting?"

Mike says that even at Harvard, antigay incidents have made
some people not as high-profile as athletes wary of coming out. A
gay tutor's door was repeatedly vandalized, the copresident of a gay

144 student organization had vulgarities drawn on his door, and posters were torn down. "So for someone who cares as much about sports as a college athlete, coming out risks a lot," Mike reiterates. "You risk losing good friendships, and possibly even playing a game you love. And there are so few gay role models in athletics, it's hard to realize that it *is* an option to come out. Most people don't know you can come out and it won't be disastrous."

Mike is glad he came out his way, on his own terms. First he explored the territory; at the same time he gave his teammates time to know him as a person and player. That way, he says, even if someone had a problem with homosexuality, it would not be a problem with him personally.

One of the most important lessons Mike Crosby has learned as an out gay athlete is that homosexuality and athletics are completely compatible. He says with conviction, "You *can* be a gay man and also play college sports. The two things don't have to conflict."

What, then, will it take for another gay athlete—or two, five, 10, or more—to come out, not only at Harvard but at places far less enlightened?

"It will take the athletic department opening up to homosexuality," he says. "They need to bring in speakers. Every year it's mandatory for athletes to hear people talk about gambling and alcoholism. Homosexuality isn't a disease, but the athletic department has to make sure that every team addresses homophobia. I was lucky enough to have a friendly team and good teammates who enabled me to come out in the open. But I know that's not true everywhere. If athletic departments really want to teach their teams and athletes about life, this is a good place to start."

As for Mike, after his own slow start, he finished with a bang. Early in his senior year he received an E-mail from a water polo player at Brown who knew of him through mutual friends. Soon they met, in an odd location: Claremont, Calif., where both teams played in a tournament. They clicked, and over the next three weekends saw each other often. Their squads competed at the same events; each night Mike and the Brown athlete spent quality time away from the pool.

"It was always my dream to date another college water polo player while we were still playing," Mike says. "It would have been weird if it was someone on the Harvard team, but this was perfect. Brown was close geographically, it's a comparable school—it was too good to pass up."

The last weekend, in Providence, was tense. The victor would advance to the Eastern championships; the losing team's season would end. Both squads thought they could win.

Harvard did. And though Mike was thrilled, as both teams made their way to the warm-down pool he saw his boyfriend and felt bad for him. They looked at each other, moved closer, embraced—and suddenly shared a long, deep, and passionate kiss.

"We didn't hold back," Mike says, relishing the memory. "At that point we just didn't care. There were tons of people around, but we took such joy in that kiss. I think it was a great way to show everyone how we felt about each other at the end of the competition."

And at the beginning of a new, exciting, and very honest relationship.

Sports Management Professor
Tom Habegger

Diving is as solitary as a sport can be. All alone, an athlete climbs the platform steps. Clad only in Speedos, he stands motionless, oblivious to the eyes of spectators, competitors, and judges trained only on him. When he is finally ready, he launches himself in the air. For one or two quick seconds, he has one crucial task: to move his body as gracefully, powerfully, and perfectly as possible. He slices through the water. Instantly, his work is done.

One excruciating moment remains, but it is no longer his alone: The scores are flashed. Though they are the diver's own, he must share them with everyone else.

That split second of truth was always the hardest part of Tom Habegger's dive. To avoid seeing his numbers—because he feared the silence that followed a poor score and because he felt so ill at ease drawing attention to himself after a good one—Tom stayed underwater as long as he could.

Eventually, of course, he had to resurface. He learned then whether his dive was successful or not—whether he had succeeded or failed. Yet because he had spent so much of his life learning to avoid interactions with people, those agonizing moments following his solitary, though very public, efforts were no different.

Tom developed a similar habit at West Virginia University, where in the mid 1980s the 5-foot-8, 145-pounder sat in sports management courses surrounded by enormous football players. By that time he had become a cheerleader—even less of a he-man activity than diving. "I placed myself in a difficult, intimidating situation," Tom acknowledges. "But I got by. I did what I had to do. I acted like class was a diving meet. I just sat there every day and didn't interact with anyone else."

Today, a decade and a half later, Tom is still in school. Now, however, he is a popular associate professor. His sports management classes at Ohio's Columbus State Community College are full. His Sexuality in Sport seminar is both groundbreaking and thought-provoking. Students research and discuss such topics as the legal and social barriers that keep gay men, lesbians, and transgendered people from full participation in athletics. For their final project, students must devise an antidiscrimination policy for use in a sports workplace.

Yet for all his accomplishments, Tom is not officially out on the 17,000-student campus. After all these years, the number of colleagues he has officially come out to is less than a good diving score. He never tells his students he is gay (although a photo of his partner sits on his desk). And when class ends, he walks out of the room without hearing any comments about his lecture. Like the diver he once was, Professor Habegger feels uncomfortable drawing attention to himself. It is an odd way for an athlete and teacher to act, he admits, but he knows why he does it. It is irrevocably linked to growing up gay.

Tom enjoyed a warm, loving, traditionally structured upbringing in the Columbus suburb of Westerville. An active athlete, he gravitated to the individual sports of swimming and gymnastics, while his twin brother Kenny opted for a team game, baseball. At 14, Tom concentrated on diving. As a senior in 1983 he qualified for the high school state meet, then accepted a full athletic scholarship to West Virginia. But he competed collegiately for only one season. Burned out, he spent the next two years cheerleading, and graduated a year early.

All along, Tom played the straight game. He can pinpoint the exact day he realized he was gay. At age 10 he walked into a high school locker room with a friend, the son of the coach. "When I saw a guy with a hairy chest, I knew right then and there—*bam!*" he recalls. He spent the next 15 years dealing with what he calls "my pain and secret."

At 25, Tom married a woman. Standing on the altar pledging "I do," he sobbed. Friends and family members smiled at the sweet emotion; Tom knew he cried because he was ruining two people's lives.

Six weeks later he told his bride he was gay. That was his only option, he thought, besides killing himself. She was angry—"She had a right to be," he says—and the divorce was nasty. It took five years to work out the finances.

Looking back, Tom sees that those 15 years were lived through the goggles of his homosexuality. A good athlete, he could have focused on any sport. He chose diving, an activity he could practice and perform alone. And, he reiterates, at diving's climactic moment—the point when everyone learns if he won or lost—he could hide underwater and be the last to know.

Diving did more than delay Tom's coming-out process; it affected his entire career path. As an average student who lacked social confidence, he felt successful in one area: physical education. At 16 he heard of a new profession, sports management. When WVU— one of 10 schools in the country with an undergraduate program in that field—offered a full athletic scholarship, he grabbed it.

At the time, he says, sports management was simply "a brilliant repackaging" of the traditional, yet much-derided, physical education major. Today, broader and deeper, it encompasses high school and college sports administration, fitness center operations, clinical health care, cardiac rehabilitation, and recreation studies.

Tom raced through his undergraduate program. He avoided friendships, even casual conversations, with the burly football players in his classes. He also never realized that his roommate, a fellow cheerleader, was leading a similar closeted, self-loathing life. The two men now live a few miles from each other. They often discuss the pain both could have avoided had they trusted **149** their friendship more.

In 1987, Tom earned his master's degree from Ohio State University. Just 21 years old, he was hired as athletic director by Columbus State, an urban community college offering 52 degree programs. His charge was to initiate an intercollegiate sports program. Today CSCC fields 13 teams. In 1993, Tom was honored as Ohio Junior College Athletic Director of the Year.

In six years as athletic director, only one other person—his assistant, Eric Welch—knew Tom was gay. A former scholarship athlete at Marshall University comfortable in his straight jock world, Eric nonetheless recognized Tom's agony and educated himself about homosexuality. "Through Eric, I found out what friendship is," Tom says with feeling. "He was the most loyal individual I've ever known. And he still is. Eric is not afraid of who he is as a man, so he's not afraid of me."

However, Tom believed there were no other Eric Welches on the Columbus State campus. While he no longer felt as if he was going to die, he was not yet ready to open up to anyone else. Not until 1995, when he entered a doctoral program at Cincinnati's Union Institute, did he trust himself to tell another colleague, "I am gay."

He selected lesbian activist and author Minnie Bruce Pratt to be part of his doctoral committee because she could provide the professional and personal challenges he needed. She did exactly that. Minnie Bruce forced Tom to come to terms with his homosexuality, write about it—and threatened to resign from the committee if Tom did not come out to Bill Sutton, his mentor and a fellow member of the committee. Like Eric Welch, Bill stunned Tom with his graceful acceptance and staunch support.

Tom wrote his dissertation on AIDS and the sports workplace. He researched case law, educational opportunities, and the demo-

150 graphics of the disease. Tom expected the results to be bad; they were devastatingly worse than he ever imagined.

"Everyone in sports management assumed everyone else was between 18 and 25, heterosexual, white, and athletic," he summarizes. "No one understood that someone working out at a fitness center could be gay or have AIDS. There's a gym here in Columbus whose clientele is 75% gay, and no one acknowledged it."

In response, Tom developed a training program for fitness providers. Slowly, area sports and recreation professionals realized their clientele is far more diverse than it looks.

Doctorate in hand, Tom moved on to teaching. He now handles all HIV classes on campus—up to six a quarter—along with his three-credit special topics course, Sexuality in Sport. Because many students arrive with little background in sexuality issues, he begins with the basics. That agitates some of the gays and lesbians, who occasionally lash out at their straight classmates. Tom explains that such lack of knowledge is similar to what they will find in the sports workplace.

The learning curve is often steep. One student, a former Ohio State athlete, wept while reading *Strong Women, Deep Closets*, Pat Griffin's study of lesbian athletes. He had not spoken to his sister, a lesbian, in five years. Tom urged him to write her a letter and send the book. A few days after receiving them, she called. The athlete—a self-described gay-bashing frat boy—quickly flew out to see her.

"I've tended to underestimate today's generation and their acceptance of gays and lesbians," Tom says of his straight students. "They're still somewhat uncomfortable talking about transgender issues, but they realize things are deeper and heavier than they imagined. They're more open-minded than even five years ago."

Because CSCC is filled with older students, however, Tom treads lightly around his own sexuality. He still feels uneasy identifying as gay with people his age and older. The fear of rejection—the same weight that held him underwater after each dive—now hangs over 151 his classroom.

In the 21st century, of course, it is nearly impossible to be completely closeted. The word is out on the Columbus streets, and gay and lesbian athletes find their way to Tom's seminar. Most, however, do not reveal themselves to him until the course is over. Fear of rejection still permeates the sport management world.

Fortunately, times change. A former National Hockey League player took Tom's class to understand the environment he grew up in. Now working as a hockey administrator, he told Tom his insights will help him become a better sports executive.

Columbus is home to an expansion NHL franchise, the Blue Jackets, and it is in that organization that Tom sees clear evidence of changes in sports management. Nationwide Arena sits just half a mile from the city's large gay district, and the Blue Jackets draw many queer fans. "The owners and management know we spend a lot of money on the team. There's a billion-dollar redevelopment project going on around the arena, and they realize where those new shops and restaurants are," Tom says. "Everyone in customer service, from executives right down to the ticket takers, has been trained about this. They handle all their fans with great care. I go to the games, I see it, and my friends in the organization tell me about it too." Some of those friends are graduates of Tom's Sexuality in Sport course.

Other graduates, he says, are quietly and effectively laying the foundation for acceptance of gays and lesbians in fitness centers, YMCAs, parks and recreation programs, and school and college physical education departments around the country. "You may not see the results for 10 years," Tom warns. "But as a wave of retirees comes about and older people are replaced by fresh thinkers, we'll have a number of professionals who support gays and lesbians in athletics. Some of them will be gay or lesbian themselves. Things

152 are going to get a lot better for gays in sports and recreation."

Pointing to himself—noting that even as the instructor of Sexuality in Sport he does not yet felt comfortable coming out officially—Tom says, "Hopefully this cycle of self-hatred can stop. I cannot imagine having my name in a book chapter like this five years ago. But I've learned I'm a hell of a lot more resilient than I thought. That's why I'm ready to put my name in print. I want people to read this. There's no reason for anyone else to go through the self-loathing I went through. No gay athlete ever needs to think, *I'm not a man*."

Or to hide underwater after a breathtaking dive, afraid to hear the cheers that are rightfully his.

Ice Hockey
Jeff Kagan, Warren Cohn, Michael Kiley-Zufelt

Stereotypes die hard.

One day in 1997, while surfing the Net, Jeff Kagan—a recent but avid convert to ice hockey—idly typed "gay" and "hockey" into a search engine. To his amazement, a long list of sites popped up. One link led him to the Toronto Gay Hockey Association, and from there to news of an upcoming tournament. Teams from six cities would play. None, however, was from New York City, where Jeff worked in HBO's programming department. Undeterred, he asked if he could be placed on a team. "Sure," the organizers said. "How about Vancouver?"

The British Columbia players were thrilled to have another player. In fact, they decided that since he was from New York City he was probably bossy. Naturally, they made him captain. Jeff laughed at that stereotype of New Yorkers. After all, he had his own misconceptions: for instance, that gay men could not play hockey.

In fact, Jeff had laced up his first pair of skates just two years earlier. His introduction to gay hockey at age 29 changed his life.

He had never felt happier, Jeff says. He always knew he was gay, but apart from a few preadolescent fooling-around experiences, he'd had no physical contact with a man until he was 27.

His first few years in New York were lonely. HBO was a great place to work—and (he learned after coming out) a very gay-friendly company—but in the beginning he felt an overwhelming need to hide. A late bloomer physically and socially, it was not until he got AOL and went online that he felt free to acknowledge his sexuality.

First, however, he had to get over his hatred of sports, an aver-

154 sion dating back to always being picked last for gym class teams. Jeff's two cousins, 13 years his junior, invited him to their youth hockey games in suburban Westchester County, so he went along. The sport seemed interesting, and the more he learned, the more he liked it. One day his cousins asked him to try ice skating. To his surprise, he agreed.

He looked like a complete idiot, flapping his arms and falling all over the place. But he wanted to prove to the young boys he could learn, so he bought skates. Watching others, he taught himself. Three times a week, he lurched around a Manhattan rink. It was the first truly athletic endeavor he ever tried, and as he realized he was accomplishing his goal, his confidence grew.

Jeff discovered that Sky Rink on the West Side had a friendlier environment than the first place. Other skaters offered tips, and no one laughed. After six months, Jeff told his cousins he was ready to try hockey.

They shopped for gear. Back in his apartment, Jeff admired himself in his mirror. He had not yet played a minute of the game—had never checked someone or been tripped, never even handled a stick—but suddenly Jeff envisioned himself as an athlete. "I had always been a fat little guy," he recalls. "Now I had muscles! It was so empowering." He realized he was capable of doing things he had always been afraid to try.

That realization helped him reach out to strangers and make friends. In the summer of 1995, Jeff enrolled in Sky Rink's instructional clinic. He learned basic puck handling, passing, and shooting. Within a few months, he inquired about team openings.

It was high school all over again. No one wanted a novice skater. Eventually, he found a Division IV team, but even those beginners gave him very limited ice time.

Yet the new Jeff was undaunted. The next year, when Sky Rink organized a Division V team for true first-time players, he appointed himself captain. Fifteen men joined; instantly, Jeff found 15 new friends.

His life grew better off the ice as well. Mastering hockey gave Jeff the confidence to deal with his sexuality more honestly and openly. That led to his fateful "gay hockey" Web search and eye-opening trip to the Toronto Friendship Tournament. He enjoyed captaining the Vancouver team so much that after returning to New York, he wrote an article about his experience for a gay hockey Web site.

He also kept in touch with his new Canadian friends by E-mail. "For the first time in my life, I was not alone," Jeff says. "I was finally happy. Before that, I knew a few gay men, and we had our sexuality in common, but that wasn't enough. We really didn't connect. All of a sudden I found gay people who also loved hockey. They understood the pleasure of skating and playing and competing. But around them I didn't have to hide my sexuality, like I did at Sky Rink. In New York I was living a double life. I was a tough guy on the ice, but then I went home to a boyfriend."

It was not as if Sky Rink was homophobic—the oft-heard "faggot" and "cocksucker" were terms of jock teasing, not antigay put-downs— but despite his joyful experience with the game, Jeff did not feel he could come out. He did not know a single other gay hockey player in New York City.

However, he realized that if they existed in Toronto and Vancouver, they were there in the biggest city in the United States. Once again he logged on to AOL. This time he searched profiles for the words "gay" and "hockey." He entered those men's chat rooms and sent E-mails, asking if they were interested in forming a team.

Through notices in gay newspapers and flyers in bars, the word spread. Several men signed up; so did four lesbians. The Ugly Americans were formed. The founders even recruited a few straight friends. Most did not realize they were joining a "gay team," however; they thought they were simply part of a new club. When the straight skaters saw that the majority of their teammates were gay, they did not care. But when they moved on to other divisions, they were replaced by gay players. Gradually, the Ugly Americans grew gayer and gayer. That means that today the Ugly Americans, as tough as they play on the ice, feel free to celebrate goals with the arm-pulling gay pride gesture of camp icon Queer Duck. Of course, Jeff notes, a bigger difference between gay and straight hockey teams has to do with the bars they head to after games.

Jeff now organizes two teams in Sky Rink's developmental league, the Ugly Americans and the Rockets. The Lions, a gay travel team, plays in competitive tournaments. Sky Rink is fully supportive of all its queer teams. "Any team that can buy ice time is welcome," Jeff laughs.

Like many men who discover a passion, Jeff cannot get enough hockey. He also joined a straight team, the Bandits. After a year and a half he was finally ready to come out to his teammates. After dropping what he thought was a bombshell at a bar after a game, Justin, a cute linemate, said, "Duh."

"What?" Jeff asked.

"Dude, you've been hitting on me for two years," Justin replied. He explained that his brother is gay; his gaydar works well. "Hey, Jeff," he laughed. "I'm on your team—but I'm not on your *team*." What a few months earlier would have been an unthinkably agonizing conversation for Jeff had turned into a joke.

More recently, he joined a predominantly straight team called Sudden Death (for some reason, though, most of the defensemen are gay). When his teammates congratulated him on a great shot, he replied, "It's not me, it's this new stick. I love it!"

One straight player countered, "Jeff, is there a stick you don't love?"

Most straight hockey players are not homophobic, Jeff has learned. The dynamics of the game—its speed, precision passing,

and tight spaces—force players to work together all the time. **157**
Individual talent is important, but there is little room for freelanc-
ing. "You have to be more of a machine than in most sports," Jeff
says. "You have to know exactly where your teammate will be every
second of your shift. It's almost like you're part of a brotherhood."

Jeff had never known that camaraderie as a youngster. He did
not grow up as an athlete, so he never felt the fear of some young
hockey players: that if their homosexuality becomes known, they
will be teased, tormented, even attacked. Jeff does not believe
hockey players are like that. Still, he has heard teammates explain
that is the reason they stopped playing in high school or college,
as well as why it took them years to get back on the ice—even with
a gay team.

But gay hockey players are returning to the rink in ever-
increasing numbers. The International Gay and Lesbian Ice Hockey
Association, an umbrella organization, lists over a dozen teams, with
names like Boston Pride, Colorado Climax, Seattle Ice Breakers, and
Vancouver Cutting Edges. There is even a gay hockey team in
Florida.

The Internet helps pass the word—just as, a few years ago, it
provided Jeff Kagan with his first entry into the gay hockey world.
In a twist on the prevailing wisdom that people adopt false identities
online, he says, "No, you really can be yourself. Before I found gay
hockey, I was hiding something. Suddenly, one day I found what I
was looking for. Now I can be free."

• • •

Like Jeff Kagan, Warren Cohn discovered the joys of hockey
relatively late. Like Jeff also, he found that mastering the techni-
cally difficult, physically demanding sport gave him self-confidence that spilled over into other areas of his life, such as dealing

with sexuality. But even more than for Jeff, hockey gives him a reason to live. "I've got a great job," says Warren, a director for a Fortune 500 company, who is also fortunate to live in San Francisco. However, he adds, "If I had a chance to move to South Dakota to play hockey, I'd do it in a second. Hockey is the most addictive thing I've done in my life." Echoing Jeff's words, Warren says, "When I play hockey, I feel completely free."

That sense of freedom was enhanced one Friday evening in December, when he and several players on his straight team went to a bar for happy hour. Nearby was a company holiday party, which they crashed. A woman flirted with Warren. To prevent any misunderstandings, he told her he was gay. She did not believe the athletic-looking executive-type man, so she turned to his teammates and asked, "Is he really gay?"

Warren—who had not yet come out to his team—simply smiled. In unison, they said, "Uh, yeah." Warren offered, "Well, now they know." But no one skipped a beat, and within seconds they were back dancing and partying.

Warren's revelation brought him closer to his teammates. They knew one more thing about him—and trust, he notes, is an important element on any successful hockey squad. One player went beyond acceptance. He had never known a gay hockey player and told Warren he thought it was cool. But he wondered why Warren had not come out before. "You never asked," Warren replied.

Even in San Francisco, a gay hockey player is unusual. And even in gay America's unofficial capital city, being out breaks stereotypes. One night at a crowded bar, someone knocked into Warren's teammate. Reflexively, the player called the other man a "homo." He had no idea what he said was wrong—until Warren spoke up. Realizing the power of words, the teammate felt chagrined. He told Warren he truly looked up to him as a player and role model. The next morning, still embarrassed, he poured out an apology in a long

E-mail. "That made me feel so good," Warren says. "If he thinks twice the next time he calls someone a name, then I'll have accomplished something."

Warren has already accomplished plenty. In addition to his corporate success, he is an ardent volunteer who works with runaway youth at the Larkin Street Center. He has an active and fulfilling social life. None of that would be possible without hockey.

Until 1999, when he moved to San Francisco from South Florida, Warren had been a closeted player. He either was not close to his teammates or liked them but did not trust them. They were, he says, "typical straight locker-room guys, with all their typical straight locker-room jokes." As much as he loved hockey on the ice, he hated the uncomfortable environment off it.

That difficult time helped Warren deal with his homosexuality. Though he was not out, simply playing the game reaffirmed his own sense of self. "As I came to terms with being gay, my big fear was that I would lose my masculinity," Warren says. "I was a big, brawny guy that people—women and men—liked. As I learned to play hockey, and as I moved from copper to bronze and now silver leagues, I redeemed my self-respect. I was playing this incredibly masculine, tough sport. I was making good plays and scoring. I had the respect of teammates who didn't know I was gay, and of friends and family who did know of my sexuality, and saw that I could play this very difficult sport that takes a lot of skill. I challenged their views of what a gay person is. I proved to them, and myself, that I was just as masculine as ever."

Hockey was not part of Warren's boyhood in Atlanta and South Florida, but many other activities were. He played baseball and soccer, was elected class president, and in high school was chosen for both Boys State and Boys Nation (where at the White House he met President Reagan). He dreamed of law school and a career in politics.

High school was also where Warren suppressed the homosexuality that he now knows was part of his entire life. He surrounded himself with friends and dated girls.

At George Washington University, Warren joined a fraternity and became its president. His frat won the intramural championship cup every year. He had only three same-sex experiences during college (two were fraternity-related). He enjoyed the college spotlight but gradually recognized that his attraction to men was not a phase. He was consumed by inner turmoil.

By the time he graduated in 1993 after having majored in communications, Warren realized that a career in politics was out; skeletons already filled his closet. He took a job with PaineWebber in Miami just as South Beach was becoming popular. He lived in that gay resort and began exploring his still-repressed feelings. Until then, he recalls, he not only knew no gay people; he also believed he had nothing in common with them. At the same time, however, he understood there had to be people like him—active, athletic, interested in politics—somewhere.

After two years Warren left investment banking to join a start-up. To supplement his income he started working at a popular club. One night a week it was gay. Soon he was running the show. He met more and more gay people, though he still presented himself as straight.

Around that time the National Hockey League Panthers franchise came to South Florida. His father purchased season tickets for the family, and Warren was hooked. He had never played hockey— he could not even stand up on ice—but he loved everything about the game.

One day his roommate, a model, returned from a shoot with a pair of Rollerblades. Warren strapped them on and learned to skate.

He was skating around the issue of sexuality too. The men he met at clubs were not like him—not athletes, not interested in politics—

and he still did not know if his feelings represented purely sexual drives or whether he might someday meet a man with whom he felt an
emotional connection.

Finally, in late 1995 he did. It happened one weekday night when
Warren was Rollerblading along the Fort Lauderdale beach. The
most gorgeous man he had ever seen—"a blond Adonis, like Leo
DiCaprio"—jogged by. Their eyes met, and for the next 45 minutes
they ran and Rollerbladed past each other. When the jogger sat
down, Warren skated up to him and struck up a conversation. They
spent the next three years together.

Connecting emotionally with another man enabled Warren to
at last come to terms with his homosexuality. He and his partner
came out to their respective families. Warren's took the news poorly. They were stunned that someone so intrigued by politics and
hockey could also be gay. His mother was heartbroken that he
would not get married and produce grandchildren. Eventually,
however, she came around. Though his parents' love never faltered,
at times he felt like a stranger.

Two years after learning to Rollerblade, Warren started ice
skating. He began playing in recreational roller and ice hockey
leagues. He had his MBA; life was good. However, when he and his
partner broke up, he knew it was time to move on physically. A
straight fraternity brother encouraged him to take a promotion he
was offered out west. "In Florida I was 'Warren who came out of
the closet,'" he says. "In San Francisco I could just be 'Warren.'"

Yet even after coming out, it was not easy being himself. Being
"just Warren" meant many things, and he was unsure how to integrate his gay and hockey lives. Even after he came out to his hockey teammates that night in the bar, he did not wear his sexuality on
his sleeve. "I wanted to be judged on my playing ability, nothing
else," Warren says. "Hockey means everything to me. When I play,
I feel a total freedom from everything. When I'm on the ice, the

162 only thing I'm thinking about is the game. I don't think about work or friends or relationships or sexuality. I focus completely on hockey, and I want the guys on my team to do the same."

But one day his team was scheduled to play the Earthquakes, a team he'd heard was predominantly gay, and Warren was intrigued. He got to the rink early, watched the players walk in, and talked with two of them. He was guarded because he was not sure they were gay; they were guarded because they had no idea he was. Afterward, the players Warren had spoken with before the game came over to him again, bringing two more teammates with them. The captain handed Warren a flier that described the Earthquakes as an "all-gay team." All watched his reaction carefully.

"You're gay?" Warren asked, feigning surprise.

The players said nothing.

Then Warren said, "Cool. So am I." Relieved laughter filled the rink.

When the teams met again, the Earthquakes tried to recruit Warren. But, he says, they were not very good. He was happy where he was and decided to stay with his straight squad.

Today, Warren is fully out and feels completely comfortable. He is, he says, "in a great place. I'm doing what I love. Hockey is a gritty bonding game in a very straight frat-type situation, and I feel very accepted there. I'm making my life here in San Francisco, working with an excellent company in a job I enjoy and volunteering with homeless youth. Sports has allowed me to do all that. Being passionate about hockey allowed me to feel good about myself, and everything followed from that. Tthat's pretty good for a boy from Florida who never held a hockey stick until he was 23."

• • •

A third hockey player, Michael Kiley-Zufelt, also came late to the game. Like both Jeff and Warren, he learned one of sport's most important yet often overlooked lessons: Teammates often come through in the clutch. Gay men may shy away from organized athletics or isolate themselves on teams because they fear they will be ostracized. But time and again, they come to realize that by stereotyping all other athletes as antigay, they judge heterosexual players as narrowly as gay players sometimes are judged.

Michael is a Delaware native. The Philadelphia Flyers won the Stanley Cup in 1974 and 1975, sparking a local hockey explosion. Michael, entering his teen years, had never played sports, but he wanted to skate like Bobby Clarke. At the same time, however, he was realizing with horror that his attraction to males was more than curiosity. He knew that words like "fag" and "fairy" were stronger than casual insults—and that he was one of "those people."

He did not take the route of many confused young boys—having sex with girls—but at the same time he was unready to accept his situation, much less tell a soul. He knew that the television images of gay people—limp-wristed men wearing big scarves and poufy sleeves who appeared only for comic relief—did not represent him. He also knew, however, that if he told anyone he was gay, that is all they would think of.

Michael sought a way to hide his homosexuality, and hockey seemed a great choice. No one, he thought, would assume that someone playing such a rough game could be gay. At 15, he signed up for a summer league in St. Petersburg, Fla., where his grandparents lived. Because he had not skated much, he was handed a pair of pads and told to play goal. Today, he notes, goalies must be able to skate as adeptly as forwards or defensemen, but back in the '70s the game was less evolved. Michael was unfazed; in fact, he thought, playing goal—trying to stop vulcanized rubber disks hurtling up to 75 miles an hour—was the butchest of all positions. His secret would be safe forever.

His summer league coach once had a tryout with the Minnesota

164 North Stars, so Michael learned skills. He enjoyed being on the ice 4½ hours a day. His skating improved tremendously. He became friendly with three players, one of whom often sat in the locker room sporting a full erection. Michael was intrigued but too scared to find out more.

Michael returned to the league the next summer but left early to attend Bernie Parent's goalkeeping school in Pennsylvania. Michael will never forget the moment the Flyers' star, one of the greatest goalies in National Hockey League history, put his arm around Michael's shoulder, talked to him in his charming French-Canadian accent, and signed his stick. Michael also remembers the older players, boys from local prep schools, who ran the drills. He had crushes on several of them.

That fall, his sophomore year, Michael tried out for his first organized team. The Chiefs, though affiliated with his high school, were not an official varsity squad. He was backup goalie and played the first game of the championship series, which they won. He benefited greatly from the head coach—another former goalie—and was named the team's most improved player.

The next year, Michael split goalkeeping duties evenly with another player. The Chiefs lost in the finals. They fell to the same team the following winter, when Michael was the starting goalie.

Throughout high school, hockey gave Michael an escape from the torment of dealing with his sexuality. He began playing as a defense mechanism but had grown to love the sport. He was a true rink rat, skating, watching, and hanging around the game as much as possible.

Because he had never played sports as a child, team camaraderie was something completely new. A quiet boy, never the most popular, Michael found that being part of a tight-knit group was appealing. He liked working toward a common goal and sharing that experience with others his age.

Equally enjoyable, Michael found, was that many players looked hot. In fact, he says, hockey players are hotter than any other athletes (he acknowledges this may have something to do with his taste in men). Yet he never came on to anyone he played with. If the truth about him got out, he feared, that precious feeling of camaraderie would shatter. So Michael repressed his sexuality. He never talked about sex, not even during the interminable locker-room discussions about it. His release came alone, at home, when he fantasized about the boys on the ice.

Many athletes enjoy parties, and that is where Michael learned to drink. Alcohol, he found, made him funnier and more popular. "I was 16, 17, getting absolutely ripped," he recalls. "It was a way to dull the pain of my repressed sexuality, and at the same time I could throw my arms around someone's shoulders. No one would think anything of it, because everybody else was doing it too."

Michael's drinking spilled into other areas of his life. He never took alcohol to school, but by senior year he was drinking several nights a week. As a junior he had started smoking pot. Soon, he says, "I was stoned more days than I wasn't."

Because the Chiefs were not a varsity team, Michael was not a true high school "jock." He fell in with the band, chorus, and music crowd. They had great parties, Michael says, offering him "one more excuse to drink cheap wine and not think about the fact that I might be gay the rest of my life."

Hockey remained important to him, which is why all the way through senior year he did not drink or get high before games. (It helped that they were played on Saturday or Sunday afternoons and not in the evenings.) If he had a game the following day, he went easy at parties.

As a freshman at the University of Delaware, Michael tried out for and made the varsity squad. However, he would have been the third goalkeeper. Used to being the starter and unwilling to sit, he quit. At the same time, he heard about a new all-star travel team ages 17 to 19 that played as far away as Baltimore and Harrisburg, Pa. He joined but did not stop partying. He and a couple of teammates downed six-packs and Jack Daniels in the parking lot before practice.

By the time Michael was 22 and playing in a men's recreation league in northern Delaware, he began to join the gay world. He ventured into bars and had his first relationships. He had not considered coming out in hockey, though he recognized the emotional tension of being close to teammates while also concealing an integral part of himself from them.

One day, he was bartending at a wedding. Though he had a game that night, he expected not to play. He knocked back a few shots, then spent the evening on the team bench thinking he had to quit playing because he was gay. He believed his teammates would never accept his homosexuality. He had never heard any antigay tirades from them—nothing, in fact, worse than typical locker-room "Stop looking at my ass!" comments. He simply assumed, from everything he had heard about sports while growing up, that it was impossible to be both a gay man and an athlete.

Michael walked out to the parking lot and wrote a note to his coach. He said he was gay, was sure the guys on the team would not accept it, and that he would not be back. He stuck it under the coach's windshield wiper and sped away. The radio was playing the Rolling Stones' "Undercover of the Night." Still half drunk, he found that to be an intense, apt metaphor for his life.

Michael thought his hockey career was over. The coach never called—exactly the reaction Michael expected. He did not hear from any teammates either. Nearly three months later, however, the coach phoned. Without preamble, he said that the other goalie might not be at that night's game; could Michael show up just in case?

"Even..." Michael began.

"No," the coach replied. "I want you there!" He added that he

had told the cocaptains that Michael had quit—though not the reason why—and they wanted him back as well.

When he returned to the locker room, he was greeted nicely.
The other goalie was there, but the coach put Michael in for the
third period. Once on the ice, he realized he never really wanted to
stop playing.

Two days later Michael called the cocaptains and explained why
he had quit. Both men independently had the same reaction:
"What's the big deal? You're still you—and you're still our goalie."
They told the other players, and several picked up the phone to call
Michael. They said it was silly for him to think they would not want
him on their team.

"That was the coolest experience," Michael says. "It reinforced
everything I'd ever felt about the importance of 'team.' Those guys
cared about more about me as a person than about any individual
aspect of my life. It was awesome."

When he returned, there were no negative reactions. "I hadn't
given them enough credit," Michael admits. "Rather than judging
them the way I wanted to be judged, I had judged them in the same
narrow way. I ascribed everything I'd read and heard about sports
to those guys, even though I knew they were better than that. I'd
written them off, and that was unfair to them."

As with any team, over the next few seasons old players left and
new ones appeared. Michael always waited for someone to say
something negative, but no one ever did. He assumes the veteran
players clued in the newcomers that his sexuality was a nonissue. He
never heard an antigay comment from an opponent either. "I guess
being gay didn't really matter," Michael says. "They realized it was
nobody's business but my own."

Michael spent 12 years in the northern Delaware recreation
league. The final couple of years, one of his teammates was gay. But
by that time it was so irrelevant, the new player did not know

168 Michael was gay, nor did Michael know about him. They found out after both had stopped playing, when they ran into each other at the Wilmington Pride Festival. The incident reminded Michael of how, when he was in his early 20s and first coming out, he'd occasionally seen men wearing hockey jackets in the bars of Philadelphia. He'd been amazed and thrilled but too scared to approach them.

He realized how far he had come when, at the 1994 Gay Games, he attended a party for hockey players and saw over 100 gay men. He was in New York as a tennis player—he had not known hockey players could sign up for the Gay Games as individuals and be assigned to teams—but watched games every day, enjoying himself thoroughly. That year, he notes with satisfaction, he celebrated six years of sobriety.

Michael quit playing hockey when he entered grad school (he's earning his master's degree in sociology), but in January 2001 he came out of retirement when his former team's goalie got hurt. He had been away for so long that many new teammates did not know he was gay. His partner, however, takes telephone messages for Michael and cheers at games. "They know what's going on," Michael says. "And once again they don't care."

Actually, he is wrong. They do care: They care about Michael as a teammate and a human being. After his team lost the final game, a young player sought out Michael's partner. "Just tell Michael he's a hell of a goalie," the man said. He paused for emphasis, then gave the ultimate jock accolade. "A hell of a fuckin' goalie."

High School Athletes
Mike Lambert, Brad

For several years, Mike Lambert had felt sexually repressed. In Rye Brook, N.Y., being openly gay was not an option for any adult he knew, so it was certainly out of the question for a 16-year-old like himself. Homosexuality was never discussed as a natural, positive part of life—not in school, at home, or anywhere else. The only times Mike heard the word "gay," it was used as a joke punch line or put-down. And at tiny Blind Brook Middle/High School, where the 35 members of each class all knew everyone else's business, it would be social suicide even to hint at coming out.

But Mike was desperate. As a three-sport athlete, he had plenty of jock friends, yet at their ritual Saturday parties he stood around all night, awkward and depressed, watching them pair off and hook up with girls. Meanwhile, he ached for guys.

After chickening out several times, Mike finally summoned the courage to walk into the Loft, a support group for gay and lesbian youth in nearby White Plains. Finally, he thought, he would find people he could connect with, boys who just happened to like other boys. He could hardly wait for "Utopia."

Instead, the Loft teenagers turned against him. "They trashed me," Mike says. "It was brutal, vicious. The fact that I played sports alienated me from them. They were openly hostile. I got no respect. To them, being a gay athlete was like collaborating with the enemy."

Mike was crushed. But drawing on the lessons he had learned through a decade of playing soccer, ice hockey, and baseball, he vowed to rally from that setback. Returning a second time, he met a boy two years older, who seemed to share Mike's interests. He had been a high school soccer player and fencer. As they talked, they clicked. Mike asked his new friend if he fit in with the others at the Loft, and the boy replied, "No way." They went out to dinner, and soon became a couple.

The relationship lasted three months. "It didn't work out romantically," Mike says. "But after we broke up we stayed very good friends."

Those three months were crucial to Mike's coming-out process. He felt guilty sneaking out to another town to see his boyfriend, and frustrated there was no one in high school to talk to about it. He was leading a double life, but it could not continue.

After their breakup, Mike asked his ex-boyfriend for advice on coming out. That spring of junior year he was planning to tell his parents, but they beat him to it. One night they sat Mike down and asked awkwardly, "Do you have something to tell us?" To this day Mike does not know how they learned he is gay—he suspects they checked his computer, an act he calls "incredibly uncool"—but a long, emotional conversation ensued.

It ended with relief. Mike's parents said all the right things: "We love you," "You're still the same person you were before we knew." Still, they quickly went into denial. They did not talk about Mike's sexuality in the days that followed; to this day, they still do not.

Desperate for an outlet, Mike recommitted himself to sports. He rebelled against the silence at home and the homophobic comments at school by trying harder than ever at athletics. He was a two-year varsity player on mediocre soccer and hockey teams and a four-year starter on a baseball team that reached the state Section C finals, but records and standings were less important than simply practicing, competing, and being a jock, day after day, week after week, season after season.

Mike's dedication paid off. When he was a senior, Blind Brook's coaches named him Athlete of the Year. That gave him a small measure of relief and joy. "I felt like, 'Yeah, this faggot throws and runs better than all of you,'" he says. "It was like, 'So fuck you all.'"

His feelings on receiving the award were tinged with anger because, by the end of senior year, nearly everyone at Blind Brook High knew Mike was gay. He never came out officially but somehow, he says, people found out. It was not an easy time.

The ostracism started slowly. Previously, the jocks called often to tell him where that night's party was. That stopped; when he phoned them, they vaguely said nothing was really going on. Then they left for the party without him. "It was all so stupid," he says. "They shut me out because they didn't want to lose their popularity by associating with a faggot."

In the entire school, there was only one boy Mike could confide in. Bursting to talk, he came out to Matt Zinman. "At the time, I didn't consider him a close friend," Mike says. "He was a football player on a pretty poor team, so he wasn't one of the real jocks, but I knew I could trust him. He was truly supportive and stuck by me the whole way. The other guys—the athletes I considered my best friends—I realize now they were just party acquaintances. The 'cool athletes' weren't my friends after all. They were phony. I guess I found out that Matt was my real friend all along."

But even if they wanted to, the jocks who talked trash about faggots could do nothing to Mike himself. A muscular 5-11, 170 pounds, he trained in three martial arts. "I wasn't about to take shit from anyone," he explains. "Only one person tried to pick a fight with me all through high school, and he backed down pretty quick. If you confront people, they're not as big as they think they are. I really believe all gay people should learn how to defend themselves. We don't have to always be victims and take abuse." The problem was that because he was not officially out to his teammates and "friends," he felt unable to fight back verbally.

Today, Mike realizes the power of words. Another Blind Brook student was effeminate. Before his own ostracism began, whenever

Mike and the jocks walked past, someone would make a comment about "that faggot." "Stereotypes are amazing," Mike says. "I was the gay guy, and he wasn't—he's a heterosexual—but no one knew the truth about either of us. He became my decoy. I really wanted to tell them off, but in that small-town situation I didn't have the courage to stand up for him." Ironically, today, that effeminate straight boy and Matt are the only two high school classmates Mike keeps up with.

Mike does not have good things to say about either his town or school. "Rye Brook seems like the smallest, most isolated place on earth," he says, even though it is part of sophisticated Westchester County, and New York City beckons half an hour away. "It's all white, all middle-class. There's no diversity and nothing to do, so all the kids have screwed-up values." In homogeneous Blind Brook Middle/High School, he says, "kids think that's all there is to the world, so that's the way the world must be. No one ever brings up the word 'gay' in a positive way. And I don't think any of the parents ever said at a PTA meeting, 'What are we going to do for the gay kids?'"

As a result, when Mike recognized he was different—at age 10 or 12 he knew he was not interested in girls, and at 14 he finally put the word "gay" to his feelings—he could not cope. "All I wanted to do was fit in," he says. "I liked the sense of team spirit, the camaraderie I got from sports. From day one in kindergarten, I played everything. But even before I knew what 'gay' meant, I heard all the negative comments. When I realized that was me, I pushed it all aside because I knew I had to avoid it. My loyalties to my teams was the number one thing for me. I didn't want to do anything that would disrupt the team. And of course I didn't want to lose all my 'cool' friends. My so-called friends, as I later learned."

Because he did not fit the stereotype of a gay person and never acted on his impulses, he was able to hide for a few years. But gradually the inner conflicts grew too strong, and by junior year Mike

knew he could not repress his feelings forever. That's when he found 173
a number of gay youth Web sites. "I was glad to see other people felt
like me," he says. "But at the same time I was too scared to do anything about it, beyond the Internet."

Then came his courageous decision to walk into the Loft, and his
near-instant rejection for being a jock. Interestingly, however, that
experience—indeed, Mike's entire athletic background—ultimately
helped, not hurt, him.

"Sports turned out to be good for me," Mike explains. "Athletics
taught me to play every game my hardest, to overcome whatever
obstacles were in my way, to never show my emotions, and to always
be tough. Ironically, those were the qualities that got me through
the hardest times and helped me realize I was a good person despite
being gay. I didn't do it with a 'team.' I had to do it all by myself. But
I did it, because I'd always been taught never to give up."

Sports—specifically, baseball—also helped Mike get into Tufts
University in Medford, Mass. His talent impressed the admissions
committee, but Mike cared more about the college's gay-friendly
reputation. As a high school senior touring universities with his
parents, he yearned to ask how safe and accepting each campus was.
But he felt uncomfortable saying the words out loud, so he would
tell his parents he wanted to sit in on a class without them, then
sneak off to the gay and lesbian center. At Tufts he met the director, who boasted that his school was one of the most tolerant anywhere. Mike was sold.

He did not play varsity baseball because the time commitment
was too great. Political science courses became his passion; he hopes
to attend law school, then work for a social justice advocacy organization like the Human Rights Campaign or ACLU.

Unwilling to give up athletics completely—he'd seen too many
inactive freshmen gain a quick 15 pounds—Mike continued martial
arts, four times a week. His main extracurricular activity, however,

174 became Tufts's Transgender, Lesbian, Gay, Bisexual Collective (TTLGBC). He began his college career with plans to be closeted, just like in high school. That decision was reinforced when he met his freshman roommate, a high school jock who, Mike assumed, would not be a real friend once he learned Mike was gay. But one night Mike decided to give his roommate credit for being mature and open-minded. With great difficulty, Mike came out. His roommate's genuine, avid support provided Mike the courage to become actively involved in TTLGBC. Within a short time he was named to the group's top post, coordinator.

Yet even leading that gay group, as a completely out man in a liberal college environment, has not helped Mike feel fully at ease. Ninety percent of his Tufts friends are straight, and at times he feels TTLGBC is just a college extension of the Loft. "I still can't relate to most people," he says. "I know there's a difference between an 'athlete'—a guy who plays sports—and a 'jock,' which is an asshole who plays. But most gay people in our group can't separate the two. I don't really blame them—they grew up being picked on, so they think all athletes are homophobic jocks—but it hurts me to hear them put down some of the things I love."

In fact, for a long time some TTLGBC members insisted Mike was bisexual. As an athlete, he did not fit their stereotype of a gay man.

Still, Mike insists, gay people's stereotypes about athletes pale compared with what athletes think about gays. When he returns to Rye Brook for vacations and summers, he sees his former jock friends. They too are in college, yet they have not changed at all. "It's pathetic to watch them cling desperately to their tiny community," he says. "They still strut, they still act like they own the world, they still spout homophobic comments. Regardless of what they feel about gay people inside, they still care more about their image. They were hot shit in high school. They're not any more, but they don't even know it. I was right all along: They're not the cool dudes they **175** think they are."

Rye Brook is not alone, Mike believes. He has met many people from similar communities, and most tell similar tales. "It's suburbia at its worst. It's all the same bullshit, for any kid who has to grow up in any place like Rye Brook."

It would not have taken much to change his childhood and adolescence, Mike says. "Affirmation, education, a program in high school that says it's OK to be gay—that's all. But homosexuality was totally taboo. If one teacher in one class or one coach on one team ever said that being gay is psychologically normal, that would have done it for me. It might not have convinced anyone else, but that's OK. It would have done me a world of good."

Mike cannot point to one specific homophobic incident or event that made its negative mark. Rather, it was the daily repetition that convinced him homosexuality was bad and he was evil: the "faggot this, faggot that" comments in the halls and locker rooms, the constant, casual use of phrases like "You throw like such a fag," and the "tacit agreement" by adults to never respond to the *f* word. "For teachers and coaches not to say anything just endorses it," he points out. "The total effect is more than the sum of its parts. After a while it just wears you down."

Mike knows he lost some important parts of his youth by being a gay athlete at Blind Brook: the opportunity to date guys, for example, and the chance to come out earlier, like many nonjock gay youths today.

So, if he had his life to live over again—knowing he was gay—would Mike prefer not to be an athlete? "No!" he answers emphatically. "Being an athlete made me stronger. It made me realize I don't have to take anyone's bullshit. If I hadn't taken such shit in high school and learned how to handle it through sports, I might not have been such a fighter. I like who I am, and I am who I am because I'm gay and an athlete. I think that's pretty cool."

Besides, if he was not an athlete, Mike might not have had an experience like the one with a hockey teammate. At Blind Brook, Mike had a huge crush on another player he was sure was gay. Doing things no other straight jock would do—like greeting Mike with a hug—he set off every gaydar sensor in Mike's body. Mike never had the guts to come out to him in high school and was always bothered by questions. What if, he asked himself, this other hockey player was "the one"? How could Mike let such a golden opportunity pass by?

His freshman year at Tufts, Mike could no longer take the torment. He wrote the player an E-mail, expressing his feelings. He sat paralyzed for five minutes, terrified to click the send key. Then he shut his eyes and went for the gold.

The player quickly replied. He was sorry, he said, but he was not gay.

Matt was devastated. He cried all day, on his best female friend's shoulder. In his mind, he had built the other player up to be a perfect match. Finally, Mike had told himself, he would no longer be lonely.

It took a week for his depression to lift. When it did, it came in the form of an epiphany. Mike realized that what he had done took more courage than he ever knew he had. So what if it didn't work out? he told himself; everyone has successes and failures in life. With that understanding, Mike suddenly felt stronger. He recognized that if he could out himself to another hockey player, he could out himself to anyone on the planet.

And at that moment, thanks to many lessons learned through sports, Mike Lambert took a giant step toward leaving his athletic past behind.

• • •

Like Mike, Brad (who asked that his full name not be used, because he is not yet out to many relatives) spent his high school years in a state of deep repression. He too dealt with his gay feelings by denying them; he too was a noted athlete who believed that acknowledging his sexuality would bring instant social suicide. He too grew up in a small town. But Brad had even more reasons than Mike to fear coming out: He lived in rural Tennessee, not suburban New York. In addition to starring on varsity basketball and tennis teams, he was president of his student council, played in the band, and had the lead role in school plays. And, to make his storybook life even more difficult, his father—a former Division I college basketball player—was also the high school basketball coach.

As the tallest student in school, there was no place for 6-foot-5 Brad to hide—physically, that is. Instead, he found a psychological hiding place: the closet. It was the only way he got through adolescence.

Sports formed an inescapable part of Brad's life; it was woven into his genes. His father was not the only one with an athletic pedigree; his mother had been an all-state high school basketball player, and his brother, two years older, was also a star. Brad learned to dribble, pass, and shoot almost as soon as he could walk; tennis, golf, and baseball followed. It seemed he was always active, and that suited him fine. "There was not a lot of entertainment in our town," he says, his voice still tinged with a Southern drawl. "Sports kept me from being idle, maybe getting involved with drugs and alcohol or whatnot."

Brad did not feel coerced into athletics. "Everything I played, I enjoyed. I was coordinated, and sports came naturally to me. I felt pride representing my school and my family. It was fun to go to other towns around the county and have people know who I was."

But life in rural Tennessee was hardly idyllic. Brad had imaginary boyfriends as far back as age 4, more than three decades ago—boys who, he admits, were players on his father's basketball team. Another defining moment was watching Jan-Michael Vincent run around in a loincloth in the Disney movie *The World's Greatest Athlete*. Despite Brad's sports prowess, he was called a sissy when he was young and was teased for being a bit feminine. But as he gained fame as an athlete, those taunts faded away. He dated just enough to quell any questions others might have; token homecoming and prom dates were difficult but necessary experiences.

"I repressed all my attractions throughout high school," Brad acknowledges. "I got involved in so many things and channeled my energy in so many directions, I didn't realize until I was out of high school how miserable I really was. I thought I had fun, but I know now I didn't. I was surrounded by hundreds of people playing basketball and cheering me on, but I was really alone."

Having earned a master's degree in social work, Brad now realizes he was a classic overachiever. He notes, "Society often stereotypes gay men as weak, so we try to overcompensate. I tried to do everything I could to be accepted. I did sports, I was the model student, Mr. High School This-and-That. I was the golden child: polite, mannerly, athletic, smart, good family. But deep down I thought that if people knew the real me—that I wanted to date the quarterback, not the cheerleader—I'd be ostracized by everyone. In a small town like that, everybody knows everybody else's business. But that kind of business…I feared the unknown."

Complicating Brad's situation was religion. His Church of Christ sect was so strict that it prohibited boys and girls from swimming together. He heard nothing positive about homosexuality from the pulpit, but Brad does not dismiss his upbringing lightly. "I think the church kept me grounded in ways many gay men don't get," he says. "I don't agree with a lot of my religion, but I don't hate it or have anger toward it."

Yet his church's influence was pervasive enough that when it came time for college, he chose a small fundamentalist school not far from home. He could have played basketball as a walk-on, but he enjoyed tennis more. Perhaps, he says, he was growing tired of 179 "playing the straight game" in the macho world of basketball, where increasingly the locker room talk involved sexual conquests.

Brad also appreciated the individuality of tennis. Every forehand winner and ace draws applause; in tennis too there are no teammates with whom glory must be shared. "It might sound arrogant, but I liked hearing those oohs and aahs," says Brad, uncharacteristically immodest. "For someone gay, that affirmation is especially important. We need accolades."

In the spring of sophomore year, however, when his older brother was killed in an automobile accident, Brad stopped playing tennis. They had been best friends. As youngsters they hit balls for hours, pretending to be Wimbledon champs; as they grew up they trained together, helping each other improve. His brother's sudden death numbed Brad. He sank into a depression that lasted five years.

His brother's death had another major effect on Brad: It drove him even deeper into the closet. For a decade he tried to fill a family void by being both his brother and himself. "My parents didn't expect me to; I just did it," he says. "I tried to be two children at once. I saw my parents' pain and knew I didn't want to add to it by coming out. The last thing they needed at that point was to hear I was gay." When he finally told them, at age 30, they looked as grief-stricken as they had that terrible day 10 years earlier. They did not say it out loud, but he got the message: Their second son was now dead too.

Yet, in his late 20s Brad found sustenance in a place from his past: sports. He began playing tennis again. He was still not out—in fact, because the only openly gay people he knew were hairdressers and funeral directors, not athletes, sports actually kept him closeted— but he began to feel better physically. He won tournaments, earned accolades, and slowly started to participate again in life.

In a roundabout way, his brother's death helped him finally come out. During his long soul-searching process, Brad realized he wanted to dedicate his life to helping others. Ten years after his brother's accident, Brad moved to Memphis to enter graduate school for social work. He learned, to his amazement, that his new profession is one of the most open-minded, gay-friendly of all. When the course work turned to homosexuality, he began gathering the courage to come out.

"God has a sense of humor sometimes," Brad says. "I was taking a class on oppression, and the instructor randomly assigned us minorities to study. I just happened to get gays and lesbians. My face got beet-red, but my partner, a straight woman, had lots of gay friends and was very comfortable with it." She was the first person Brad came out to. That night, his life changed.

The gay community in Memphis is not very large or vocal, and Brad is no activist. He has never marched in a gay pride parade; he prefers to come out quietly to friends, an approach he says can be more effective than militancy. He has come out that way to several tennis partners, and has been delighted at their near-universal acceptance.

Athletics, he now believes, may even be beneficial for gays by providing an effective way to come out. The interpersonal skills he learned through basketball and tennis have served him well. In fact, he says, gays who lack sports backgrounds may be hampered in coming out or may overdo it by being too in-your-face. He explains: "Because sports is such an important part of our society, gay men who are nonathletes might feel ostracized and react with anger. It's a positive experience to mix and mingle with people, and sports forces you to do that. I feel that because I participated in sports, I never felt as isolated as some gay men do."

In the six years Brad has been out, he has met only a few gay athletes—but that is more than he once dreamed existed. Growing up in small-town Tennessee, he had no idea any gay man could play an

"aggressive, masculine" sport like football or basketball. Yet most of 181
what he has learned about gay sports comes from the Internet. The
gay community in Memphis is not large, and few of its members are
athletes.

Brad, however, is undeterred. He knows gay athletes exist, and in
his low-key way, he is looking for them. "So far, of course, that
means a lot of my athletic friends are lesbians," he jokes. "But that's
great too. I like lesbians. Even if they do kick my butt on the softball field."

ESPN
Bill Konigsberg

In May 2001, Brendan Lemon, the editor in chief of *Out* maga-zine, ignited a sports firestorm by revealing his affair with an unnamed East Coast major league baseball player. Most media out-lets handled the situation well. There was little of the knee-jerk "There are no gays in baseball!" reaction that would have occurred just a few years earlier. Few columnists and radio show callers pre-dicted the demise of civilization as we know it. As it grew, the story focused on three important angles: the ethics of a journalist teasing-ly revealing his love life, the reasons this professional baseball play-er needs to remain closeted, and the result if he (or any other pro athlete) came out.

At ESPN.com, however, Bill Konigsberg wanted to do more. The 30-year-old assistant editor, who spent his days feeding baseball news to obsessive online sports fanatics, suggested that the site devote a package of stories to the ongoing controversy. A senior edi-tor told him the idea was already in the works. So Bill returned to his computer and in 10 minutes banged out his own contribution.

"It's easy for people to play 'What if' games when dealing with an issue such as homosexuals in sports," he wrote. "The fact is, since no male figure in one of the four major team sports ever has revealed himself to be a gay, at least while still playing, we simply don't know, and guessing is the only tool we have."

Why, he wondered, is professional sports still mired at "step one, with nary a gay male athlete to look up to?" He answered his own ques-tion: "It's scary to step out on a ledge where no one has been before."

And then he personalized the issue, with words as sharp and strong as a home run flying off Barry Bonds's bat. Bill wrote: "As a gay man who has worked in sports since 1994, I know something **183** about this."

At that point Bill was out to exactly five of the thousands of people who work at ESPN's high-tech headquarters in Bristol, Conn., a few miles west of Hartford. If his words went up on ESPN.com, they would be read not only by everyone he had worked with for over two years, but hundreds of thousands of sports fans around the globe.

He printed out a copy and dropped it on the senior editor's desk. The man—one of the five who knew Bill was gay—read it, then looked up. "Great," he said. "We'll run it right as it is." He slotted it in with the rest of the four-story gays-in-sports package, and scheduled it to be posted at noon the next day. Bill went back to his cubicle and waited.

Baseball was Bill's life. As a boy growing up in New York City, he lived for two things: sports and statistics. At age 5, he wrote a fan letter to *Baseball Digest*, enclosing reams of made-up stats. In high school he played baseball and loved it—until 12th grade. That was the year it became too difficult to try to figure out how he could be both gay and an athlete. In late-1980s New York, the only gay men he saw were "stereotypical," he says. He could not understand where in that world he would fit in. But with the help of a teacher he came out to, he began accepting himself.

As a high school senior Bill became politicized. "I was angry—at injustice, my parents, everything," he recalls. "I was proud to be gay, but my life was still not meshing. I thought the only way I could be gay was to give up sports."

At Oberlin, one of the most liberal colleges in the country, he was ready to return to baseball, and eager to piece the diverse parts of his life together. Very quickly, however, he realized that the school was too liberal for him. He was progressive, but Oberlin was radical. *Most* of Oberlin, that is. He met a football

184 player who, upon learning Bill was gay, challenged him to a fight.

Bill felt caught in the middle. He did not want his baseball team-mates to learn he was gay. He is certain now that they knew, and he thinks they might have accepted him, but at the time he convinced himself they did not know and would not have approved. The tensions grew too great, and he made the same decision as in 12th grade: It was more important to be gay than to play baseball.

Confused, he left Oberlin in May of his first year. He fell into a deep depression. When he felt better he transferred to Columbia University. The city atmosphere was good for him. He discovered a gay softball league and wrote sports for the *Columbia Daily Spectator*. In 1994 he graduated with honors as a literature major.

Bill had no idea what to do next, and he spent hours playing computer simulation baseball games in the apartment he shared with his boyfriend of three years. The big news that summer was the major league strike. Bill had a brainstorm: simulating the rest of the season and describing each game as if it actually happened. He sold the idea to the New York *Daily News*, *San Francisco Chronicle*, and *Miami Herald*. For two months he was the only baseball writer in the country "covering" major league games. It was the most fun he has ever had—and he made the best money. (The one downside: The *Daily News* told him the Yankees "had to win" the World Series, so he kept playing until they did. He compares their tainted victory over the Cincinnati Reds to the 1919 Black Sox scandal.)

Bill's intriguing work garnered plenty of attention. ABC's *World News Tonight* did a feature; so did *Dateline NBC*. When the NBC crew arrived at his boyfriend's small studio apartment, the producer became suspicious. He asked questions about where Bill lived, but Bill deflected them. The producer's tone made Bill anxious, which is how he thinks he appeared when the piece aired. The incident taught him an important lesson: Mixing sports and his sexuality was going to be very difficult.

So he decided not to pursue a sports-related job. He was hired as
a beat reporter by a New Jersey newspaper, but once again he grew
unhappy. He did not care about the stories he was assigned, yet he
was spending so much time on them he felt he had no life. On a
whim he moved to Denver, where he freelanced for the *Post*. For the
first year and a half the novelty was fun, but still he felt unfulfilled.
Finally, he had an epiphany: He was *meant* to be in sports. The *Post*
assigned him to high school games. Although he had never cared
about high school sports, he had a great time.

Eight months later he heard about an opening at ESPN.com and
applied. He passed an excruciatingly difficult sports test, and in
February 1999 began work as a production assistant. He cut video-
tapes and wrote highlight film scripts. It was highly stressful, imme-
diate-deadline work, but millions of people saw the results every day.

He loved his work, but there was one problem: The environment
was rabidly homophobic. To anyone driving by on Route 229, the
low-slung glass buildings and lush lawns make ESPN headquarters
look like a modern office park or college campus, (or, if one focuses
on the dozens of satellites arrayed in front, a NASA space center).
Inside, however, the atmosphere more closely resembles a locker
room. Nearly every employee is white, male, and young. Jock
humor abounds. And because everyone assumes everyone else is the
same, the air is rife with antigay comments, innuendoes, and slurs.
In that atmosphere, there was no way for Bill to come out.

One day he discovered a pitcher had set a National League
strikeout record that no one else noticed. Bill was promoted to
ESPN's research department, a much better job, where he especially liked writing and designing "Did You Know…" features.

It was not an easy year. Every day he heard homophobic comments in the screening room. He heard things in less-expected
places too. Once, in a high-level meeting with anchors and pro-
ducers, the talk turned to the Ladies Professional Golf

186 Association's "lesbian problem." An anchor kept the conversation going; then someone asked about the "gay problem" on the men's tour. "It sounded like 50 years ago, when people talked about the 'Jewish problem,'" Bill says. With difficulty, he kept his temper in check. But when he left the meeting he wanted to put his fist through a wall.

That environment is not found in most American workplaces today. Bill attributes the reason to ESPN's work force. "Ninety-five percent of them are guys, and there's a lot of ignorance," he says. "There is diversity of geography, but almost all of them have athletic backgrounds. Anyone who's ever been on a high school or college sports team knows that antigay stuff is prevalent. Until they meet a gay athlete—and not many of them have—they're not aware of what's out there."

Finally, in July 2000, Bill had enough. He came out to a coordinating producer and said he would no longer tolerate inappropriate behavior. She was very supportive, as was another producer, but their suggestion that he involve the human resources department turned out poorly. "HR handled it in a professional but worthless way," Bill reports. "They wanted names. Well, no! I didn't want to get people fired. I wanted honest communication."

Bill also came out to two friends in the research department. Though conservative, they knew and liked him as a human being. That demonstrates the other side of ESPN, he says. "This place is very much like a sports team. Sports people are very loyal to teammates; that's how teams work. So even if they don't understand homosexuality, they understand what it's like to be a 'good teammate.'"

When the opportunity arose a month later to move over to ESPN.com, he took it. He was fed up with the homophobia he encountered in research. Besides, the pay was better.

The atmosphere definitely improved. The Internet side attracts more educated people, and for nine months he heard no antigay comments. When the Brendan Lemon story broke, Bill was finally **187** ready to come out.

Before the posting of Bill's piece, John Marvel, the head of ESPN.com, told him to expect hate mail and obscene phone calls. Bill said that would not bother him; if anyone tried to harm him or his property, however, he expected ESPN to take action. John assured him he would be protected.

A few minutes before noon, two friends (one so straight that, Bill says, he'd never met a gay man before in his life) took him to lunch. When Bill returned to his desk, his story—the teaser read "Konigsberg: It's Scary Out on the Edge"—was up. Already, 80 E-mails filled his in-box. Eagerly, yet filled with trepidation, he read them all. Not a single one was nasty or even negative.

"I got so much mail, and all of it was positive. It was one of the most unbelievable days of my life," Bill says. Most of the reaction came from inside ESPN. Colleagues in production told him what a great piece it was; many complimented him on his "courage." A friend with whom he competes in a fantasy baseball league said, "Great article, man. More importantly, are we still going to do our weekly trades?" Someone from research wrote, "I have to admit I was a little taken aback when I read this. I had no idea, and I don't understand that kind of thing. But I applaud what you did." Considering the source, Bill says, "that was the nicest, most touching E-mail of all."

The on-air personality who had talked about the "lesbian problem" in the golf meeting—and had continued with his antigay comments long afterward—approached Bill in the newsroom. "Terrific!" he said. "I'm proud of you." He added that one of his best friends is gay and they play golf together all the time. Bill refrained from rolling his eyes.

Bob Ley, who joined ESPN three days after its founding in 1979, had recently examined the Brendan Lemon controversy as anchor of

188 *Outside the Lines*, the highly acclaimed series focusing on issues beyond the playing field. He called Bill's piece the most eloquent of any he had read on the subject, and quoted an old saying: "I don't care what people do, so long as they don't do it out in the streets and frighten the horses." Bill notes, "Bob is a very conservative man, but he has lots of heart."

Bill plays in two softball leagues—one a day league for ESPN employees, the other a night league in the nearby town of Plainville—and he worried how teammates and opponents would react. He had no problem in either league, and jokes that he knows the reason why: "I'm their cleanup batter. What were they going to do?"

Outside of ESPN, Bill heard from a number of people who said they were helped by his piece. Many described their own stories, adding that they were glad to know they were not the only gay men who loved sports.

But although he faced no overt hostility, not everyone at ESPN was pleased when Bill came out. After his story, whenever he walked into the newsroom he sensed a chill. "For a year and a half, that had been a friendly place," he says. "I'm a nice guy and people liked me. Now I feel like I'm looked at like an alien in that room. Things have totally changed. One guy, who I used to consider a friend, does not even acknowledge that I'm there."

Bill sees parallels between his own coming-out experience and that of a professional athlete who might in the future do the same— perhaps Brendan Lemon's lover, perhaps another man. "I'm not sure a major leaguer would necessarily have it bad—unless the media *made* it bad," he says. "Unless you're really a bigot, if you have a teammate who's going through strife, you're not going to turn against him and pound him into the ground."

He sees the Brendan Lemon story—and his own, on ESPN.com—as positives. "The more the media does to educate themselves, the better it will be for everyone when a player does come out." Of course, he realizes, much will depend on who that athlete is. "Not on his stats, but *him*," Bill emphasizes. "What kind of person, what kind of citizen he is. Take me: I'm an easygoing, friendly guy. The reaction probably would have been a lot different if I was a jerk."

While Bill Konigsberg is glad that millions of Americans are learning the same lesson he did, after difficult experiences in high school and college—"there is absolutely no correlation between the ability to hit a baseball and a person's sexuality"—it may take years for someone to take the next step at ESPN headquarters. Among the thousands of employees, the only one to come out following his ESPN.com piece was a staff member for *ESPN: The Magazine.* "But he's in New York, so that really doesn't count," Bill points out.

Meanwhile, back in Bristol, the one known lesbian avoids him. So does the one married man who, Bill knows, fools around with guys. Just as before he came out, Bill gets the feeling that ESPN is simply a big workplace version of a small-town high school locker room.

Baseball Fan
Dug Funnell

Baseball is a reflection of life in America. Not only straight people enjoy this sport, but gay people do as well. I am a gay man with pride and dignity in myself, my career, and my friends. I am respected in my community. Baseball is my passion, hobby, and interest. I realize that baseball isn't ready to accept us yet, as it took a long time to accept black men in the sport. But we are all people on this planet. When will we accept those who are different from ourselves?

I wanted desperately to like sports, especially baseball. But when you are the last one picked for "choose-ups" in high school gym class and the teams argue over who has to take you, a nonwelcoming flag goes up. I love baseball, but the majority of baseball hates a faggot.

At times I feel like a motherless child in a world where I don't fit in. Perhaps that is why I cling to my passions like baseball, because it makes me feel that I deserve to have a place where I can find myself and enjoy something meaningful. I don't think I have a hunky, macho personality to offer, but I can be kind. So why does baseball hate me? Many of the players are men that I want to emulate. They have the talents I wish I had. They are the men I want to identify with. I desire affirmation from them.

I may be 39 now, but it's not too late for someone's kindness. Please, world of baseball, accept us. We are your brothers, your sons, your cousins, your friends. We are human beings. Please, people in the baseball field, please care.

For more than a century, baseball has occupied a spot in the American psyche unlike any other sport. It is our national pastime; along with mom and apple pie it centers us, defines our most traditional values, explains who we are as a people to ourselves and the

rest of the world. More than any other sport, baseball cuts across 191
lines of race, ethnicity, and class; unites people of disparate backgrounds, and gives us a national sports identity. From summer camp
to company picnics, baseball is everywhere. In the United States,
diamonds are everywhere—and forever.

Dug Funnell knows all that. So, for nearly two decades, he has
fought to make sure that whenever an umpire shouts "Play ball!" gay
men are welcome pieces of that all-American mosaic, on the dia-
mond and in the stands.

It is no easy task. And, at first glance, Dug would seem a most
unlikely fighter. But he is every bit as feisty as another pioneer,
Jackie Robinson. And, Dug believes, his battle is every bit as
important.

Dug grew up in Cleveland, the youngest of five children. He was
born blind in one eye, and poor coordination left him at the mercy
of his school's in-crowd, the jocks. When they were not ostracizing
him or leaving him off teams, they were calling him names. A naturally outgoing and friendly boy, Dug developed nonsports interests.
He organized variety shows for hospitals and old-age homes. But
deep down he desperately wanted to play sports, and be accepted by
the jocks. The more he longed for their attention and affirmation,
however, the more they scorned him.

Dug always felt like an ugly duckling. He spent years seeking his
niche. By the 11th grade he suspected he was gay, but he didn't come
out until his first year at Bowling Green State University, when a
counselor told him it was OK to be gay and feel good about it.
Graduating with a degree in special education, Dug went to work in
the Mayfield, Ohio, public school system. For over 20 years he
taught multihandicapped and hearing-impaired youngsters. His
favorite activities were plays. He was as thrilled as his students when
they acted, danced, and received applause. Naturally, he delighted in
producing *Damn Yankees* and any other baseball show he could find.

Today, nearing 50, Dug teaches only part-time. He also does social service work for gay people.

His dream of being an athlete lay dormant past childhood and adolescence, well into adulthood. Finally, in his 30s, he found a few friends—all straight—who were patient and kind. Learning of his passion, they taught him how to throw a baseball, and hit. Gratefully, he formed and sponsored a team to play in the Euclid, Ohio, men's softball league. Everyone knew the owner was gay—the team name, the DugOuts, is a clever word play on several levels—but it was never a problem. Dug made out the lineups, warmed up with the squad, coached the bases, and lived vicariously through his team.

"I was fully accepted," he says. "I was not a mascot or someone nobody wanted to be around. This was the first time I'd ever been able to go to a ballpark with guys and not feel as foreign as if I was doing brain surgery. I was so glad I hadn't let that part of my life be taken away forever."

When talking about baseball, Dug grows rhapsodic. Bowling Green had had a great, exciting ice hockey team, and Dug attended games, but that sport and football never drew him in. He did not care to watch athletes attack each other. Baseball, however, was in a class by itself.

"Baseball requires brains and intelligence, along with skill," Dug explains. "To complete a double or triple play, twisting in the air, is almost like ballet. It takes incredible talent to know what to do in every situation, and have the skill to do it. There are so many options every time the ball is hit. And think about a batter who hits .400. He fails six times out of every 10, yet that's considered a brilliant performance. Baseball is all about the human ability to fail yet have another opportunity to succeed next time. In life, we don't always hit the ball right. It should be OK to think succeeding three out of 10 times is wonderful. It should be OK to miss. There's always another inning or day."

Of course, Dug also likes watching baseball players perform. 193 "They look damn good out there!" he says. "A nicely designed uniform shows off the male form very well. Baseball players are not gruff or animal-looking, like in other sports where they have to draw blood. To my mind, baseball players look exactly the way a handsome male athlete should look. I guess it's like heterosexual men watching women gymnasts—it's easy on the eyes."

Dug's baseball obsession developed gradually. In college he began searching for his male identity—missing, he says, since childhood—and found it through baseball. After graduation he became friends with a pair of straight men, Little League coach Billy Rohwer and former Notre Dame University baseball player Gary Sasse. Over beers, both taught him about the game. Patiently, they answered his most "embarrassingly silly" questions, like "What is a suicide squeeze?" Eventually, Billy took him outside and made him throw a ball.

"My entire life, one phrase had absolutely torn me apart: 'You throw like a girl,'" Dug says. "Hearing it still rips me to shreds. But now I know that many girls throw pretty well. The phrase really should be, 'You throw like someone who's never been taught.'"

Dug met Gary through a mutual friend, who was intrigued by Dug's baseball memorabilia collection. (His artifact-filled home, Dug says proudly, is "like Cooperstown.") As they got to know each other, Gary told Dug, "You're one of the strongest people I've ever met."

The remark stunned Dug. "I'd always considered myself weak, and here this handsome straight athlete called me strong!" he marvels. "I told him he was someone I always wanted to be: a college baseball star." That Christmas Eve, a few minutes before midnight, Dug was home alone when he heard something being wedged between his two front doors. Opening it, he found a paper bag containing Gary's college glove. "He knew how much that meant to me, and what I meant to him," Dug says. "Now, at night, whenever I feel lonely, I pick that glove up off my mantel and hold it. I've got plenty of things in my house—autographs of Babe Ruth and Lou Gehrig, you name it—but if it was burning down and I could save only one thing, it would be Gary's glove. That's something I could never replace." Dug's will stipulates that he be buried with Gary's baseball glove.

A third major influence was Dave McMillan. Dug describes Dave as "a beautiful man but a tough, kick-ass athlete, the type who would have beat the shit out of me when I was a kid." Dave played left field on the softball team. One day soon after Dave joined the squad, Dug made a nice catch. Dave casually said, "Hey, nice snag." That simple comment—the affirmation Dug never heard as a boy— sent him soaring.

Several weeks later, Dave learned that Dug was gay. "Because of his background as a hockey player and jock, he had a tough time with it," Dug relates. "He tried to work through it. I offered not to be around the team when he was. That touched him. He realized he had to come to terms with what he was feeling."

At the time Dave was a master's degree candidate in family therapy at John Carroll University. That incident with Dug led him to choose homophobia as his thesis topic. In a paper titled "Homophobia: Homosexuals as Human Garbage," he wrote:

I myself have had the personal experience of witnessing how discrimination is taught, how fear and ignorance moves on from generation to generation unquestioned. Growing up as a "preppy jock" I looked at the band members and drama students as fem, sissy, queer, faggots. Anyone with a lisp or feminine qualities was labeled a homosexual. I recall one conversation with my friends vividly. The question was, "What would you do if you caught two faggots butt-fucking?" My response was to beat them to a pulp with a baseball bat, snap the bat in half, and shove half up each of their assholes, leaving them bloody to be exposed. I actually held **195** *the stance that I could kill another human being based solely on his sexual orientation.*

When I moved to Cleveland a year and a half ago, I met Dug Funnell. After two or three encounters I was told that he was gay. At first I was shocked. "But he's so normal," was my response. I had always expected some grotesque monster with whom I would be incompatible. Dug taught me to question the beliefs with which I had grown. He taught me to look beyond outward appearances, even prejudgments foisted on myself by others' intolerance, and see to the heart of a person.

Dug taught me that for gay men to be healthy they need affirmation, especially from straight men. I now have the education and understanding to be able to give this affirmation to a new group of people, people who at one time were not worth my effort. Dug opened my eyes to a whole world of prejudices and discrimination that were inside myself and taught me how to question these fears and educate myself against them. I have paid over $15,000 throughout my education, yet have learned more from a homosexual man than any course could ever teach me. I want to thank my new friend for being Dug, I want to thank him for being homosexual, and I want to thank him for making me the person I am today.

Incidents like those prodded Dug to move from baseball fan to baseball activist. Three handsome men, all comfortable in their heterosexuality, had another friend who, like them, happened to love baseball, but also happened to be gay. Dug had found the affirmation he had long been seeking, and now wanted to use his newfound confidence to help others.

Around that time Dug saw *Field of Dreams.* The popular movie's message resonated with him. He realized that life was no different from baseball: To be happy, a man must take his dreams and run with them. He sent that revelation—along with its relevance to him as a gay man—to W.P. Kinsella, who wrote the novel on which the film was based. Dug soon received a handwritten reply. The author told him his letter contained many truths, and urged him: "Go the distance!"

"I'd always been effective with words," Dug says. "I knew if I spoke from my heart about my pain and my hope, people would listen." So he used words. He began sending letters to Major League Baseball club owners, managers and players. They were the people he most looked up to, the ones he most wanted to reach. He asked them, in words similar to those that begin this chapter, to recognize that some of their fans were gay. He urged them to respect people who were different; to understand them, and affirm them too.

The first responses came in agonizingly slowly. A pair of rookies, the Chicago Cubs' Turk Wendell and Cleveland Indians' Jerry Dipoto, were two of the few players to reply. Both thanked him for his letter, agreed that baseball players could be insecure and thoughtless, but urged him to stay true to himself and retain both his passion and pride.

Though Dug was discouraged by the lack of responses, those replies pushed him forward. He flooded the mail with more letters. This time, more wrote back. He was thrilled.

After hearing from former major league baseball commissioner Fay Vincent and several owners and top executives, many of whom thanked him for opening their eyes to diversity and invited him to their ballparks, Dug redoubled his efforts with players. Within a few years he had mailed over 5,000 letters. This time, he got more reactions.

Dug separates the responses from players and management into several categories. Some said that Billy Bean, the journeyman outfielder who came out after he retired, was not the only gay professional athlete. Some said that baseball mirrors society. Others

went further, expressing the wish that baseball could be a positive 197
force for social change. Only two players, both well-known,
responded negatively. They said that God condemned Dug and he
would go to hell.

Despite the strong support, Dug notes that words do not always
match reality. In 1998, for example, a former clubhouse worker filed
a lawsuit against the New York Yankees, claiming he was the victim
of gay bashing by players, threatened with a baseball bat, and fired
because he has the AIDS virus.

"It's still there," Dug says of homophobia in baseball. "It's still a
very tough door to break down. People wrote letters to me, but
they're still afraid to speak out publicly. It's still seen as something
that could kill a career. Think about that Yankee clubhouse: How
could a gay person, or even someone who speaks up for gay people,
survive in that environment?

Dug admits that Major League Baseball has taken forward
steps. One of his favorite correspondents is Peter A. Magowan,
president and managing general partner of the San Francisco
Giants. In 1994 that organization became the first professional
sports organization to stage a benefit game for AIDS research,
education, care and services. "Until There's a Cure Day" is now an
annual event, raising hundreds of thousands of dollars as well as
heightening awareness. Players have embraced the cause, even
forming a red ribbon on the field.

But progress is slow. Few clubs have added sexual orientation to
their antidiscrimination policies. And when Dug approached his
hometown team, the Indians, with an idea for their own "Until
There's a Cure Day" event, he was told Cleveland was not ready for
it. A team spokesman said, "Don't expect us to form a red ribbon
on Jacobs Field. People come out to the park to forget their trou-
bles, not be reminded of them." When Dug pointed out that AIDS
was not just a disease of gay men but also affected women and

babies, he was told the Indians do not support any medical cause.

"That's backward and ignorant," Dug—who helped raise over $50,000 for an AIDS hospice by organizing auctions of autographs, uniforms and other sports memorabilia—fumes. "I love baseball, but because of the way that team is run, I can't be an Indians fan."

He compares the Indians—and much of Major League Baseball—to another conservative institution: the Catholic Church. "They both have a long way to go before they accept all people humanely and compassionately. There is still a lot of fear, ignorance and hatred about gay people, and in both cases it's there because that's the way people have been taught."

Dug has a solution. He wants to travel from team to team, meeting players individually for an hour, telling his story. He would say that, like all of them, he had a dream when he was young. The players' dream was to play professional baseball; Dug's was to be picked by guys like them for their team. "I know they would respond to that," Dug says. "It's real hard to hate someone who looks you in the eye and speaks from the heart." For added effect, Dug would travel with Dave McMillan, the former homophobe whose life was changed by meeting a gay man.

Although those team meetings are only a dream, Dug believes baseball will change sooner than other sports. "There's a better chance of acceptance in baseball, because of the high level of intelligence needed to play," he says, slipping back into fan mode. "You don't need brawn to be a good baseball player; you need a smart mind, to think quickly."

Good baseball players know that their sport is timeless. There is no clock, and the season stretches well past 150 games. Progress—winning games, building leads, then capturing pennants—does not happen overnight. Though he is not a professional player, baseball fan Dug has learned that lesson well. He understands that the progress he desires—raising consciousness, erasing 199 prejudice, bringing baseball into the 21st century—also takes time. He is committed to his crusade for the long haul. So he continues writing letters, hoping to effect change one player, one manager, one owner at a time. Finally, Dug Funnell has found his own field of dreams.

Gymnastics
Brandon Triche

When Brandon Triche was young, his gymnastics coach ordered him to remove an earring from his right ear. It looked gay, the coach said. And that reflected badly on him and his gym.

His coach's fears were well-founded, Brandon admits. Many parents will not send their children to a "gay gym." They fear homosexuality and worry that their youngsters will turn gay.

He laughs. "Well, gymnasts *do* wear leotards. It *is* a very artistic sport. A lot does depend on form and grace, like ballet. To some people, I'm sure it seems pretty soft." He pauses, his dark brown eyes intense. "But it really is one of the hardest sports in the world."

Brandon should know. As a varsity gymnast at Southern Connecticut State University, he honed his talent under Abie Grossfeld, one of the sport's most legendary coaches. In 2001, Brandon ended his college career on a high note at the NCAA Division II national championships, turning in one of his best performances ever.

Brandon knows firsthand exactly how grueling gymnastics can be, and not just because he spent up to eight hours a day perfecting his sport. Brandon can compare it to football, which he played in high school, and baseball, his other favorite activity, where he squatted inning after inning as a catcher in the broiling sun.

And anyone who doubts that gymnastics is tough—or that Brandon is a tough young man—should examine the road he traveled. It is a long way from Texas, where Brandon was adopted by rigidly religious parents, to Connecticut, where he moved with his boyfriend to pursue college gymnastics. But the journey was made even longer and more treacherous by detours including substance abuse, psychiatrists and pastors who tried to "cure" his homosexuality, and years of estrangement after his parents threw him out of the house.

Compared with all that, vaulting over a pommel horse or catching a high bar is a piece of cake.

Brandon, who is half Native American and half white, was adopted as an infant. His parents, devout Catholics, brought him to church every Sunday. At an early age he learned that sins such as homosexuality would bring condemnation to hell. But from an equally early age he knew he was gay. Muscle magazines enthralled him, and he had his first same-sex experience before he could ejaculate.

When he came out at 15, his parents sent him to a series of counselors. He was also put on Ritalin. His parents and therapists reasoned that declaring his gayness was a cry for attention, so he must be suffering from attention deficit disorder. His parents' reaction drove him back into the closet—when he was around them, anyway. His friends and teammates, by contrast, did not care; the students at Klein High School, in the Houston suburb of Spring, seemed far more tolerant than many adults.

Brandon played baseball and football at Klein because, four years earlier at age 11, he had quit gymnastics. He had loved gymnastics from the moment he watched Mary Lou Retton and Bart Conner star at the 1984 Olympics, but his father never cared for it. "He probably thought it was a sissy sport," Brandon says. "He had been a minor league catcher for the Yankees, and I think he really wanted me to experience his world."

At age 11 too, Brandon was training with a coach who was a poor role model—the gym was filled with drugs and strippers—so Brandon stopped competing and took up baseball. He loved hitting as well as controlling the game from behind the plate. He found his teammates cool too, especially in high school, when he came out and no one cared. In addition, he discovered that when he played baseball, his father paid more attention to him.

But baseball and (for two years) football were only part of Brandon's high school life. At the same time he was partying very, very hard.

He graduated, however, and enrolled at Abilene Christian University, several hundred miles away. He played baseball his first semester there. But a few weeks before school began he watched the Olympics gymnastics competition on television and realized he missed the sport. So at Abilene he took a one-credit gymnastics course and rekindled his love.

The school was not a good fit for Brandon, and after one semester he dropped out. He joined a gymnastics club in Houston, where a "hard-core" coach trained him. Brandon, by then a muscular 5-8, 165-pounder, picked up where he had left off eight years earlier. He went back to school (this time a two-year college), trained on the side, then transferred to Southern Connecticut.

The New Haven school appealed to him for two reasons. A cousin was nearby, at Yale University, but more important, the Owls were coached by Abie Grossfeld. His long career included three stints as head of the U.S. men's gymnastics team; in 1984 he led them to their only first-place medal ever. At Southern he coached 29 individual NCAA champions, 135 all-Americans, and 12 national team members. The college even named a street after him. In the gymnastics world, Abie Grossfeld's name was gold.

Brandon arrived at Southern planning to start life over. He would not be out; he went so far as to date a female gymnast. But even if he had wanted to be open, Brandon would have faced difficulties. There were few gays on what he calls a "thuggish" campus. He was too young to go to clubs. He did not even have AOL.

Yet toward the end of his first year at Southern, Brandon did go on the Internet. In a gay Texas chat room he found a man 10 years his senior. Scott was a policeman, which Brandon found hilarious, but they hit it off online. Back home for the summer, the college student sneaked out of his house and met the older cop at the mall. Brandon was impressed. Scott looked just like he had in his photo; he hadn't lied.

They continued to see each other, but Brandon soon tired of lying to his parents. He started a journal, and after two weeks of entries (and one night at Scott's home) he handed it to them. He began by saying the journal described all his friends and explained every lie. The family talked about his life, and Brandon thought things were OK. The next morning, however, his father told him to leave. He didn't care where Brandon went, he said; the important thing was that he go.

Brandon spent two "horrible" weeks on his own. He was homeless and penniless. Finally, he moved in with Scott. The two men have been together ever since.

For a year Brandon did not speak to his parents. Back at Southern, he injured himself while training. He sunk into a "deep hole," finding solace only in drugs. He took cocaine, ecstasy, special K, and crystal meth. He was so out of control, not even Scott—who had moved to Connecticut to be with Brandon—could help. Once again, Brandon dropped out of school.

"I was lost," he admits. "I didn't know what to do with my life, or how I was going to do it." He maxed out his credit cards and slid even further downhill. He was 20 years old.

Finally, Scott lost patience. At his insistence the couple moved back to Texas, and Brandon entered a rehabilitation program.

Three people helped him get through that harrowing time. One was Scott; the other two were his parents. "The thing I needed most was to know they still cared for me," he says. "They did. They were there for me every moment." As his parents came to terms with Brandon's homosexuality, he learned to accept them for what they were too. The ordeal also proved the depth of Scott's love for him. As awful as that period was, it led to tremendous growth and self-awareness.

When Brandon completed rehab—aided by a counselor who told his parents their views on homosexuality were wrong—his mother and father helped him return to Southern Connecticut. He and Scott moved to New London, 50 miles east of campus, to avoid the temptations of New Haven and New York City.

Abie Grossfeld gave Brandon his full support too. That did not change when the gymnast came out. He did it by telling a teammate, who he knew would tell everyone. Although Brandon was the first athlete ever to come out while actively competing for Abie, the coach did not blink. "He's from New York," Brandon explains. "He's seen it all." For the rest of Brandon's time on the team, Abie made sure to include "guys for you, Brandon," whenever he talked about "chicks." And he did it in the same joking manner he used with his straight athletes.

"New teammates usually wig out when they hear I'm gay," Brandon says. "It's like, 'Holy crap, I can't seem cool with this kid or everyone else will think I'm gay.' But when they see everyone else is cool with it, including Abie, they're fine." Brandon attributes some of that acceptance to the fact that he never showed fear or concern. By speaking honestly and happily about his own life, he showed he was cool with himself. He believes, "You only get in trouble when you worry about what other people will say or do. Now I'm just like, 'I love being gay!'"

Other teams are not as cool as Southern Connecticut's, however. The night before a meet against Temple University, gymnasts from both squads hung out together. The Temple athletes were "a bunch of assholes, ragging about gay guys." Brandon said nothing; his teammates could not stop laughing. Finally, Brandon said, "By the way, I'm gay." The Temple athletes sat in stunned silence.

The next day one of them confided in Brandon that he too was
gay. "I told him everyone already knew and that he should be real.
He was only hurting himself," Brandon recalls. "I don't know if he
wanted to hear that, but it was obvious to me his team knew."

It takes a special person to be a gymnast, Brandon says. The
sport attracts people who are mentally tough. "You've got to like
pain. Physically, most people's bodies can take a lot. But the willing-
ness to work incredibly hard—that's mental."

Gymnasts also face a variety of challenges—so many skills to
learn, so many ways to organize a routine—while facing simultane-
ously the constant specter of injury, even death. And in the end, at
the ultimate moment of accomplishment, hardly anyone applauds.
"You've busted your ass for so long, and no one has any idea what
you went through. No one even remembers most people from the
Olympics," Brandon says. On top of all that, he says, it is virtually
impossible to make money from gymnastics.

Though it would seem those qualities would bond gymnasts
together, Brandon believes the positive reactions of his Southern
Connecticut teammates are rare. More typical is the homophobic
taunting of the Temple team, or the knee-jerk worry of his Houston
coach that an earring brands an athlete as "gay."

"There's a lot of fear that gymnastics is a 'gay sport,'" Brandon
says. "But who really cares if there are gay people in a sport? How
can an athlete's sexual orientation have anything to do with a sport?"

He is concerned that so many good male gymnasts drop the
sport, as he did, when they enter high school. "It's not respected at
that age," he laments. "It's all about football and basketball then. But
I know it's one of the roughest sports around. It's too bad people care
so much what other people think."

Returning to gymnastics and successfully completing rehab gave
Brandon the opportunity to compete at the 2001 Division II national championship, near the end of his senior year. The arena at the

206 University of California, Davis, was beautiful, filled with flowers—but again the sport's aesthetic pleasures came at a cost. The pollen aggravated his already severe allergies. He felt sick the entire time. His parents stood by his side, however, nursing him back to health, and by toning down his routine Brandon gained confidence. He settled down, vaulted excellently, and finished his college career with a flourish: He caught the high bar perfectly.

His elation was great; even better, his parents kept saying how proud they were of him. It was a storybook ending to his gymnastics career—just the way, Brandon Triche says, he always dreamed it would be.

Soccer
Jeffry Pike

From the very first day of practice in 1987, sex hung in the air. It was clear that certain members of the Boston Strikers Soccer Club were attracted to others; it was obvious too that players were hooking up.

For the most part, dating and sexual encounters stayed quiet. Bragging and gossiping would have been rude; besides, there were practices to concentrate on and games to play. However, off the field—traveling to and from matches, and socializing—decorum flew out the window. One favorite pastime was a guessing game: A player revealed how many teammates he'd had sex with, then everyone tried to figure out who they were. Though one couple established a long-term relationship almost immediately, it was far more interesting to dish players like the one who had slept with two thirds of the Strikers squad.

Over the following years, several players gained renown for their promiscuity. They were not outcasts; in fact, the attention they received combined good-natured humor with jealousy. A highlight of the Strikers' yearly Thanksgiving dinner was the Tournament Tramp Award, given to the player perceived to have had sex with the most men at the annual international tourney.

In 1993, however, the Strikers' executive board and several veteran players felt things were getting out of hand. Celebrating only sexual conquests, they realized, could be misinterpreted. It also perpetuated the stereotype of gay men as piggish dickhounds.

That Thanksgiving, self-appointed social coordinator Phil White (alias Jewel-Lee) adapted her awards. With great flair she unveiled several new awards, including one for monogamy, that

208 reflected a more balanced range of Strikers sexual behavior.

During the next few months, the club went even further. Cofounder Jeffry Pike organized a discussion group where players could talk about sex and relationship issues. Though it met only a few times—the setting felt artificial, so members decided spontaneous discussions over beer and pizza were better—it accomplished its goal. The personal nature of those conversations made Jeffry realize the Strikers had created a safe, secure environment for a broad range of gay soccer players. That, in fact, had been one of his goals when he helped start the team. (Another was to find a boyfriend.)

Unlike most gay sports leaders, Jeffry does not run away from the *s* word. "I put it out front: It's OK to have sex on the team, just as it's OK to have relationships on the team or use the team to gain confidence to come out."

Through his father (an athletic trainer at the University of Connecticut) and the influence of excellent coaches at E.O. Smith High School, Jeffry was raised to believe that sports build character. But as he got older, he watched gay men fall through the athletic cracks. "They *didn't* find a safe space; they *were* oppressed by other athletes," he says. "So it's important for a club like the Strikers to provide a fun, relaxing, recreational environment where we can talk about all kinds of issues."

At the same time, Jeffry says, it is important for people to recognize the power of sex. To deny sexual attraction on a soccer team—or pretend it is not one of the reasons for joining—is to perpetuate the lies and deceits that have been a part of gay life for far too long.

Yet those concepts lay far in the future in January 1987, when Jeffry—who, as president of Team Boston, was preparing athletes for Gay Games II in San Francisco—received a phone call from Erik Andersen. Erik longed to re-create the camaraderie he had felt on his college soccer team (and perhaps find a boyfriend as well)—but the only places he knew to meet gay men were bars. Jeffry's soccer background consisted of being an average player on an undefeated high school team and a stint on an adult recreational squad with players from Europe, South America, and Africa. He also organized gay softball and volleyball leagues. He agreed to help if Erik would plan the first practice, and on May 27, 1987, the Boston Strikers were born.

At the time, gay sports teams were a new and little-noticed phenomenon. Loosely organized basketball, rugby, softball, volleyball, bowling, and swimming teams were scattered throughout Boston. "Sports were not considered a gay thing," Jeffry remembers. In addition, there were no leaders: Most talented athletes were not out, and the ones who were did not want to be activists.

The gay press was no help. None of Boston's several newspapers covered gay teams. "They connected sports with homophobia, with obnoxious, stupid jocks," Jeffry says. Because gay sports were relegated to the fringes of the community, it was hard for interested athletes—many of them closeted—to learn about teams and participate.

With such a small pool of players, tensions were bound to arise. Early problems surfaced when it became clear that some team members had little experience with soccer—or organized athletics of any kind. To keep newcomers interested and motivated and to create a safe environment for nervous, self-conscious gay men who as youngsters had had negative sports experiences, Jeffry and other leaders devised a Sunday afternoon novice program. Players learned not only skills, rules, and strategies, but also such basics as how to stretch before working out. A positive side effect of the novice program was that advanced players were encouraged to join in and teach. The result was tremendous team unity, a feeling of shared pursuit of a common goal.

By 1989 the Strikers had enough players for two teams, based on skill level, and a new controversy erupted over the division of

210 Sunday practice time and space. Many advanced players openly disrespected those with less skill. The lower-level players, who had been encouraged by the Strikers to believe that every person had a place and a value, refused to be put down or shoved off the field. As tensions escalated, Jeffry announced a two-hour open meeting. More than 20 players spoke, many emotionally. In time, the better players came to appreciate the lesser-skilled athletes' efforts to improve; the lower-level players, for their part, began to understand that intense competition gave the better players pleasure. Developing—and maintaining—club camaraderie continues to be one of the Strikers' most formidable challenges.

From the club's start in 1987, a family atmosphere was one of Jeffry and Erik's goals. They hoped to create a safe place for gay men, an alternative to bars, bathhouses, and cruising spots. For some players, that "family" concept represented more than a buzzword; the Strikers became a literal replacement for the parents and siblings from whom they were estranged. In addition to social activities such as surprise birthday parties, potluck dinners, dances, and AIDS fund-raising walks, there were true family events like Thanksgiving dinner. The tradition began at the end of the first season, when David Austin and his landlord opened their home to the team.

In 1990, after the feast, Jeffry asked players to speak, Quaker meeting–style, about what the club meant to them. That expression of thanks became an important part of the Thanksgiving ritual. One year, over 60 members spoke. For an hour and half, the entire team (and "extended family") laughed and cried together.

Also in 1990, the Strikers inaugurated Friends and Family Day. This event, held every September, begins with family members and friends attending a regular Sunday practice and scrimmaging with team members. Players and guests divide up by age for a game pitting those under 30 years old against those who are older. Later everyone gathers for a mix-and-mingle potluck dinner. One year Jeffry's brother, niece, sister, and brother-in-law all came. "I was so proud to introduce them to my team," Jeffry says. "And it felt so good to get my two families—my blood family and my Boston Strikers family—together."

Jeffry and Erik's parents, avid Friends and Family Day supporters from the start, now talk each year with club members who are concerned about coming out to their own parents. "It's fun to see them talk to people who are sure they'll get kicked out of their family if they come out or that their parents will have heart attacks," Jeffry says. "Then the next year we see those same parents at Friends and Family Day, advising other players to come out."

But any discussion of the Strikers' safe, loving environment invariably returns to sex. As more players joined the club, more dated, had sex, and developed relationships. Couples began showing affection at practices and social events. That was a challenging time for Jeffry, who yearned to find a monogamous relationship on the team. He grew angry at the players who found pleasure showing off their sexual conquests. It took him a while to recognize that monogamy is not for everyone. It was all part of his growth as a team leader and a human being. Today, he says, "judging from the smiles and body language, sex still goes on quite regularly."

As leaders, he and Erik learned that some players joined the team to sleep with the coaches. When he stepped down from a leadership position, Erik said that one reason for his decision was that he had no time to spend on relationships. On the other hand, another coach easily entered into two long-term relationships with players. He balanced his leadership and lover roles well, becoming a positive role model for the team and Jeffry.

Jeffry's leadership abilities are put to the test whenever relationships between players end. Sometimes one man tells him what has happened and asks him to be aware of tensions at practice. Jeffry often

212 puts the two men on the same team, forcing them to work together (and preventing them from hurting each other). A soccer team, he notes, thrives only when people share the same expectations and goals—a situation no different from a romantic relationship.

On the other hand, some breakups have actually helped the Strikers. "Sometimes after you work through the anger and resentment and grief, a different level of communication occurs," Jeffry says. "In my own case, I've noticed that in moving forward we have to find a different understanding of and respect for each other and ourselves. It's gotten to the point where I sometimes can't wait to play soccer with someone, because I still feel close to him."

Jeffry notes that the diversity of relationship types on the team—from monogamous and long-term to single sexual encounters; from friendships that include sex to bisexuals enjoying support from various partners—demonstrates that the Strikers have matured. They have developed an ability to live with many complexities of intra-club relationships.

All this talk about "family" and sex leads to the inevitable question: When Strikers hook up with each other, is it incest? "There is an incestuous quality to it," Jeffry admits. "People do grow close on the team, and when they start having sex it is with someone they're pretty familiar with." However, he notes, there may be less sex among teammates now than in the past. Part of the reason has to do with the team's success. As players have grown more comfortable with themselves and their sexuality (thanks in part to being on a gay team), they have become more open as human beings. That allows them to feel comfortable in a variety of settings, leading to more opportunities to meet a wide range of people. So they rely less on other Strikers to fill their sexual needs.

Sex is not the only issue the club has faced since its founding, of course. The same social issues that buffet the nation—including homophobia, racism, sexism, and economic inequality—have intruded onto the soccer field. And just as with sex, members and directors have faced those problems head-on.

Homophobia has arisen in a variety of ways: jokes among players, reactions to men in drag, the inclusion of bisexual and straight players on the squad, being out to mainstream teams, even the choice of the club logo. It was there, in fact, from the very first practice. Players made jokes about flamboyant characteristics, limp wrists, swishing, and drag. At times those comments were made about, and in the presence of, less butch players.

"It goes back to the old idea that it's bad to be flamboyant or queeny, because then you can't really be an athlete," says Jeffry. "In the beginning, so many players wanted to be butch that they were quick to put down any signs of stereotypes." As the club grew, and grew up, the jokes were replaced by camp. Now some players make fun of their own butchness.

Today, the Strikers even sponsor drag parties. Players and friends bring dresses, heels, makeup, and accessories. They spend the night changing outfits and lip-synching to favorite divas. One night before a gay pride parade, six Strikers who had sworn they would never wear women's clothing took off their trousers and joined in the fun. That party lasted longer than any other. Jeffry explains, "The thought of doing drag is no longer about gender; it just means having fun. It is less about stereotypes than about being whoever we are. Some players have really come a long way in dealing with their own fears and anger."

Homophobia was also part of the reaction to including straight players on the squad. For many players, this evoked horrible memories of being put down or humiliated by elementary school jocks. For others, it raised the specter of being replaced. After all, they reasoned, aren't straight athletes always better than gay ones?

These were not always unwarranted fears. Some of the straight men were good players; they had been invited by skillful gay players, impatient with the low ability level on the team. Had the straight

214 players been novices, they would not have been asked. "Not only was it clear that the straight players joined for the soccer only, but that the advanced-skill gay players were willing to sacrifice the club goals of learning soccer and building community just to get a crisp return pass," says Jeffry.

The situation came to a head the day a gay player felt that the aggressive practice style of a straight player—including bumping and incidental contact—was motivated by a homophobic intent to hurt a gay man. The gay player started an argument. The straight player retaliated with a head butt, opening a large cut that gushed blood. Both players needed to be restrained as the rest of the squad watched in horror.

"As a group we never imagined the volatility of the feelings we harbored," Jeffry says. He talked with both players and learned their perspectives. The gay man felt betrayed that Jeffry even listened to the story of the straight man, whom he was certain intended to hurt him. Neither man returned to the Strikers.

Things have changed, Jeffry says. Many gay players are now far more willing to use their bodies aggressively. The reason is simple, and has nothing to do with sexuality or upbringing: "We've learned if we don't, we'll get knocked off the ball."

There are, of course, humorous gay-straight stories. When one player who was not out to his family invited his straight brother and two straight friends to play on an indoor team, the Strikers decided not to come out to them. They knew the importance of their teammate's bond with his brother—and fear of a violent reaction. However, behind the straight players' backs—and sometimes in front of them—they enjoyed seeing how campy and cruisy they could be. "We tested our abilities to be our true selves," Jeffry says. The brother did not come back for the next season. Now, however, after the gay player came out to him, he and his girlfriend enjoy hanging out with the Strikers.

These days, straight friends and siblings, as well as bisexuals, are integral parts of the team. Club members no longer hide their sexuality from new players. When someone wonders why straight players would want to stay on a queer team, Jeffry says the answer is clear: "Because this is a good group of people."

In a farewell letter published in the club newsletter, one straight man wrote, "Being a Striker helped me better understand my own beliefs and feelings about homosexuality. Prior to joining the team, my experiences with gay men had been limited to isolated individuals in college and graduate school who were cautious, confused, and tentative. It was a powerful experience to have the tables turned, to be the minority for a change. It was also moving to discover a community that drew its strength not only from the common bond that defined its members but also from the diversity that each contributed to the community's character. Being a Striker gives me hope that things can and will change for the better. Most important, as a teacher, my experience has helped me understand why I must become an advocate and friend to those students who are discovering they are gay. Being a Striker has allowed me to walk a bit in another's shoes, and for this I am truly grateful."

Even the team's logos have evolved. The original design—still in use—includes a red (not pink) triangle, but the ball receives the greatest emphasis. Two years later, when the club hosted the third international gay and lesbian soccer championship, Jeffry (whose full-time job is as a graphic designer and photographer at Harvard University) and another man designed a typeface in which the *b* in Massachusetts Bay Championship could be misread as a *g*, making it Massachusetts Gay Championship. The cleverness of the design outweighed any fears players had about being found out.

That tournament, in fact, was a turning point in many ways. The support of the Massachusetts Institute of Technology, where the tourney was held; the presence of gay and straight elected officials at the opening ceremony, and press coverage in the gay paper *Bay Windows* provided positive affirmation to players who had been unsure of the wisdom, safety, or importance of playing gay soccer.

Another team issue was racism. In the first year, when every player was white, this did not seem problematic. When several players told racist jokes, others laughed; those who felt uncomfortable said nothing. By 1989 several nonwhites had joined the team, and a year later Rodney Byrd—a skilled, intelligent black man with strong character and a good sense of humor—was elected club president. Yet racist jokes continued, Jeffry said. Unconfident talking about the issue, yet wanting to do something, Jeffry used his artistic talent to design a T-shirt that showed black legs kicking a soccer ball. Most players loved the shirt, and several thanked him for opening the subject for discussion.

Whatever racism now exists on the Strikers, Jeffry says, is institutional. Club members make well-intentioned plans to reach out to minorities, yet their methods—hanging posters in gay clubs and gay businesses, putting notices in the gay press—do not work well. Those are not the places or papers patronized or read by most gay minorities. And, says Jeffry, "we as a club do not look further. We have accepted the quiet racism that separates out the people of color in Boston. Our gay community here is still fairly racist."

Further, he has noticed that players whose English is weak are barely tolerated by the group. "We've even had gay Latinos say about us, 'Soccer, no way.' That would be like an American saying no to football. That's not a very good perception of us, and it means we've still got a long way to go." Another player offers an explanation that it may be easier for white men than blacks or Hispanics to come out as gay. Thus, even for minority men who love the sport, joining a gay soccer team is a daunting task.

Another minority—if not numerically, then culturally—is women. When Jeffry played in the Beantown Softball League he watched men drive women away and vowed that would not happen in soccer. When the first females came to practice, some men felt they could not compete with men. But in the early 1990s Kathy Mahoney, an advanced player, followed her brother onto the team, and men quickly realized just how good women could be. In 1993 Kathy traveled with the Strikers to an international tournament in Berlin and more than held her own.

In the beginning most female players were lesbians. When the P's and Q's, a lesbian team, was formed, many women left the Strikers. The two teams sometimes trained together, mixing their squads for scrimmages in order to bridge the gender gap.

For the Massachusetts Bay Championship in 1989, the Strikers added a women's division. Several players, even some committee chairs, wondered why women needed to be included. Jeffry and Erik tried to make them see that they were as guilty of stereotyping as any homophobe who had ever put them down. At the tourney's opening ceremony, Jeffry spoke directly to the importance of bringing together all soccer players, gay and lesbian, and how that idea was central to the club's vision of inclusion.

One final Strikers issue involved money. Initially, there were few fees for club activities. Many players were students or young people starting out in jobs. Social activities were chosen for their affordability.

In 1989 the first dues requirement was imposed: $10. Players who could afford it helped subsidize, anonymously, those needing help with trips and activities. The club has stood by its commitment to keep dues affordable. But as league and tournament fees rise, along with travel expenses (the international gay and lesbian championship rotates throughout North America and Europe), finances have become a major club challenge.

Looking back on a decade and a half of obstacles, growth, opportunities, and fun, Jeffry feels quietly satisfied. "This club has seen

218 periods of great sport, community building, and family," he says. "We have also endured times of loss, frustration, and disinterest. We've had no model of mainstream sports organizations to copy. Often we have set the example for other gay sports teams. Along the way, as we have tried to find the right structure to fit the many needs of club members, the broader gay and lesbian community changed and now satisfies those needs. We were once the exclusive safe environment for members, but now alternatives exist."

They may not have won many championships, and chances are soccer fans will never confuse them with the Brazilian national team. But in a number of important ways—community building, inclusion, and that time-honored sports tradition, "creating a family"—the Boston Strikers are indeed a World Cup champion squad.

Tennis
Billy Wilkinson

The small city of Abilene, Tex.—west of Dallas, on the way to nowhere—is known for two things: religion and tennis. There seems to be a church on every corner (even the two major universities, Hardin-Simmons and Abilene Christian, have religious affiliations); the spaces in between churches are filled with tennis courts. Billy Wilkinson, an Abilene native, has no idea why that is so. But when you grow up in a certain environment, you don't question it; you simply accept it as the way things are. For years the church and tennis were the primary parts of Billy's world.

When he was 13, however, that world began to unravel. His father, a personable man who owned a paint contracting company, died of cancer. His four older sisters—including one who played tennis at Baylor University—were out of the house; three were already married. Billy was left with his mother, a cashier at a car wash who earned $14,000 a year. It was time to decide what to do with his life.

Billy buckled down in school. He also concentrated on tennis. He had been a good golfer, and although not a particularly gifted team sport athlete, he had won a seventh grade basketball shooting contest, and one of his last memories of his father is showing him the trophy.

By the time he entered Abilene High School, Billy was one of the top students in his class and the best young tennis player in the city of 100,000. He traveled throughout the huge state of Texas, as far away as Corpus Christi, earning points for a national ranking. It was a heady period, but a troubling one too. Billy noticed he was attracted to other boys. He convinced himself everyone had those feelings but that as a Christian his job was to push his thoughts aside and live life the "right" way. He threw himself into tennis. During the school year he practiced twice a day; in the summer his mother dropped him off at the courts at 8 A.M., on her way to work, and picked him up at the end of the day, when she was through. At night, he worked at Baskin-Robbins.

Billy thrived on the grueling schedule. He loved everything about tennis. "It's such an individual sport—so much one-on-one," he says. "You either survive those two hours of a match, or you don't. I could do so much with a tennis ball. The quick movement on the court, the pace, the challenge—I didn't care if it was 110 degrees out there." Doubles—which, like singles, he played at the number one position in high school—was fun too. It is a spectacularly fast game, and Billy ate up the action.

Interscholastic tennis was particularly enjoyable. The team traveled far, spending nights in different cities. After dinner the coach would hold a meeting. When he left, players shut the door, turned off the lights, and wrestled. The air was filled with homoerotic jokes and innuendoes. That, Billy admits, was difficult to deal with; he wanted to join in the fun but never did.

One night, sharing a bed, he woke up to find a teammate's leg straddling his body. Billy was so petrified, he thought he would vomit. He knew what he wanted to do but had no idea how to go about it. Finally, he made what he calls "the nerve-racking decision" to drape his arm over the other boy's leg. The initial touch was, he says, "outrageous." Billy will never forget that moment. It confirmed for him everything he thought he had been feeling, and pointed with clarity the direction his life was headed. At the same time, he had no idea what any of that meant.

The high school team won the Texas 5A state championship. Along with his teammates, Billy dated girls. "In Abilene in 1990, that's what you were supposed to do," he says. "By the time you were

16 there, you were getting pressured to marry a good Christian girl
and settle down. I wanted that for me, but over time I started understanding I didn't want it to be with a girl."

Adding to Billy's torment was another player on the team, a
younger boy he thought of as a little brother. On weekends Billy
smoked cigarettes and drank with him and told him all about girls—
"all the time wishing it was him," he says. "I was no mack daddy, but
I did all right."

Billy followed his sister to Baylor, though the men's team was
not good. He lived in a jock dorm. The gang showers posed special difficulty. Billy had always shied away from them in high
school; in addition, he had hit puberty quite late, at 17. "So I'd see
all these hot guys," Billy says. "Nothing ever happened, because I
was deathly afraid. When my roommate went out of town I'd have
a session by myself. That was it. I had no confidence in myself. I
really didn't understand what was going on. I penned everything
up inside, and I had no one to talk to. I was thinking about my
mom, money, working, school, maybe going to law school, and I
also had this incredible burden in the back of my head. There was
a lot going on, that's for sure."

When friends from Abilene told Billy that Schreiner College in
Kerrville, in the hill country outside San Antonio, needed tennis
players, he applied to transfer. He was accepted and granted a full
ride. Billy calls that the best decision of his life. The new atmosphere
was much better, for personal as well as academic growth.

He and two friends became inseparable. They joined the local tennis community and met a very popular man seven years older who,
Billy says, was "kind of nelly. Everyone said he was gay, but they also
said he was a great guy." One night Billy and his friends got drunk and
went to a gay bar. The gay man was there and invited Billy to ride
home with him. Billy was nervous, but as they talked he started figuring things out. Nothing happened between them that night.

Over time they became good friends. Once, after they had been drinking, they started fooling around. Though Billy was not physically attracted to the man and not ready to kiss him, he enjoyed the sexual contact. The next morning, however, he went into "absolute denial." Once again, Billy says, "I had no idea what was going on."

He played tennis with renewed vigor. He and his best friend— one of the inseparable trio—rose every morning at 4:30 to run wind sprints, then showered together in the gym. Though Billy was not attracted to him either, he began shying away. He spent more time with the older tennis player. They would drive to San Antonio, have a nice dinner, get drunk, and the other man would tell Billy how much he cared for him. Billy never reciprocated.

But through that man, Billy met other gay people, and things started to click. He realized it was silly to hide his attraction to males. He even started having fun.

That summer, back in Abilene, Billy attended a meeting of a small church group he had once belonged to. He saw a young man he had gone to high school with. Drawn to his short, stocky build, great eyes, and kind heart, Billy invited him to Austin for his sister's law school graduation. During the weekend, Billy planned to come out for the first time to someone he knew.

The night before they left, they shared a bed in Billy's mother's house. He was so nervous, he didn't sleep at all. Not until several years later did Billy to learn that his friend had not slept either.

Sitting by an Austin lake, Billy told him about his experiences with the older man. His friend asked why Billy was telling him the news. "Because I think you have the same feelings," Billy said. Indeed he did: Ten years before, he had told his parents he was attracted to males. His parents sent him to therapy, and he never acted on his feelings.

Back at the hotel, dressed only in boxers, Billy was nervous. Tentatively he rubbed his friend's head. In an instant, he was all over

Billy. "It was the first mutual attraction I'd had," Billy says. "He was
extremely good-looking, good-hearted, and he came from the same
hometown and had the same morals I did. That's when I knew
things were OK."

When Billy returned to Kerrville, he told his older friend they
could not continue what they had been doing. Billy had not yet
resolved all his internal dilemmas—he still thought about marriage
to a woman—but at the same time he acknowledged his desire to
learn more about the gay world.

Billy's life at Schreiner College was going well. Billy played
intramural softball, flag football, volleyball, and basketball, and
his teams invariably won. He was the number 1 singles and doubles player, made the tennis Academic All-America team, was elected president of the student body, met the former and future
President Bushes, and even found time to party.

With so much going on, Billy felt there was no way he could
come out. "I'd always wanted acceptance," he says. "Whether it was
shooting pool or driving a car, I always wanted to be the best and be
recognized for it. That's just my nature. And now I had it. I couldn't
imagine coming out in the middle of all that."

By senior year he was no longer a plaid-wearing, conservative kid
from Abilene. His professors had taught him to think for himself;
life experiences had taught him that people are not always what they
seem. He wore a bandanna and grew a goatee. He started understanding that it's OK to be different from other people. The more
he became himself, the more respected he became. Yet Billy was not
ready to come fully out, and he continued sleeping with women. "It
was partly for show and partly for animal instincts," he explains. "If
you can't get it any other way, you get it that way. But if I was getting it that way, I was always drunk as could be."

Billy's San Antonio friend told someone in Kerrville about him.
The man brought Billy out of his final stages of denial. They spent

nights in the hills above town drinking beer or wine, listening to George Michael, joking, dancing, then going to sleep. It was the kind of innocent friendship he needed. The man did not force Billy to admit he was gay; rather, he gave Billy the time and space to say so on his own terms, in his own way. By June of 1996, Billy was ready.

The next step involved coming out to family and friends. His mother's reaction was, in retrospect, funny: "Please don't move to San Francisco!" (Ironically, his sister lives there now, and his mother loves the city.) It was even more difficult to come out to his former tennis pro, a man 13 years his senior who had taken Billy in as a son after his father had died. They had chopped wood and talked about girls together; he helped Billy with his homework, and his wife cooked Billy dinner. Coming out to the tennis pro, Billy felt, would be like coming out to his father, had he lived.

As it happened, Billy did not have to come out to the man; he already knew. An old high school friend of Billy's had told the tennis pro's wife, who then told him. He had a hard time with the news at first, Billy learned, but came to accept Billy fully. The two men now play golf together—and his wife has accompanied Billy to gay bars.

Why golf and not tennis? During his last semester in college, Billy stopped playing tennis. For nine years, every day of his life had revolved around the sport. He got up at 4:30 A.M. to train, sometimes six hours a day. Every trip he took was tennis-related. Even his days off were filled with tennis thoughts. He had always wanted to be the best, but in Kerrville he was—and that was the end. He realized he would never play the pro tour; the end of the competitive line had come.

Quitting the game had nothing to do with being gay, Billy says. "Homosexuality never affected tennis. At that point, I was just ready to move on with my life. My coach was pissed, but there was no camaraderie on the team and no reward for me. It was time to get on with my life."

But Billy will never give up tennis completely. A couple of years 225 ago, after he quit his job as a stockbroker, and before he started his own financial annuities marketing company, he taught tennis and enjoyed it. Now, to get away from the demands of his business, he has started playing competitively again. His doubles partner is a former teammate from middle and high school. The man knows Billy is gay; it is no problem at all. "It's all in the way it's presented," Billy declares. "I live my life normally, and he respects me for it. In fact, the other day we were talking, and he asked if I could find him a girlfriend."

Basketball Coach
Dave Garcia

Dave Garcia was 12 years old the first time he saw Isiah Thomas. The Detroit Pistons guard was already an NBA sensation. In 1989 and '90 he would lead his once-sorry team to back-to-back championships, but on that day in 1986 he awed young Dave with a last-second shot to beat the Atlanta Hawks. Dave never forgot that scene, nor the celebration that followed when the 6-foot-1 Thomas jumped into teammate Rick Mahorn's enormous arms.

"I just loved seeing this little guy in a sea of monsters and tall trees slice and dice," Dave recalls. "He seemed to be the smallest guy out there, but he was trying the hardest. And he was so tough, but he was always smiling."

From that day on, Dave wore his hero's number, 11. He plastered his wall with Thomas posters (and, intriguingly, an X-ray of Thomas's hand that was given to Dave by a nurse who knew he idolized the star). Up to that point Dave played two sports, baseball ("not very well") and track. But, inspired by Thomas, he tried basketball. The harder he worked, the better he got; the better he got, the more his confidence grew. That confidence soon spilled into other sports. He started the baseball season batting a dismal .050; he was scared of the ball, and it showed. But he ended the year with a sizzling .364 average.

His life changed almost overnight. Dave no longer hoped for walks; he did not care if he got hit by the ball. From that spring on, Dave says, he "attacked" sports. "I was no longer afraid of messing up. And in middle school, that makes all the difference in the world."

Middle school is a difficult time in many boys' lives. It is especially tough for those struggling with their sexuality. Dave grew up in a strict Catholic family and was an altar boy. In first grade his father, a Mexican who worked on an automobile assembly line before getting into computer management, moved the family from the tough east side of Flint, Mich., to Gaines, a predominantly white suburb. Though Dave is lighter-skinned than his older brother, it was not easy being half Mexican.

Sex was never mentioned in the Garcia house. By the time he was in middle school in the Swartz Creek District, Dave knew he was attracted to men, but he had no one to confide in. He coped by spending most of his time playing basketball. He always managed to have girlfriends, but he cared more about shooting hoops until dark. He even stole floodlights from his theater class and hooked them up in trees so he could play through the long summer nights.

"When I was on the court, I was in the moment. I didn't have to think about other things," Dave says. "Being good at basketball helped my confidence and my schoolwork. I made more friends, joked around more, and argued more with teachers I didn't like." Although he beat high school players one-on-one, he was strictly a backyard player. Being cut from his high school team was devastating. He realizes now the others made it because they spent their summers working with the coach at his summer camp. At the time, however, Dave had no clue about all that; he did not even know the coach's name.

So he took his basketball and returned to downtown Flint, where his grandparents still lived and where, he says, "the real competition" in Genesee County is. He was the only non–African American on the city courts and by far the smallest. But he loved it. "No one in Swartz Creek could slam," he says. "These guys could. And I was just a point guard, but I could play with them." When he went back to Swartz Creek he challenged established players to games of one-on-one. Dave made plenty of money.

228   At Northern Michigan University he played basketball intramurals. But the activity that turned his life around was a freshman year coaching class. Instructor Mike Geary, the head women's basketball coach, noticed Dave's enthusiasm—he arrived at 7 A.M., an hour before class, to work on free throws—and asked him to serve as team manager. Dave performed the usual tasks of fetching water, preparing practice facilities, and taping games, but the most important aspect was taking notes for the coach. That taught Dave the subtleties he had never known, like the importance of "seeing the ball," learning to look at the big picture, and motivating players.

The summer after freshman year, while playing the best basketball of his life, he broke his ankle. He spent eight weeks on crutches, mad at the world. His mood darkened even further when X-rays revealed that his ankles and knees were weakened from his years on concrete surfaces. The doctor advised him to stop playing. "The way he said that, so nonchalantly, killed me," Dave says. "Basketball meant so much to me. I started crying right there. The doctor couldn't believe how upset I was. 'You can take up swimming,' he said. Swimming!"

Wearing braces, Dave could not get back to where he was. "When you're short and your skills and mobility fade, you're dead," Dave says. "I was never again as good as that summer. It was frustrating because I'd worked so hard to get there."

He turned his competitive fire to mountain biking, flag football, and ultimate Frisbee. They were sports he could master. Having trained hard to become a good basketball player, he was not content to once again be one of the crowd.

Dave had entered Northern Michigan on a musical theater scholarship but changed his major to communications. The school, in Marquette on the Upper Peninsula, was predominantly white. Dave got involved in campus racial issues and became president of NMU's Mexican organization. He received criticism from two sides:

from white students for his insistence that the college hire Mexican faculty members, and from members of his own club because he "did not look Mexican enough." His work with the multicultural department brought him into conflict with the university president over policies regarding the recruiting and retaining of minority staffers.

During the 1994-95 school year the head of NMU's lesbian, gay, and bisexual group asked the Mexican and African-American organizations to help sponsor a dance. Dave was not out but helped with the plans. Death threats rolled in. "You've said enough about the spics," one caller admonished. "Now you're helping the fags. You better stop."

"Fighting for Mexicans was easy for me," Dave relates. "It was the honorable thing to do. I had my family and church behind me. That Mexican fight made me feel like a young, strong prizefighter jumping into the ring." At the same time, he knew a more difficult, perhaps truer fight loomed ahead, and it would begin only when he confronted his sexuality.

Dave was not yet ready for that fight. For years he had been taught that his family and faith came before himself. He had learned that "sexual deviance" was anathema to the church and that to come out as bisexual would bring shame and disgrace to his family's name. So at the same time he fancied himself a prizefighter, he considered himself a coward.

That year he was dating a woman he had known since high school. She knew of his attraction to men, as did his brother and parents; all urged him to make the "right" decision. But what was right for them was wrong for him, and one night he talked to his girlfriend, attempting to end their relationship. She could not do that, she replied. She was pregnant.

Abortion was not an option for either of them. Yet marriage was also out of the question; it would be too dishonest. Though he was (and still is) attracted to women, his feelings for men are stronger.

230 He knew that to be whole he had to be in a committed, loving relationship with a man.

But for the sake of the child, they worked on strengthening their bonds, and on July 26, 1996, Dave's son, Gabriel, was born.

Fatherhood brought major changes to Dave's life. He left school and took three jobs. One was as buildings supervisor for the Swartz Creek School District. To keep his hand in sports, he signed on as assistant coach of the seventh-grade boys' basketball team at a local parochial school, St. Mary's Queen of Angels. The head coach respected Dave's basketball knowledge and saw how well the boys related to him. The following year, when the players were in eighth grade, he asked Dave to step up to head coach. That spring Dave added St. Mary's baseball team to his coaching duties.

Meanwhile, he was promoted to community services coordinator, a new Swartz Creek position aimed at bridging the gap between the city and school board in community and educational events. Included were activities as diverse as a muscular dystrophy fundraiser, Gamblers Anonymous meetings, Easter egg hunts, services for abused women, teen anger management programs, and gun, water, and fire safety. He also helped develop and coordinate recreational programs such as fishing, guitar playing, karate, and chess. He planned a radio show where teenagers could talk about important issues.

Several gay students approached Dave with horror stories about harassment in the school halls. Matthew Shepard had just been killed; the Boy Scouts of America was embroiled in controversy over its anti-gay policies (Dave, a former scout, speaks highly of his experiences with that organization). Gay issues were in the news, and that visibility was causing problems for Swartz Creek students. "They were having bottles thrown at their heads, and they were dropping out of school," Dave says. "They came to me because they knew I'd grown up there, they thought I was cool, and they needed help."

At the time, Dave had never heard of any organizations that 231 could help gay youth. But his job was to build bridges between community and outside agencies, so he began to research them. He discovered Parents, Families, and Friends of Lesbians and Gays and the Gay, Lesbian, and Straight Education Network. GLSEN was about to hold its national conference in Chicago. A workshop would focus on organizing gay youth groups, and Dave asked permission to attend.

Up to then, Dave had received positive press. To promote programs, he cultivated good relationships with the local papers. In July 2000, Swartz Creek mayor Dennis Allen told a *Flint Journal* staff writer, "Dave's doing a great job. He's a very personable guy, and he's good at solving different people's problems." The story mentioned a minor squabble—a woman was irate that a new community education magazine designed by Dave contained a phone number for the area's gay and lesbian switchboard—but also carried his matter-of-fact response. He listed it "for the same reason I included the NAACP. This program is all-inclusive."

Two months later, however, the coverage brought Dave into the middle of controversy. On Sunday, September 24 the Flint paper carried a story headlined "Swartz Creek Official Hopes to Help Gay, Lesbian Students." The article began: "He was everybody's idea of the perfect son: good-looking and popular, outgoing and athletic. Honor student, basketball player, altar boy at the Catholic church. Now Dave Garcia, Swartz Creek's community services director, wants to launch an effort to reach out to people who are just like the boy he used to be. But the programs Garcia wants to create aren't aimed at that idealized stereotype. They're aimed at the boy who was hidden inside—the one not even his family knew."

Near the end of the piece, reporter Elizabeth Shaw wrote, "Going public with his own sexual orientation was not an easy decision, Garcia said, but he felt it was necessary if the program he

232 envisions is to become a reality. 'For the focus to be on me and my coming out is wrong. I want these youth to believe it's OK to be open and honest about who they are. I can't do that honestly without letting the community know I am gay,' he said. 'I have a responsibility to truthfully represent myself if I'm encouraging youth to do the same.' "

He acknowledged that his basketball and coaching positions might be at risk.

"If they're still willing to call me once this is out there, I'd be happy to coach again," he said. "I'm a damn good coach. While I'm coaching, I am talking about basketball and certainly not my sex life. It angers me that men can coach female teams, and nobody thinks twice about it. Sexual orientation should be seen as just one of many personal characteristics. I may be gay, but I'm also Catholic and Mexican-American and dark-haired and a basketball player and a whole list of other things."

Though Dave placed the need for a gay youth support group in the context of Matthew Shepard's murder, and the assistant superintendent of schools seemed to acknowledge the importance of such a group, the story ignited a firestorm of opposition.

Four days later, the *Journal* reported that the city council wanted to review Dave's job description. Councilman Richard Abrams wondered if Dave had "stepped a bit too far for his position." Mayor Allen said the action was unrelated to Dave's coming-out. "I would hate for people to think we're doing this now because he's gay," he claimed. "I know that's what it looks like, but it's not true. We've been talking about needing an evaluation for at least a month. It's just a shame he came out publicly with this when he did. The timing is just unfortunate."

"As in sports, I knew once I stepped up to the plate I was prepared to fight the battle," Dave recounts. The battle raged on all sides. When his extended family learned he was gay, some supported him.

Others did not. His grandmother urged him to become a priest. "In a Mexican family, that's the honorable way out for a gay man," he says.

Almost overnight, Dave's work environment changed. He did not move as scheduled to a new office upstairs; his desk was placed in the middle of a lobby. His supervisor sent a memo ordering him not to leave the building. "Seventy percent of my job was outside," Dave says. "I had meetings, supervision duties, you name it. If I left the building I couldn't do my job—and then they'd write me up for that." His flexible hours were altered, putting him in direct conflict with a second job he was working to help support his son.

His request to attend the GLSEN conference was denied too. "They said part of the reason was financial," Dave reports. "They told me if parents removed their kids from programs like day care because I was allowed to go to the conference, their federal funding might be in jeopardy."

Garcia—who earlier had been encouraged to speak freely to the press about the programs he was promoting—was also ordered to comply with a school policy forbidding employee communications with the media without prior approval.

That same week, the St. Mary's athletic director came to Dave's office. Dave had coached the man's son in both basketball and baseball, even provided private training. The athletic director praised Dave for doing such an excellent job. He said Dave was the reason his son loved basketball. The coach had been a profound and positive influence.

Then, as his wife sat in the corner and cried, the athletic director told Dave he was no longer welcome around his son. "I don't want him to be gay," he said bluntly.

That was Dave's darkest day. He knew a Catholic school could fire him because of his sexuality. All he could do was tell the athletic director he was sorry he felt that way and hoped the man would educate himself about homosexuality.

234   When the athletic director and his wife left, Dave cried. Then he got mad.

He began following his job description—which called for him to leave the office to supervise programs—to the letter. A Flint lawyer who specialized in antidiscrimination cases warned Dave that the longer he did his job, the more reasons his superiors would find to cite him for insubordination. Dave talked to the media during his free time, but was written up for that too. On his lawyer's advice, Dave signed a letter of resignation. In it, he said he did not want to leave, but felt the administration was forcing him out.

Because Dave lived in Michigan—one of nearly 40 states without civil rights protection for gay, lesbian, bisexual, and transgendered citizens—he had few legal options. A lawyer agreed to take the case as a First Amendment issue only. The trial was set for late 2001.

Swartz Creek felt less and less like home. When he took his young son, Gabriel, to a restaurant, Dave was conscious of averted eyes and whispered conversations. He moved to Ann Arbor and took a programming job at the University of Michigan's Office of Student Activities and Leadership.

Dave became an activist of sorts too. In December 2000 he walked 60 miles in two days from Swartz Creek High School to Lansing. There, on the steps of the capitol, he delivered a powerful speech. America will not stand, he said, for "the exclusion of brilliant and beautiful young gay and women from full and equal access and participation in our schools, in our military, in our places of work, in our social service organization, any more than we would accept in today's society the exclusion of blacks from our churches, Jews from our schools, or women from our voting booths. No more exclusion, no more shame or hiding. Not one more student should die in secrecy or in vain. Absolutely not one more."

When his fiery talk ended, a woman shook his hand. She said she was a former Swartz Creek student. Although she had never known

Dave, she followed his story closely in the Flint newspapers. She 235 called her experience at their shared alma mater "pure torture." It's about time, she said, that someone stood up for gay civil rights— "especially at Creek."

Many months after leaving Swartz Creek, Dave returned. In the interim, he had received several E-mails of support from former players. "You're still the same coach as before," the boys said. Others, however, never talked to him—either of their own choice, or because their parents forbade them to. On this day, however, there was a softball game, and four players attended. They were now sophomores in high school. Dave had not spoken to them since his forced resignation.

After the game, Dave talked to them alone, along the third-base line. He told them that it is important in life to choose battles wisely. Once the choice is made, however, one must always fight as hard as possible. Just as in athletics, a person should always do his best. The boys did not say much, but Dave thinks he made his point.

"Most kids are not going to be professional athletes," Dave Garcia notes. "But as a coach, you have the opportunity to use the field or the court to teach them something they will remember for the rest of their life. As coaches, we can teach team building, character, and determination that will last beyond the locker room. I did that when I was coaching, and they got it. Hopefully, I'll get the chance to do it again."

He does not know, however, when that opportunity will come. And he is certain it will not be in his hometown. "In Swartz Creek, I'm now 'the gay guy,'" he says. "And in a place like this, to some people, that means more than anything that's really important."

Adventure Racer
Rodger McFarlane

"You swim. You ride camels. You paddle 50 miles. And then, when you're utterly exhausted, they tell you you're supposed to go through desert gorges and catch horses. And *then* they point at the highest peak in Africa, where you've got to do all this. At that point, even the most elite teams start sobbing.

"There is nothing macho about adventure racing. It's just a lesson in humility. You learn about life. You either put one foot in front of the other and keep going, or you stop. So you keep going. And when you do that and you finally get to the other side of the mountain, all you have to do is ride a bike 120 miles to Marrakech. And that's a breeze."

Adventure racing, as explained by Rodger McFarlane, is not pretty. His description of the 1998 Eco-Challenge Morocco makes *Survivor* seem like a Brady Bunch picnic. But Rodger seeks neither praise nor glory. He recounts that grueling, body-breaking, mind-twisting eight-day trek across rivers, deserts, and mountains matter-of-factly. And it was not even the most important undertaking of his life.

Picking one highlight from Rodger's 45-plus years is impossible. He is a U.S. Navy veteran and graduate of the Nuclear Power School. He served as a nuclear reactor operator on seven North Pole submarine expeditions, one of which still holds the world's under-ice navigation record. He is internationally certified in alpine climbing, ocean kayaking, land and ocean navigation, rescue swimming, touring and off-road cycling, ultra long-distance running, and arctic survival. He has set numerous Ironman course records.

But those are mere sidelights to his day jobs. Rodger has written books on subjects ranging from caring for seriously ill friends and 237 family members to an insider's guide to Broadway. He has worked for Internet medical firms; served as executive director of Broadway Cares/Equity Fights AIDS; and been project director for an AIDS professional education program. As executive director of Gay Men's Health Crisis, he led the nation's first and largest community-based AIDS service organization.

Rodger has lectured nationally at places like the Harvard Law Forum, Johns Hopkins School of Public Health, and Yale University. He has been interviewed by every media outlet, including the major broadcast networks and CNN, NPR, and the BBC, and print sources such as *The New York Times* and *Esquire*. He has been honored by President Ronald Reagan, Gov. Mario Cuomo, the Black Leadership Commission of New York, and the Hetrick-Martin Institute for the Protection of Gay Youth.

Oh, yes. Rodger has also been photographed by Robert Mapplethorpe and acted in commercials directed by Woody Allen. He was the first arrested member of ACT UP. He won a Tony Award. And in 2001, while caring for his agent who had pancreatic cancer, his brother with end-stage AIDS and his good friend Larry Kramer, suffering from liver failure, Rodger was also organizing an all-gay team to compete in the 2002 Eco-Challenge.

Not bad for a man who, 30 years earlier in rural Alabama, felt so clumsy and "different" he wondered what would become of his life.

Rodger confronted those questions early in Theodore, a small town just south of Mobile near both Mobile Bay and the Gulf of Mexico. He was close to all three brothers. One was nationally ranked in tae kwon do; another starred in football, then embarked on a distinguished Army career. Rodger calls his gay brother, David, "a flawless machine and a great recreational athlete."

"They all had physical gifts," Rodger says. "I was the freak show." By seventh grade he stood 6 foot 6 but weighed a skeletal 130

238   pounds. He and David were both aware, as early as age 2 or 3, that they were unlike anyone else they knew. However, neither boy had words to describe that differentness.

Alabama in the 1960s was surreal, Rodger says. On the one hand, he was surrounded by images of George Wallace and attack dogs; on the other, he saw blacks working hard on nearby farms and for his father's construction company. For a long time, Rodger did not know how to make sense of his world.

Football, even more than Christianity, was Alabama's true religion, and Rodger tried it for two years. "I wanted to prove I wasn't a sissy, that I could do it," he says. "I ran blindly into people and nearly killed them, but any time I got hit I buckled at the knees like a twig." To this day, he despises low-center-of-gravity sports.

Because of his height, everyone expected Rodger to play basketball. But he was too awkward to be any good. Besides, he says, "being 'different' made me not much of a team player. And I never felt comfortable in the locker room."

At the University of South Alabama, Rodger did pick up a sport: tennis. "It was something a gay guy could do," he says. "There was no macho bullshit, and I was good at it. After one lesson I could serve anyone off the court, and if I ever lumbered my way to the net, no one could pass me."

But he left college before graduation, and to avoid being drafted he enlisted in the Navy. Because of his aptitude in science and math, he was sent to nuclear engineering school. There he learned to prepare for covert operations. "Being a farm boy helped. I was not a great athlete, but I wasn't scared of critters, and I could find my way through a swamp. I didn't have a macho streak about me, and that was good."

An important accomplishment was completing a 150-mile over-ice rescue along the remote Siberian coastline. With each step, Rodger realized that he owned and commanded his body. "Gay or

straight, that joy and endorphin rush gives you great confidence," he   **239**
says. "Mastering your body for the first time is a wonderful thing."

Though Rodger had never had a sports coach who taught him
confidence—"I'd gone to third-rate schools with not-nice human
beings," he says bluntly—his father and airplane pilot–sailor mother had always urged their four sons to accomplish anything they
wanted. That helped Rodger when, with 100 men, his nuclear submarine traveled more than 30,000 miles and spent more than six
months without surfacing, setting a world under-ice record.

Not once that entire time, Rodger says, was he made to feel
uncomfortable because of his sexuality. "No one there had any sex
life, except with themselves," he points out. "We were impeccably
trained, very professional, and fully respectful of each other. In that
situation, you had to be. If anyone did anything amiss, it would kill
us all." And, he adds with pride, "All those superstraight *Top Gun*
nuke guys told me they wanted me to run their reactor again, even
if I was wearing a dress."

After leaving the Navy in 1978, Rodger returned to South
Alabama. He played tennis and rowed—both sports where his enormous wing span and newly developed muscles were advantageous—
but left before graduating.

He headed to New York City, where an opportunity to study at
the American Ballet Theatre awaited. The men Rodger met there
were the most incredible athletes he had ever seen. They moved
with grace, power, and passion. Best of all, the "locker room"
atmosphere was queer-friendly.

However, after helping start and run Gay Men's Health Crisis
at the dawn of the AIDS epidemic, Rodger lost his excellent conditioning. Spending all day behind a desk, chain-smoking while
surrounded by the horror of disease, he slid into "dreadful shape."
Concerned for himself, he sought out Mike Motta, a noted personal trainer and fitness adviser. Within six months Mike got

240 Rodger in highly competitive shape and onto the triathlon circuit.

With his enormous aerobic lung capacity, sternwheeler arms, and Special Forces experience, coupled with a boyhood spent swimming in oceans, lakes, and bayous, Rodger was a natural. Mike introduced him to sponsors. Cannondale customized a nickel cadmium-frame bike for him. He proved as powerful a bicyclist as he was a swimmer. And although running was not his forte, Rodger's knees and hips were strong, and his long strides ate up ground.

Rodger dove into training with the same enthusiasm he showed for every other endeavor. Each week he swam 24,000 yards, biked 200 miles, and ran 50 more. He entered several major races, won a bit of money, met intriguing people, and regained the all-important sense of mastery of his body that he first discovered in the Navy, then honed in ballet. He returned to work with new vigor.

But all that was a prelude to Eco-Challenge '98. The event, first held in 1995 in Utah, is an outgrowth of New Zealand multisport and European endurance races. However, it differs from them in substantial ways. The courses are longer, there are no assistance crews, and organizers send a strong environmental message.

Each team of four men and women races nonstop for six to 12 days over a rugged 300-mile course. Skills include mountain biking, river rafting, horseback riding, mountaineering, fixed ropes, swimming, kayaking, and navigation. No team knows, until they complete each segment, what the next challenge will be. Any team losing a member, whether to illness, injury, fatigue, or disagreement, is disqualified.

Rodger first heard of the Eco-Challenge from an exercise physiologist. Competition to enter the Morocco event in 1998 was fierce, but Rodger put together what he calls a "scary" team. They trained by running 50 kilometers in the dead of winter, riding bikes, and climbing up the snow-covered Catskill Mountains. But "Team Urban Edge" qualified: "A faggot, a Gulf War Marine Corps vet, a black sistah Eagle Scout instructor, and a Jewish girl who grew up in the Congo but was trained by the Israelis," Rodger says. "We looked 241 like a Benetton ad."

After a year and a half of training that changed Rodger's life ("Endorphins are sweeter than Zoloft and a lot more dependable," he jokes), the group traveled to Morocco. There they joined 56 other teams from 27 countries. The race began with camel riding. Then came ocean swimming, beach running, coasteering (hiking and swimming through ocean waves, tides, and wildlife), and kayaking. After two days competitors headed into the Atlas Mountains, where they hiked, rappelled, and canyoneered. On the fifth day they mounted wild Arabian horses, galloping over huge desert fields and through tiny villages. Then it was back into the mountains, this section far higher and longer than the first. Finally, utterly exhausted but eager to finish, they climbed on mountain bikes for the final leg through steep hills and cactus-studded plains. A police escort provided a welcome finish in Marrakech.

Team Urban Edge performed poorly. In the first 24 hours the marine was felled by hypothermia. Though they knew they would be disqualified, the other three pushed on, earning the respect of all the participants. "Everyone's first race is like that," Rodger says. "And we felt good that we upheld New York's reputation just fine."

The disqualification did not prevent Rodger's team from garnering the lion's share of publicity. They were featured prominently in the Discovery Channel's documentary, and Rodger became an inspiration for other gay extreme sports athletes. He was invited to elite races around the world. "That's the last thing a sissy faggot from Alabama ever imagined," he marvels.

So where does the gay piece enter into extreme competition? "Nowhere, really," Rodger says. "This is not anything like team sports, where the financial stakes are so high that every competitor's masculinity is all wrapped up in every game and the fans treat statistics like the Holy Bible.

"But that's macho bullshit. Great athletes, the people to really respect, are the ones who aim for excellence in whatever they do. On the racecourse, on the track, the only thing that should count is what you can do. Gay, straight, black, white, male, female—it all comes down to who can do what on that particular day."

Rodger finds traditional sports to be "the last bastion of homophobia, like the military. Everyone is so worried about upsetting 'team balance.' Well, the fact is, you play better—you do anything better—when you're real. And when you're real, you have integrity. I don't buy bullshit. I've been on your submarine, I've run and swum next to you. I've always been there, and nothing bad has ever happened. So when I hear about some ballplayer who earns $8 million a year and can't tell his mommy he sucks pee-pee, I just find that reprehensible."

But extreme sports are not like that, and that is why Rodger is so excited for the future. "Gay people are in every adventure sport I know of, and no one cares," he says, his voice pulsing with enthusiasm. "We're so far ahead of the game. But, you know what? The last dinosaurs are going to die. Twenty years from now, all this talk about gay men in all professional sports is going to seem as outdated as keeping blacks out of sports does now or worrying about whether women are getting a fair shot. We've won the war. This is a great time for any gay man to start a sports career."

Crew
Chris Martel

Of all the sports in the world, crew might be the most difficult. Competitive rowing mixes two of the most important physical elements—strength and endurance—in the most painful, grueling manner imaginable. Rowers race at full speed for 3½ long miles. Just as important as power, however, are technique and cooperation. Eight individuals must meld into one cohesive unit. Each athlete's oar must strike the water at the same moment; each must pull his oar through the heavy water at precisely the same angle, with exactly the same form.

A boat is no place for individual stars. One man does not amass better statistics than his teammates; no one "carries the ball" more than any other. Each depends fully and completely on the other seven—and the coxswain—for success. Anyone who eases up lets down seven other people who, he knows, have given everything they have for him.

Those marital-like bonds are tightened through discipline unheard of in most other sports. Rowers routinely rise at 5 A.M. to run, lift weights, and train. They hit the roads and rivers well before sunrise, undeterred by rain, fog, snow, or bitter cold. The only thing that stops them is ice, and that merely drives them indoors to rowing machines.

It's not unusual for competitive oarsmen to spend nearly every minute of their lives together. In college they share houses and meals. When they party, they rely on each other for a good time—and to make sure no one else in their boat has too much of one. They are each other's teammates, best friends, and confidants. As difficult as it is to row, it is also a wonderfully secure life. Crew offers

244 both a physical and social outlet. It also provides an identity at a time many young men are seeking one.

Chris Martel embraced that identity. He felt happy and comfortable to be known as a member of the Marist College rowing team. He wore the "crew jock" label with pride.

At the same time, however, Chris was miserable. Spending every spare second with his teammates meant pretending to be someone he was not. Chris is gay, and to avoid upsetting the delicate harmony all had achieved, he felt the need to hook up with women. His teammates' thumbs-up was important—not only to him but, he believed, to the success of all. Crew is ultimately about balance, on the river as well as off, and Chris was terrified of being the one to rock the boat.

Freshman year was his low point. Rowing was the one activity that made him happy; in fact, it was the only thing that kept his mind off the ever-present knowledge that he liked men. When he was on the water, Chris's mind was crystal clear. The rest of the time, however—the countless hours he spent eating, studying, and hanging out with other rowers—he was in agony. Crew came to be Chris's greatest strength as well as his gravest worry.

It was not that way at the start. Chris grew up in Simsbury, Conn., a small, affluent, and homogeneous Hartford suburb. He played youth soccer and Little League baseball, but his competitive juices did not kick in until freshman year of high school, when he discovered crew. He knew nothing about the sport, but that was part of its appeal. None of his friends rowed, so it became a chance to start something completely new. The high school program was excellent, and Chris was hooked. The sport's physical demands challenged him; the camaraderie pulled him in. Winning the prestigious Head of the Charles race in Boston as a senior capped off a marvelous high school career.

At the same time, though, Chris realized he was drawn to males.

The attraction was not to teammates; they were too much like brothers. But, he says, "put me next to another team's boat…"

In high school in the mid 1990s, Chris heard very little about homosexuality. There were a few comments about how "they" walked, talked, and acted, but he had no positive images or role models—and certainly no one to talk to. He dated girls while suffering silently through his first same-sex crush and ultimate disappointment. His infatuation was not reciprocated. "How could it be?" Chris asks wryly. "I was too scared to say or do anything. He never even knew I liked him!"

Talented, experienced high school rowers are rare, so Chris was heavily recruited by colleges. He ended up at Marist, a small, conservative, and "jockish" Catholic school in Poughkeepsie, N.Y. Though not Catholic, Chris felt he could fit in there (his $4,000 scholarship was also a factor). Marist also recruited a Simsbury High School teammate, so while Chris was starting fresh at a new place, he did so alongside someone who thought he knew all about Chris's past.

Chris entered Marist with "homophobic" feelings. He desperately wanted not to be gay, and he saw crew as a way of "beating" homosexuality out of his body. The tension simmered close to the surface, but he could not quite articulate or even admit to himself what he was feeling. "I guess I thought if I worked really hard at crew, I wouldn't be gay," he says.

Delightedly, he found his new teammates to be great guys. From day one, they gave crew their full time and energy. They trained together six days a week, beginning at 5:45 A.M. For two hours each fall and spring they rowed on the Hudson River; in the winter they went inside. Every afternoon they lifted weights and ran. Weekends were filled with races up and down the East Coast.

Chris earned a reputation as one of the hardest-working, most dedicated rowers of all. Meanwhile, on the river, his teammates urged one another on: "Hey, homo, is that the best you can do?" The weight room echoed with similar comments: "Don't be such a fag—lift it!" Chris was confused. On the one hand, he was held up as an exemplar; on the other, his teammates had no idea that he was one of the "fags" being derided.

He is quick to note, however, that his teammates were not anti-gay. Because they had never been exposed to gay people, certainly not gay athletes, they simply did not know better.

By spring of freshman year Chris had never held hands with another male; he certainly had not come close to kissing one. But one day, after a very tough Saturday practice, his coach brought the team to his house for a cookout. He also invited a coxswain from an East Coast school, a young man on spring break who had grown up in Poughkeepsie. Chris found him adorable. "I've always been attracted to guys with rowers' qualities. We don't drink or smoke ourselves into oblivion; we're focused, down-to-earth, athletic, and have no time for bullshit. I've also always had a thing for coxswains." (A coxswain—commonly called a "cox"—is a boat's undisputed leader. He steers, calls out the stroke rate, and motivates the oarsmen, all of whom are much bigger than he. Because a cox does not row and is thus essentially "dead weight," a small build is important.)

Chris and the coxswain were introduced, shook hands, and talked briefly. When the party was over, Chris went back to his dorm room. His very difficult first year was winding down. More and more, he believed he would spend the rest of his life alone.

That summer, back in Simsbury, Chris entered an AOL rowing chat room. Another rower who liked his profile sent an instant message. After chatting a while, the other person asked if Chris had a "gf/bf" (girlfriend/boyfriend). Chris replied, "I can go for anything right now."

"What does that mean?" the other rower asked. For an hour the two athletes—both shy and new to gay identity—danced around the

subject of sexuality. When they admitted they were attracted to 247
guys, they moved on and eventually told each other where they
rowed. There were strong similarities. Each had put himself in a difficult situation: Chris by choosing a small Catholic school, the other
by joining a fraternity. And then, spectacularly slowly, it emerged
that they had already met. They had been introduced to each other
by the Marist coach at his cookout.

"It was amazing!" Chris marvels. "We each needed the other
person very badly at that point. I wasn't suicidal, but the thought of
being as alone as I was was horrible. The idea of meeting someone
like me—and someone I already knew—was incredible."

For several weeks they chatted online every night. Chris left parties early, then rushed home to go online. It took two months,
though, before they spoke on the phone. Chris's parents were going
on vacation, and he asked "Brad" (not his real name) if he wanted to
come to Simsbury.

"That flipped him out," Chris says. "He stopped talking to me. I
guess it was just too real. I think he thought if we met again, our lives
would change forever."

The rest of the summer was excruciating. Chris returned to
Marist, and when he began rowing again, welcomed the distractions
the sport provided. Suddenly, in September, Brad called and said he
would be in Poughkeepsie that weekend. He apologized for his
behavior over the summer and asked if they could meet.

Chris felt terrified and vulnerable because Brad knew his coach.
At the same time, he was electrified, and instantly agreed. At an early
Saturday practice, Brad joined Chris's coach on the launch. For a
nerve-racking hour, the young man watched Chris row.

When they got off the water, their eyes met. But the coach
ordered the team to run hills, so it was several hours later before
they were together again.

They met at a mall. Both were uncomfortable. After a while they

248 said goodbye and shook hands. But later in the week they talked, and the following weekend Brad returned.

As a Poughkeepsie native, Chris knew a make-out spot by the river. There, in the dark, they spent hours edging closer together. At last their legs touched. It took longer still before they gathered the courage to hug. When they did, they held each other tight for 10 long, luxurious minutes.

"We each needed it so-o-o bad," Chris says. "That feeling of not wanting to let go was the neatest thing in the world." Finally, they kissed.

It wasn't long, however, before the two young men heard a car pull up. Feverishly, Chris tried to zip up his pants. All of a sudden they came face-to-face with another Marist rower—the same one who, earlier that evening, Chris told he was going to the library.

"What are you doing here?!" the teammate asked.

His date—a local high school girl, who knew Brad from town—asked Brad the same thing. The scene, straight out of a bad sitcom, would have been humorous to Chris had it not been so terrifying.

Later that night, when Chris returned to the suite he shared with two other rowers, they confronted him. He said Brad was just a friend. Chris did not know whether they believed him or respected the fact that he was not ready to come out. No one said anything more, and he assumed the matter died. (Only later did Chris find that for months thereafter his suitemates followed him and Brad around campus, in a game-like way. When Chris finally came out, one said, "Too bad. Now the fun is over. We kind of liked not knowing!")

The next semester, Brad—whose family was having financial problems—transferred to Marist and joined the crew team. Though he lived at home, he and Chris spent time together. They were happy to finally be near each other, but keeping a discreet distance on the team strained their relationship. Occasionally Brad said hurt-

ful things about Chris; he was critical of Chris's rowing and made a **249**
concerted effort to hang out with other rowers, in order to fit in. As
coxswain, he was Chris's "boss," which introduced another level of
difficulty. Adding to the dynamic was the fact that Chris—6 feet tall,
180 pounds—was never afraid of or subservient to the other rowers.
Brad, however—just 5-9 and 130 pounds—always felt at the mercy
of the bigger men. As coxswain, he commanded the boat—but by
tradition he also had to fetch the rowers' shoes and water. The
volatile situation took its toll on everyone.

One day Brad mocked Chris's performance. Chris said something back under his breath. Everyone in the boat let out a collective gasp. Chris, who did not realize the team understood something
was going on between the two athletes, was taken aback. He had no
idea how to react. No one said anything. Slowly and only temporar-
ily, the tense atmosphere dissipated.

"At that point I was really in love," Chris says. "I had nothing to
be ashamed of, because I was ready for people to know."
Subconsciously, he tried to come out. He spent nights at Brad's
house—the only place they could be alone—having great sex in
Brad's room, directly underneath his mother's bedroom. Chris
would get up at 5 A.M., say hello to Brad's mother, and go off to practice. "What was I thinking?" Chris wonders in retrospect.

He answers his own question: "Your first relationship is hard, but
you figure a lot out. I guess it was that the crew team had been my
haven. Here comes this college transfer, the best cox we ever had,
popular. I'm in love with him, yet I can't tell anyone, and I can't sit
next to him more than anyone else could. When we travel to meets
he shares a bed with one of my teammates, so I'm insanely jealous."

Still, youth being what it is, there were wonderful moments.
On a bus heading to a race, with 50 other people, Chris and Brad
managed to sit next to each other. They placed a pillow strategi-
cally across their legs and went to work. Well, not all the way: In

250 deference to the team's "no masturbation 48 hours before a race"
rule (it allegedly decreases leg drive), Brad refused to let Chris
ejaculate.

The following fall Brad returned to his first college. Chris visited him often. No one at Marist was certain of their relationship, but
when Chris's father asked if Brad was more than a friend, Chris told
him everything. He began to feel better.

As a junior, Chris rented a house with 11 teammates. Only one
was a nonrower, but he was the person Chris shared a room with. In
order to talk openly on the phone with Brad, Chris came out to the
nonrower. In his self-appointed role as Chris's "watchdog," one day
he told Chris that one of the others, searching for scissors, had
found a drawer full of pictures, letters, and cards from Brad.

Chris acted quickly. He spent that afternoon and evening
telling each housemate, individually, that he was gay. Two of them
asked questions about oral and anal sex; Chris calls that "their way
of letting me know it was OK." The most common response—and
the one given by his former Simsbury High School teammate—
was "There's nothing to talk about. There's no problem. It's fine."
Some wanted to know why he had waited so long to come out. All
added that they knew Brad, liked him, and hoped the two were
happy together.

Chris was now an openly gay athlete—the only one at Marist
College. It was, on the one hand, almost a nonevent. At times, however, it was an eye-opener. One day, working out intensely on the
ergometer (a rowing machine that measures energy expended), a
new rower said to another freshman, "You pull like a fag." Without
missing a beat, an upperclassman pointed to Chris and said, "*That* is
how you pull like a fag." Chris was moved. He felt even better a few
weeks later, upon learning that was not an isolated incident.
Frequently, his teammates had defended him when football players
called rowing a "fag sport."

Chris had had no idea the reaction would be that supportive. He was already committed to spending the spring semester in Italy, and followed through with the plan. He learned Italian, traveled throughout Europe, and for the first time lived life the way he wanted to. He was out to his roommates there and became good friends with a lesbian.

When he returned to Marist the following fall, rowing faded in importance. Part of the reason was his experience overseas; part was because he was student-teaching history at a local high school and writing his senior thesis. He was ready to explore different dimensions of his personality. That made some of his housemates a bit apprehensive—they were still fully committed to crew—but they were always friendly to Chris and Brad. That relationship foundered, however, when Chris realized he wanted to be more open than Brad.

Student teaching made Chris less of a college student and more of an adult. He was never officially out to his students, but he took them to a lecture by Judy Shepard (the mother of slain gay man Matthew), and in the classroom he encouraged debates on topics like the First Amendment rights of antigay rapper Eminem.

As is true for many recent college graduates, the first months in the "real world" were wrenching. Chris moved to Boston and E-mailed his former teammates and friends frequently, but it was not the same. He realized he missed rowing, and joined the Community Rowing Boat Club. He hesitated coming out there, however. The Marist rowers had known him well and realized his being gay was just a small part of who he was. Chris was not sure his new teammates would see things that way. He did not want them to scrutinize his every move through a "gay" lens.

But one day, chatting online, he met a man who had just moved from San Francisco, where he had rowed with the gay Bay Blades team. The man was appalled there was no similar gay rowing team in Boston. He and Chris decided to put one together, and the Boston Bay Blades was formed.

Chris's teammates on the Community Rowing team now know he races for another club too, but do not know it is a gay team. They have no clue how many gay men row in the Boston area, Chris says. Competing for the Community Rowing team in a big race, he was astonished how many boats had at least one man who also rowed for the Bay Blades. He felt like yelling out, "Look at the 7 seat there! Look at 6 in that boat!" so every oarsman in Boston would know they were surrounded by gay men.

Chris enjoys rowing for both teams. With practice every day at 5:30 A.M. and 6:30 P.M., he is in even better shape than in college. He appreciates living in a city "filled with beautiful guys." He thinks often of the intersection of his rowing and gay lives.

The grueling sport of crew helped make him the man he is today—but being gay did too, perhaps to a greater degree. "Being gay helped me not quit," he says. "My mission was to prove everyone wrong. In high school but also college, so many people in society let me know subtly that what I was feeling was wrong. I wanted to prove *them* wrong."

He quotes one of his favorite music groups, Rage Against the Machine: "Fuck you, I won't do what you tell me!" For years, Chris had a similar rebellious image in his mind. Whether he was right or wrong, he had to keep rowing—and keep being gay.

"If everyone else was lifting 80 pounds, I had to lift 85," he says. "Everyone else could say they had a shitty run because they'd had too much to eat or not enough sleep. For me, it was because I was thinking about guys and couldn't concentrate—but I couldn't say that. I punished myself for that. For so long I constantly battled myself. It was almost like I spurred myself on by calling myself a faggot."

But when he came out, Chris learned that even in a painful, grueling sport like crew—perhaps, in fact, *because* it is such a difficult

sport and thus binds teammates so tightly together—a person's character is far more important than the gender of his partner. One of
the scariest, yet also proudest, moments of his life occurred not far
from the scene of so much of Chris's pain and joy, the Hudson River.
It was Marist College's senior formal dance, and Chris took a male
date. As the couple walked in to the country club, they were welcomed to a table filled with all the men he'd rowed with for four
years. Chris and his date danced every dance together, including the
slow ones. Moving slowly on the dance floor, his head resting on
another man's shoulder, Chris glanced up. His oldest teammate, the
fellow rower from Simsbury High, gave an approving nod.

By that point Chris was way out, but the dance represented a
coming-out of sorts for his crew team. Since his freshman year, the
tight-knit group of men had shared everything with Chris. Now,
after he shared his heart and soul with them, they opened their arms
publicly to him.

If there was ever any doubt that he had done the right thing, it
was confirmed toward the end of that memorable night. A teammate
approached Chris, looked him square in the eye, and said, "In four
years, this is the day I'm most proud to say I go to Marist."